Eleme ML Programming

Jeffrey D. Ullman

An Alan R. Apt Book

Prentice Hall
Englewood Cliffs, New Jersey 07632

Library of Congress Cataloging-in-Publication Data

Ullman, Jeffrey D., 1942-
    Elements of ML programming / Jeffrey D. Ullman.
      p.   cm.
    "A Alan R. Apt book."
    Includes bibliographical references and index.
    ISBN 0-13-184854-2
    1. ML (Computer program language)   I. Title.
QA76.73.M6U45 1994
005.13'3--dc20   93-34273
                                                 CIP

Publisher: Alan Apt
Production Editor: Mona Pompili
Developmental Editor: Sondra Chavez
Cover Artist: Luca Cardelli
Cover Designer: Violet Lake
Production Coordinator: Linda Behrens
Editorial Assistant: Shirley McGuire

© 1994 by Prentice-Hall, Inc.
A Paramount Communications Company
Englewood Cliffs, New Jersey 07632

Printed in the United States of America

10 9 8 7 6 5 4 3 2 1

ISBN 0-13-184854-2

PRENTICE-HALL INTERNATIONAL (UK) LIMITED, *London*
PRENTICE-HALL OF AUSTRALIA PTY. LIMITED, *Sydney*
PRENTICE-HALL CANADA, INC., *Toronto*
PRENTICE-HALL HISPANOAMERICANA, S.A., *Mexico*
PRENTICE-HALL OF INDIA PRIVATE LIMITED, *New Delhi*
PRENTICE-HALL OF JAPAN, INC., *Tokyo*
SIMON & SCHUSTER ASIA PTE. LTD, *Singapore*
EDITORA PRENTICE-HALL DO BRASIL, LTDA., *Rio de Janeiro*

Preface

I became interested in ML programming when I taught CS109, the introductory Computer Science Foundations course at Stanford. It was used by several of the instructors of this course, including Stu Reges and Mike Cleron, to introduce concepts such as functional programming and type systems. It was also used for the practical purpose of introducing a second programming paradigm, other than the Pascal or C that students learned in the introductory programming course. Reimplementing algorithms and data structures in another paradigm often is an aid to understanding of basic data structure and algorithm concepts.

I first learned ML from the notes that Reges and Cleron had written for their students. Initially, I was intrigued by the rule system, which gave me much of the power of Prolog, a language with which I had worked for several years. Yet ML did not introduce the semantic complexity that comes from the use of unification and backtracking in Prolog. However, I soon discovered other charms of ML: the type system, the use of exceptions, and the module system for creating abstract datatypes, among others. From the Reges and Cleron notes I also picked up the utility of giving the student a fast overview, stressing the most commonly used constructs rather than the complete syntax.

In writing this guide to ML programming, I have thus departed from the approach found in many books on the language. As an outsider, I had the opportunity to learn the language from the standpoint of the typical reader of the book. I have tried to remember how things struck me at first, the analogies I drew with conventional languages, and the concepts that I found most useful in getting started. I hope that my selection is accurate and the book will facilitate the reader's transition from conventional languages to ML.

Organization of the Book

The book is thus divided into three parts. In the first part, I wish the reader to have fun with ML. Explore its remarkably powerful ways to express algorithms and data structures, but do not yet worry about the general cases and principles of the language.

In the second part, things get a bit tougher. There are some very advanced programming language concepts in ML, such as polymorphic functions, a powerful type system, and a module system for encapsulation. We'll tackle these ideas in Part 2, still concentrating on the usual case rather than the general case.

Finally, the last part fills in the gaps of the first two parts and gives the general cases. There are some useful tables of built-in functions and diagrams of the complete language syntax.

Language Dialect

The implementation of ML used in this book is Standard ML of New Jersey, or SML/NJ. This compiler was written by Andrew Appel and David MacQueen to run under UNIX. It is one of several similar implementations of ML. However, there are occasional differences among their dialects, and we try to point out every feature that is implementation-dependent.

Features of the Book

The test of a language is not the best or most succinct examples of its use. Rather, a language will only be adopted widely if it can handle everyday programming chores well. Thus, I have considered in this book many of the most common data structures, such as trees and hash tables, and many of the most common algorithms, such as sorting or Gaussian elimination. I think the reader will be impressed by how well ML handles these standard tasks that were selected because of their ubiquity, not because they exhibit special features of the language.

To focus the reader's attention, I have inserted bullets at various places in the text. These bullets are interruptions from the main train of thought, but they are sufficiently important that I want to make sure they are noticed. On the other hand, footnotes are also interruptions to the main thread, but they are there only "for the record" rather than as an aid to understanding.

Important terms and concepts are indicated in two ways. Some get their own section header. Others appear in marginal notes at the left of the page.

Exercises

There are over 330 exercises or parts, and almost all the chapters have exercises at the end. Following Chapter 26 are solutions to about half the exercises. In some cases, these solutions serve as additional useful examples, and the reader should spend some time looking at the solutions. In the text, we indicate that an exercise or part of an exercise has a published solution by following the exercise or part number by a star.

Exercises are graded by difficulty. Harder exercises are indicated by an exclamation point in the margin, and a few of the hardest exercises have two exclamation points.

Use of the Book

The book as a whole is a tutorial and reference for the person who wants to program productively in ML. Although there are occasional references to conventional languages like C or Pascal, I believe the book is sufficiently self-contained that it could be used to teach ML as a first programming language.

When we teach students ML in the CS109 course at Stanford, the material covered corresponds closely to what appears in Chapters 1–13. The book can be used as a supplement to a programming language concepts course, in which case Chapters 14 and 15 would surely be included, possibly along with others of the more advanced chapters.

Acknowledgments

I would like to thank Andrew Appel and David MacQueen, both of whom carefully critiqued two iterations of the manuscript. They are tied for the title of "world's greatest referee."

I value a number of important pointers on ML from John Mitchell. Also, Henry Bauer, Richard LeBlanc, Peter Robinson, and Jean Scholtz have my appreciation for their work as referees of the manuscript.

Alan Apt, the series editor was a pleasure to work with. The manuscript was ably edited by Sondra Chavez. Errors in the text are mine, however, not hers or the referees'.

Cover Art

Special thanks go to Luca Cardelli, who volunteered to create original art for this book. The result is on the cover.

On-line Access to Code

You can obtain copies of the major pieces of code in this book by anonymous ftp to host `ftp-cs.stanford.edu`. Login with user name `ftp` or `anonymous` and give your name and host as a password. You may then execute

```
cd emlp
```

where you will find the programs from this book.

J. D. U.
Stanford, CA

Table of Contents

PART 2. ADVANCED FEATURES OF ML   89

Chapter 10. Polymorphic Functions   90

Chapter 11. Higher-Order Functions   99

Chapter 12. Defining New Types   115

Chapter 13. Programming with Datatypes   129

Solutions to Selected Exercises   280

◊◊◊ 0 A Perspective on ML and SML/NJ

ML is a recently developed language that has some extremely interesting features. The designers of the language incorporated many modern programming-language ideas, yet the language is surprisingly easy to learn and use. Among the most important of these features are:

Functional language

- ML is primarily a *functional language*, meaning that the basic mode of computation is the construction and application of functions. Functions can be defined by the user as in conventional languages, by writing code for the function. But it is also possible to treat functions as values and compute new functions from them with operators like function composition.

Side-effect freedom

- A consequence of the functional style is that computation proceeds by evaluating expressions, not by making assignments to variables. There are ways to give expressions *side-effects*, which are operations that permanently change the value of a variable or other observable object (e.g., by printing output). However, side-effects are treated as necessary aberrations on the basic theme. In contrast, languages like Pascal or C use statements with side-effects as a matter of course. For example, a Pascal assignment like `a := b+c` has a side-effect, since the value of variable `a` is changed after the assignment is executed. Surprisingly, ML programs would typically evaluate `b+c` but not permanently store its value anywhere.

Higher-order functions

- ML supports higher-order functions — functions that take functions as arguments — routinely and with great generality. In comparison, languages like Pascal or C support functions as arguments only in limited ways.

Polymorphism

- ML supports *polymorphism*, which is the ability of a function to take arguments of various types. For example, in Pascal or C we may have to create different types with similar properties, such as "stack of integers," "stack of reals," "stack of pairs of integers," and so on. We would then have to define operations like "push" and "pop" for each different type of stack. In ML, we can define one notion of a stack, one push function, and one pop function, each of which works no matter what type of elements our stacks have.

Abstract data types

- ML supports abstract data types through: an elegant type system, the ability to construct new types, and constructs that restrict access to objects of a given type so all access is through a fixed set of operations defined for that type. An example is a type like "stack," for which we might define the push and pop operations and a few others as the only way the contents of

1

a stack could be read or modified. These datatypes, which are essentially the "classes" used in object-oriented programming languages like C++ or Smalltalk, are considered very important for such programming goals as modularity, encapsulation of concepts, and reuse of software.

Recursion

- ML strongly encourages recursion, since iterators like for-loops or while-loops in Pascal or C are extremely limited in ML.

Rules

- There is an easy way to do rule-based programming, where actions are based on if-then rules, in ML. The core idea is a pattern-action construct, where a value is compared with several patterns in turn. The first pattern to match causes an associated action to be executed. In this way, ML has much of the power of Prolog and other languages that are thought of as "artificial intelligence languages."

Strong typing

- ML is a *strongly typed* language, meaning that all values and variables have a type that can be determined at "compile time" (i.e., by examining the program but not running it). A value of one type cannot be given to a variable of another type. For example, the real value 4.0 cannot be the value of an integer-valued variable, even though the integer 4 could be the value of that variable. Many other languages allow confusion of types. For example, C allows a value to change its type arbitrarily, through the "cast" mechanism, while Lisp and Prolog do not try to constrain types in general. Strong typing is a valuable debugging aid, since it allows many errors to be caught by the compiler, rather than resulting in mysterious errors when the program is run. Interestingly, although most other strongly typed languages require a declaration of the type of every variable, ML tries hard to figure out the unique type that each variable may have, and only expects a declaration for a variable when it is impossible for ML to deduce its type.

ML is not the only language to possess these features. For example, Lisp (or its popular dialect, Scheme) is principally functional, supports higher-order functions, and promotes the use of recursion. Prolog also promotes recursion and supports rule-based programming naturally. Smalltalk and C++ offer powerful abstract-data-type facilities, and so on. However, the combination of features found in ML offers the user a great deal of programming ease. At the same time, ML allows one to use a full palette of modern programming language concepts.

A Historical Perspective on ML

While there are a number of medium-scale production systems written in ML, much of the recent interest in the language has been from the research and education communities. Part of the reason the number of applications written in ML is relatively small is that, until recently, ML has been primarily an interpreted language, and interpreted languages tend to offer substantially slower execution speed than compiled languages. However, a number of ML implementations, including SML/NJ — which we use in this book — have a compilation capability.

ML is still a young language, whose basic approach differs from that of the most popular languages of the day. It is common for such languages to have a lengthy phase where they are used primarily for experimentation. For example, Lisp went through such a phase but is now routinely compiled and used for production code. Thus, we expect a future in which ML, or an enhanced language now on the drawing boards called ML-2000, will become a commonly used language for application programming.

The SML/NJ System

In this book, we shall assume that the SML/NJ, or "Standard ML of New Jersey," interpreter/compiler is used. It is an implementation of "Standard ML," which is the basis of most implementations of the ML language. SML/NJ was implemented by David MacQueen of ATT Bell Laboratories and Andrew Appel of Princeton University. It runs under UNIX, and is available gratis, by arrangement with ATT Bell Labs. There are several enhancements to standard ML found in SML/NJ (and most other ML implementations). We shall point out in this book when a feature is "nonstandard" in this sense.

Interactive mode

To run SML/NJ in *interactive mode*, in response to the UNIX prompt type

```
sml
```

SML/NJ will respond with:

Standard ML of New Jersey ···
val it = () : unit
—

Here, as throughout this book, we shall use italic font to indicate ML's responses, while text typed by the user will be in the "teletype" font, as `sml` above.

Without going into detail now regarding the ML language, some interpretation of the above response is in order. First, `val` stands for "value," and `it` is the name of a variable whose value is always that of the last expression evaluated. In this situation, there have not been any previous expressions, so `it` has a "null" value, denoted (). The colon (:) is a symbol that ML uses with all values it prints, to indicate the type of the value. Here, ML is saying that the type of () is *unit*, a special type for this value only. Types are very important in ML, and we shall use the colon operator frequently to specify types ourselves.

Unit

The dash on the third line is ML's prompt. The prompt invites us to type an expression, and ML will respond with the value of that expression. We can make definitions and enter expressions indefinitely, and SML/NJ will respond to each with the resulting value.

● To terminate an SML/NJ session, type <CTRL>d.

**Program
execution**

It is also possible to get SML/NJ to execute a program in a conventional way. For example, if our ML program is in file **foo**, give the **sml** command with that file as standard input:

```
sml < foo
```

Using files

Another option is to issue the **sml** command to UNIX, which gets us started in interactive mode. Then, in response to the prompt, read and execute a file **foo** that contains an ML program. We do so by typing to ML the expression

```
use("foo");
```

Any quoted UNIX path name can appear in place of **"foo"**. This mode is handy when we are debugging a program and want to read in its definitions and then try them in interactive mode.

Prerequisites for the Reader

We assume the reader is familiar with programming in a conventional language like Pascal or C. Occasionally, as a matter of interest, we shall compare ML constructs with those of Pascal or C, but familiarity with one or both of these languages is not essential.

It is also assumed the reader is familiar with the process of writing and debugging programs in a conventional language. We expect that the reader has written at least a few recursive programs and has some comfort with that style of programming. However, our first recursive examples will be covered in sufficient detail that the style may be learned here. In addition, we assume the reader is familiar with simple data structures and data structure concepts such as records, pointers, lists, and trees. The author immodestly recommends *Foundations of Computer Science*, by A. V. Aho and J. D. Ullman, Computer Science Press, New York, 1992 for the reader who desires further background on these subjects.

References

The formal definition of the language ML is found in *The Definition of Standard ML*, by R. Milner, M. Tofte, and R. M. Harper, MIT Press, Cambridge MA, 1990.

An elaboration is in *Commentary on Standard ML* by R. Milner and M. Tofte, MIT Press, Cambridge MA, 1991.

The original reference manual is *Standard ML*, by R. M. Harper, D. B. MacQueen, and R. Milner, ECS–LFCS–86–2, Laboratory for Foundations of Computer Science, Edinburgh University, Dept. of CS, 1986.

This document has evolved into the reference manual for SML/NJ: *Standard ML Reference Manual (Preliminary)*, by A. W. Appel and D. B. MacQueen, ATT Bell Laboratories report, 1991, distributed electronically with the SML/NJ system.

Also distributed electronically is the *Standard ML of New Jersey Library Manual* by A. W. Appel, and D. B. MacQueen, ATT Bell Laboratories, 1993. This and other material, including the SML/NJ system itself, is available by anonymous ftp from directory `dist/ml` at host `research.att.com` or from directory `pub/ml` at host `princeton.edu`.

A. W. Appel and D. B. MacQueen, "Standard ML of New Jersey," *International Symposium on Programming Languages, Implementation, and Logic*, pp. 1–13, Springer-Verlag, 1991 is a technical article describing the SML/NJ system.

PART 1 | *Introduction to Programming in ML*

◊◊◊

Part 1 is an extended tutorial, whose goal is to give the reader a feel for ML programming. Topics include: program variables; types; simple data structures such as tuples, lists, and strings; functions; patterns; exceptions; and simple input/output. Perhaps most important, we introduce the functional style of programming that is characteristic of ML. There is much more to ML than is found in Part 1, and there are better ways to do certain things than we show here. Part 2 will cover more difficult features of the language, and in Part 3 we summarize the complete language.

◇◊◊ 1 Expressions

When we are in interactive mode, the simplest thing we can do is type an expression in response to the ML prompt (–). ML will respond with the value and its type.

Font convention

◇ **Example 1.1.** As mentioned in Chapter 0, "teletype" font will indicate what has been typed by the programmer, and the system's response is shown in italics. Here is an example of an expression that we may type and the ML response.

```
1+2*3;
```
val it = 7 : int

it

We type the expression $1 + 2 * 3$, and ML responds that the value of variable **it** is 7, and that the type of this value is integer. Recall **it** is the variable that receives the value of any expression that we type in interactive mode. □

There are a number of points to observe from Example 1.1.

- An expression must be followed by a semicolon to tell the ML system that the instruction is finished. If ML expects more input when a <return> is typed, it will respond with the prompt = instead of –. The = sign is a warning that we have not finished our input expression.

val

- The response of ML to an expression is: the word **val** standing for "value"; the special variable name **it**, which stands for the previous expression; an equal sign; and the value of the expression (7 in this example). Then a colon (the "type of" symbol) follows, and last are one or more words that denote the type of the value.

Constants

As in any other language, expressions are composed of operators and operands, and operands may be either variables or constants. At this point, we have not yet discussed the way values may be assigned to variables, so it does not make sense to use variables in expressions. However, syntactically, variables present no surprises; you may think of Pascal identifiers (letters followed by letters or digits) or the identifiers in your favorite language as names for ML variables.

There are four basic types of constants in ML:

Integers

1. *Integers* are represented as in other languages, with one exception. A positive integer is a string of one or more digits, such as 0, 1234, or 11111111. A negative integer is formed by placing the unary minus sign, which is the tilde (~), not a dash, in front of the digits, such as ~1234.

Reals

2. *Reals* are also represented conventionally, with the exception that minus signs within reals are represented by ~. An ML real thus consists of

    a) An optional ~,

    b) A string of one or more digits, and

    c) One or both of the following elements:

        i) A decimal point and one or more digits.

        ii) The letter E, an optional ~, and one or more digits.

As in other languages, the value of a real number is determined by taking the number that appears before the E and multiplying it by 10 raised to the power that is the integer following the E. Examples are ~123.0 (the negative real that happens to have an integer value -123), 1.23, 3E~3 (whose value is .003), and 3.14E12 (3.14×10^{12}).

Booleans

3. *Booleans* may only have the values **true** and **false**. Unlike Pascal, ML is case-sensitive, so these constants must be written in lowercase, never as **TRUE**, **False**, or any other combination involving capitals.

Strings

4. *Strings* have values that are quoted character strings, like "foo" or "R2D2". Certain special characters are represented as in the language C, where the backslash (\) serves as an escape character. In particular:

Newline

    a) The two-character sequence \n stands for the "newline" character.

Tab

    b) \t stands for the tab character.

Backslash

    c) \\ stands for the backslash character.

Quote mark

    d) \" stands for the double-quote character, which otherwise would be interpreted as the string ender.

    e) A backslash followed by three decimal digits stands for the character whose ASCII code is the number represented by those three digits, in base 10. This convention allows us to type characters for which there is no key on the keyboard. For example \007 is the "character" that rings the bell on the console.

Control character

    f) Those characters that are control characters can also be written by the three character sequence consisting of a backslash, the caret or uparrow symbol ^, and the character itself. For example, \^d stands for <CTRL>d.

g)   Finally, if a string is too long to be written conveniently on a single line, it may continue it over several lines if all but the last line end with a backslash, and all but the first line begin with a backslash.

◇ **Example 1.2.** The text of item (d) above could be written as a string extending over three lines as follows:

```
"\\\" stands for the double-quote character, \
\which otherwise would be interpreted \
\as the string ender."
```

In the first line, the first quote is not part of the string but indicates that a string follows. The first two backslashes represent the character \. The third backslash and the quote represent the character " (the second character of item (d) above). The backslash at the end of the first line indicates that the string continues on the next line. Note that the space after the comma is shown explicitly on the first line, because the newline is not part of the string. If that space were missing, the printed string would look like ...`character,which`....

For another example, the string `"A\tB\tC\n1\t2\t3\n"` would be printed as

```
A       B       C
1       2       3
```

Here we see uses of the tab sequence `\t` and the newline sequence `\n`. □

Arithmetic Operators

The arithmetic operators of ML are similar to those of Pascal or C. There are:

1.   The low-precedence "additive" operators: `+`, `-`,

2.   The high-precedence "multiplicative" operators: `*`, `/` (division of reals), `div` (division of integers, rounding down toward minus infinity), and `mod` (the remainder of integer division), and

3.   The highest precedence unary minus operator, `~`.

However, note the following.

Unary minus

•   A unary minus sign is always denoted by a tilde (`~`), never by a dash. Thus, we write `~3*4` and `3-4`, but never `3~4` or `-3*4`.

•   ML is case-sensitive, so the operators `mod` and `div` must be written in lowercase.

•   Associativity and precedence is like Pascal; higher precedence operators are grouped with their operands first, and among operators of equal precedence, grouping proceeds from the left. Grouping order can be altered by parentheses in the usual manner.

◇ **Example 1.3.** Here are some expressions and their responses from the ML interpreter.

>   3.0 - 4.5 + 6.7;
>   *val it = 5.2 : real*

Note that grouping of equal precedence operators is from the left. This expression is interpreted as $(3.0 - 4.5) + 6.7$, not $3.0 - (4.5 + 6.7)$, which has value -8.2.

>   43 div (8 mod 3) * 5;
>   *val it = 105 : int*

All three operators `div`, `mod`, and `*` are of the same precedence, but the parentheses force us to use the `mod` first, then group from the left. Since `mod` calls for the remainder when its left argument is divided by the right, the value of `8 mod 3` is 2. We thus evaluate (`43 div 2`)`*5`, or 105. □

String Operators

We may not apply the arithmetic operators to string operands. There is, however, one operator that applies to strings and only to strings. The operator ^ stands for concatenation of strings; it has the precedence of an additive opera-

Concatenation   tor. When we *concatenate* two strings s_1 and s_2, we get the string s_1s_2. That is, the resulting string is a copy of string s_1 followed by a copy of s_2.

◇ **Example 1.4.** Here are some examples of string concatenation.

>   "house" ^ "cat";
>   *val it = "housecat" : string*
>
>   "linoleum" ^ "";
>   *val it = "linoleum" : string*

Empty string   Notice in the second example that "" represents the *empty string*, the string with no characters. When we concatenate the empty string with any other string, either on the left or right of the ^ operator, we get the other string as a result. □

Comparison Operators

The six comparison operators that we find in Pascal are also part of the ML repertoire. These are =, <, >, <=, >=, and <>, representing, respectively, the comparisons $=$, $<$, $>$, $\leq$, $\geq$, and $\neq$. They can be used to compare integers, reals, or strings. In the case of strings, < means "alphabetically precedes," <= means "equals or alphabetically precedes," and so on.

- Note that the result of applying a comparison operator is always a value of Boolean type.

- The precedence of the comparison operators is less than that of the arithmetic operators, so $2 < 1 + 3$ is correctly interpreted as $2 < (1 + 3)$.

◇ **Example 1.5.** Here are some examples of expressions involving comparison operators.

> `2 < 1+3;`
> *val it = true : bool*

Notice that the result of the comparison is the Boolean value **true**.

> `"abc" <= "ab";`
> *val it = false : bool*

Here, we have compared two strings, **abc** and **ab**. In lexicographic order, the latter precedes the former, so it is false that **abc** "is equal to or precedes" **ab**. □

Logical Operators

ML has operators that apply to Boolean values. These operators are similar to the operators **AND**, **OR**, and **NOT** found in Pascal (**&&**, **||**, and **!** in C), but with some important differences. **NOT** has the usual Pascal meaning, but must be lowercase, as **not**.

andalso, orelse

AND and **OR** of Pascal are replaced in ML by **andalso** and **orelse**. Unlike their Pascal counterparts, the right operand of **andalso** and **orelse** is evaluated only when the left operand does not determine a value (i.e., only when the left operand of **andalso** is true, or the left operand of **orelse** is false).

The precedence of the logical operators in ML agrees with C, but not with Pascal. The logical operators are of lower precedence than the comparison or arithmetic operators, and **andalso** is of higher precedence than **orelse**.

◇ **Example 1.6.** Consider the following expression.

> `1<2 orelse 3>4;`
> *val it = true : bool*

ML does not evaluate the second condition $(3 > 4)$, since the first being true is sufficient to guarantee that the whole expression is true. Remember that the result of a comparison is a Boolean, so it makes sense to connect two comparisons by a logical operator such as **orelse**. In the following expression:

> `1<2 andalso 3>4;`
> *val it = false : bool*

it is necessary to evaluate both conditions. Had the first condition been false, then there would have been no need to check the second, because the whole expression could only be false. □

Side-effect

Incidentally, one might wonder why it matters whether the second operand of a logical operator is evaluated, if the result of the entire expression cannot depend on that operand. The reason is that in some special cases, an ML expression can have a *side-effect*, which is an action whose effect does not disappear after the expression is evaluated. The most common example of a side-effect is when something inside an expression causes information to be printed or read. We have not yet seen any ML construct that has a side-effect, and indeed it is in the ML style to avoid side-effects normally. However, side-effects are possible, as we shall see in Chapter 9 and elsewhere. When they occur, it is essential that we understand the conditions under which part of an expression will not be evaluated and its side-effects consequently not performed.

- Remember to use `andalso` and `orelse`, never `and` and `or` for the logical operators. There is no special meaning for `or` in ML, but `and` has another meaning entirely, having nothing to do with logical operations.

The If-Then-Else Operator

There is a *conditional* operator `if` E `then` F `else` G. We compute the value of this expression by first evaluating expression E, which must have a Boolean value. If that value is `true`, then we evaluate expression F (and never evaluate G); the value of F becomes the value of the entire if-then-else expression. If the value of E is `false`, then we skip F and evaluate G, which becomes the value of the entire expression.

◇ **Example 1.7.** Consider the following conditional expression:

```
if 1<2 then 3+4 else 5+6;
val it = 7 : int
```

We begin by evaluating the expression between the `if` and `then`. In this case, the expression $1 < 2$ evaluates to `true`. Thus, we evaluate the second expression, $3 + 4$. The result, 7, is the value of the entire expression. We do not evaluate the expression $5 + 6$, and if in its place there was an expression with side-effects, those side-effects would not be executed. □

Here are a few important points about the conditional operator.

- The conditional, or if-then-else operator, is one of the rare operators that takes more than two operands. There is, however, a similar three-operand (*ternary*) operator in C, using the characters `?` and `:` in place of `then` and `else` (nothing in place of `if`).

- The if-then-else operator forms an expression. It is *not* a control-flow construct that groups statements together, as we find in most languages.

- There is no `if` $\cdots$ `then` construct in ML. Such an expression would not have a value if the condition was false. This point emphasizes the difference between if-then-else as an operator and as a control-flow construct. There is no harm in having a control-flow construct if-then, since it simply executes no statements if the condition is false.

Exercises

1.1: What is the response of ML to the following expressions?

a)* `1+2*3`
b) `5.0-4.2/1.4`
c)* `11 div 2 mod 3`
d) `"foo"^"bar"^""`
e)* `3>4 orelse 5<6 andalso not 7<>8`
f) `if 6<10 then 6.0 else 10.0`

1.2: The following ML "expressions" have errors in them. Explain what is wrong with each.

a)* `8/4`
b) `if 2<3 then 4`
c)* `1<2 and 5>3`
d) `6+7 DIV 2`
e)* `4.+3.5`
f) `1.0<2.0 or 3>4`

! **1.3***: Write a string that when printed creates the displayed text on lines (3)–(5) of Example 1.2. You may assume that the indentation of the lines is made by a single tab character. Your string should be written over several lines so there are no more than 80 characters appearing on any one line.

◊◊◊ 2 Type Consistency

We now come to an aspect of expressions that is sufficiently important to deserve a chapter of its own. ML requires that types of operators and operands be consistent without exception. Certain operators take operands of one particular type only. Examples are /, which requires operands of type real, div, which requires operands of type integer, and ^, which requires operands of type string.

As we saw in Chapter 1, when such an operator is given operands of the proper type, it responds with the result. However, when one or both operands are of the wrong type, we get an error message.

◊ **Example 2.1.** Suppose we try to use real division with an integer for the second operand, as

```
5.3 / 4;
```
Error: operator and operand don't agree (tycon mismatch)
*   operator domain: real * real*
*   operand: real * int*
*   in expression:*
*   5.3 / 4*

Let's see what ML is telling us. The first line of the response says that the operator expects operands of types other than what it saw.[1] ML refers to this

Tycon
situation as a "tycon" (type constructor) mismatch.

The second line of the response tells us that the operator / expects an "operand" whose type is a pair of reals. The * operator in this context is not multiplication, but rather an operator that applies to types and produces

Product type
a *product type*, that is, the type of a pair, triple, or so on. In particular, **real * real** is the type of any pair of reals, for example, of the pair (1.2, 3.4).

This response makes us aware of a rather dogmatic view ML has of operators and operands. Strictly speaking, all operators in ML are *unary*, that is, they take a single argument. A binary (two-argument) operator like / is perceived by ML as taking a single argument that is a pair. In most situations there is no problem with viewing a binary operator as if it had two operands, but there are some differences that we shall address in Chapter 21.

The third line of the response tells us what ML saw as the operand of the operator, namely a pair whose first component (the left operand) is the real number 5.3, but whose second component (the right operand) is the integer 4.

---

[1] SML/NJ also tells us about the line number and position in the line where the error occurred. We omit this information.

14

The remaining two lines have an obvious meaning, showing us the expression in which the error occurred. □

The situation is more complex when we have an operator like + that applies to operands of different types. In the case of +, ML is happy if the operands are both integers or both reals, but we cannot mix the type of operands even if it makes sense to us.

◇ **Example 2.2.**

```
1 + 2;
```
val it = 3 : int

```
1.0 + 2.0;
```
val it = 3.0 : real

```
1 + 2.0;
```
Error: operator and operand don't agree (tycon mismatch)
    *operator domain: int * int*
    *operand: int * real*
    in expression
        1 + 2.0

Notice that ML has looked at the first operand 1 and decided that the operator + must take two integers as operands. Thus the second line of the response tells us ML expected a pair of integers and the third line tells us it found a pair consisting of an integer and a real. □

Another place where type mismatches may occur through carelessness is in an if-then-else expression. The rules regarding types for this expression are simple:

- The expression following **if** must have Boolean type.

- The expressions following **then** and **else** can be of any one type, but they must be of the same type.

◇ **Example 2.3.** Here is an illustration of what happens when the then- and else-parts do not agree in type.

```
if 1<2 then 3 else 4.0;
```
Error: rules don't agree (tycon mismatch)
    expected: bool → int
    found: bool → real
    rule:
        false ⇒ 4.0

This error message is rather mysterious. Obviously, it is saying something about finding a real (i.e., 4.0) when it expected an integer to match the value 3 that followed the **then**. But what's this about "rules"? The explanation lies in the fact that the if-then-else expression is really a shorthand for a more general kind of expression: the case expression. We shall cover the case expression in Chapter 19.

For the moment, let us just note that ML's view of the if-then-else is that it involves two "rules," each of which takes a Boolean value and produces a value of some one type. The first of these rules associates the Boolean value **true** with the integer 3. This rule expresses the principle that if the condition is true, we use the value of the expression that follows the **then**. The second rule associates the Boolean value **false** with the value following the **else**, namely 4.0 in this case. However, ML expects to find another integer-valued expression following **else**, which it will then associate with **false** in the second rule. ML is unhappy that it has found a real-valued expression, because ML will not tolerate groups of rules that produce values of different types.

We can see the underlying case expression and rules more clearly in the response to the following erroneous if-then-else expression, which has the expression 2 after the **if**, where a Boolean-valued expression must go. The response appears in Fig. 2.1. At the end of the response we see the two rules, which associate 3 with **true** and 4 with **false** respectively. ML looks after the **if** to find which case applies, but there it finds the value 2 instead of an expression that evaluates to a Boolean. There is no "case 2" among the rules, only cases **true** and **false**. Thus as the first line of the response explains, the "case object" 2 is not matched by any of the rules. □

```
if 2 then 3 else 4;
```
Error: case object and rules don't agree (tycon mismatch)
> *rule domain: bool*
> *object: int*
> *in expression:*
> > *case 2 of*
> > > *(true ⇒ 3*
> > > *| false ⇒ 4)*

Fig. 2.1. This erroneous conditional statement has a non-Boolean condition.

Coercion of Types

Sometimes we have a reason to convert (*coerce*) a value of one type to an "equivalent" value of another type. Thus ML provides certain built-in functions that do the conversion for us. Perhaps the clearest case is when we want to **integer-to-real** convert an integer to a real with the same value. The function **real** lets us do just that.

◊ **Example 2.4.** Applied to an integer, **real** produces the equivalent real value as:

```
real(4);
```
val it = 4.0 : real

As another instance, we can fix Example 2.1, where we tried to divide a real by an integer, if we first apply **real** to the integer. The expression and response:

```
5.3 / real(4);
```
val it = 1.325 : real

shows the correct version of Example 2.1. □

Real-to-integer

When we try to convert a real to an integer, it is not so clear which integer we want, since the real may not equal any integer. ML provides three ways to convert: **floor**, **ceiling**, and **truncate**. Each produces the integer with the same value when given a real that happens to be an integer; for instance, 4.0 is converted to 4 by each of these three functions. In general, given a real number r, **floor** produces the greatest integer that is no larger than r, and **ceiling** produces the smallest integer no less than r. The **truncate** function drops digits to the right of the decimal point.

◇ **Example 2.5.** Here are the responses of the three functions for converting reals to integers on a positive and a negative number.

```
ceiling(3.5);
```
val it = 4 : int
```
ceiling(~3.5);
```
val it = ~3 : int

```
floor(3.5);
```
val it = 3 : int
```
floor(~3.5);
```
val it = ~4 : int

```
truncate(3.5);
```
val it = 3 : int
```
truncate(~3.5);
```
val it = ~3 : int

Notice that **floor** and **truncate** do the same thing on positive numbers, but **truncate** agrees with **ceiling** on negative numbers. Remember that -3 is "larger" than -3.5. □

Character-to-integer

ASCII

It is also possible to convert from characters to integers, just as we do in Pascal, using the **ord** function (which, however, must be lowercase in ML). A character in ML is just a character string of length 1; for example, **"a"** is the character a. Each character has an internal code used by the machine; all modern machines use the ASCII code. If we apply **ord** to a character, the result is the integer that the ASCII code assigns to that character.

◇ Example 2.6.

```
ord("a");
val it = 97 : int

ord("a") - ord("A");
val it = 32 : int
```

The latter example computes the difference between the ASCII codes for lower case **a** and capital **A**. This result is no coincidence. Every lower case letter has an ASCII code that is 32 more than its corresponding capital letter. □

Integer-to-character

Similarly, we can convert integers in the range 0 to 255 to characters, that is, to strings of length 1. The function **chr** performs this task as:

```
chr(97);
val it = "a" : string
```

Exercises

2.1: Write expressions to make each of the following conversions.

a)* Convert 123.45 to the next lower integer.
b) Convert −123.45 to the next lower integer.
c) Convert 123.45 to the next higher integer.
d)* Convert −123.45 to the next higher integer.
e)* Convert "Y" to an integer.
f) Convert 120 to a character.
g)* Convert "N" to a real.
h) Convert 97.0 to a character.

2.2: The following expressions contain type errors. What are the errors and how might we fix them?

a)* `ceiling(4)`
b) `if true then 5+6 else 7.0`
c)* `chr(256)`
d) `chr(~1)`
e)* `ord(3)`
f) `chr("a")`
g) `if 0 then 1 else 2`

$\diamondsuit\!\!\diamondsuit\!\!\diamondsuit$ 3   Variables and Environments

Variable

Identifier

In most languages, such as C or Pascal, computing takes place in an *environment* consisting of a collection of "boxes," usually called *variables*. Variables have names and hold values. The name of a box is an *identifier*, which is a string of characters that the language allows as the name of a variable.[1] There is usually a type associated with a variable, and the contents of a "box" can be any value of the appropriate type. Pascal, C, and most other languages allow variables of types integer, real, and many other types.

Store

Value binding

At any given time the set of values stored in the variables' boxes constitute the *store*. In conventional languages, computation proceeds by side-effects, that is, by changing the store. One of the interesting things about ML is that it is impossible for the store to change, with two exceptions — arrays and references (see Chapters 16 and 17). Rather, ML does its computing by adding to the environment new *value bindings*, which are associations between identifiers and values. The above brief overview of the chapter is heady material, so let's start again from the beginning.

Identifiers

Identifiers are character strings with certain restrictions. Most languages allow identifiers that are letters followed by any number of letters and digits. ML allows these too, along with many other strings that are not identifiers in most other languages. In ML, identifiers fall into two classes: alphanumeric and symbolic. There is no difference in their use, with the exception of type variables, as described below, which are alphanumeric identifiers beginning with an apostrophe. The *alphanumeric* class of identifiers consists of strings formed by

**Alphanumeric
identifier**

1. An uppercase or lowercase letter or the character ' (called apostrophe or "prime"), followed by

2. Zero or more additional characters from the set given in (1) plus the digits and the character _ (underscore).

Type variable

However, identifiers beginning with the apostrophe ' are *type variables*. They can only be bound to values that are types, not to an ordinary value.

$\diamond$ **Example 3.1.** The following are examples of alphanumeric identifiers:

---

[1] Identifiers should be familiar from any language the reader knows. For example, Pascal permits them to be letters followed by any sequence of letters and digits.

```
abc
X29a
Number_of_Hamburgers_Served
a'b'c
```

The following is a legal alphanumeric identifier: 'a. However, it cannot be bound to values like 3, 4.5, "six", or any of the values we normally think of as the values of variables. It can only be bound to a type. In fact, ML often chooses the identifier 'a to represent the type of something whose value can be of any type. For instance, 'a might in some contexts be given the type integer as its "value." Note that being bound to the type integer is quite different from being bound to a particular integer like 3. □

Of all the characters we can type with a conventional keyboard, there are only ten that cannot appear as part of some sort of identifiers. These ten characters are the three kinds of pairs of parentheses (round, square, and curly), double quote, period, comma, and semicolon. That is, the only characters that always stand alone and cannot be part of an identifier are

```
( ) [ ] { } " . , ;
```

Of course the "white space" characters — blank, tab, and newline — also are not part of identifiers. These do not have a meaning by themselves, but they serve to separate the elements of a program.

Symbolic identifier

The remaining 20 keyboard characters that cannot appear in alphanumeric identifiers can be used to form *symbolic identifiers.* To be precise, the set of characters for symbolic identifiers is

```
+ - / * < > = ! @ # $ % ^ & ` ~ \ | ? :
```

Many of these symbols by themselves are names of operators. For example, we have seen the use of +, ^, and several others. ML interprets the identifier + as a special function that adds either two reals or two integers. More precisely, ML initially binds the identifier + to the addition function. Similarly, ML initially binds any other symbolic identifier that stands for an operator to the function implementing that operator.

Unlike most other languages, we are free in ML to form our own identifiers from strings of the 20 characters listed above. These identifiers might be used to name new operators that we define, but they can also be used routinely to name integers, reals, and so on.

◇ **Example 3.2.** The following are legal symbolic identifiers: $$$, >>>=, and !@#%. However, !@a is not a legal identifier because it mixes the characters ! and @ (which may only appear in symbolic identifiers) with the character a (which can only be part of an alphanumeric identifier). □

• We suggest that the reader not use symbolic identifiers for common types such as integers or strings. Besides looking strange, they often cause trouble because they must be surrounded by white space to prevent them from "attaching" to operators like + and forming unintended identifiers that confuse the ML system and cause an error.

The Top-Level Environment

When we invoke ML, we are given the *top-level environment* in which to work. In this environment, the identifiers that have meaning to the ML system are bound to these meanings.

In Fig. 3.1 we suggest some of these identifiers. Environments will be represented as a table, with a left column for identifiers and a right column for the associated value. At the bottom of Fig. 3.1 is the top-level environment.[2] We see an entry for the identifier ^ to represent the function that concatenates strings, and we see another named **floor** that represents the floor function discussed in Chapter 2. There are other entries for all the operators and functions that we have learned and those we have yet to learn.

Identifier	Value
foo	3
bar	490
pi	3.14159
. . .	. . .
^	function to concatenate strings
floor	function to compute the floor of a real
. . .	. . .

Top-level environment

Fig. 3.1. The top-level environment and some added user variables.

In addition, we have shown some other identifiers to which common values have been bound as additions to the top-level environment. In particular, we have the identifier **foo** bound to the integer 3, an identifier **bar** with value equal to the integer 490, and an identifier **pi** that is bound to the real number 3.14159.

---

[2] The top-level environment will always be at the bottom of environment diagrams, which grow upward as new value bindings are made. The term "top-level" is thus unfortunate, but we hope the reader will find the convention of adding new bindings on top of old ones intuitively appealing.

An Assignment-Like Statement

Val-declaration

It is possible to add an identifier to the current environment and bind it to a value. To do so we use a "statement" called a *val-declaration*, whose simplest form is

val <identifier> = <value>

That is, we use the keyword **val**, the identifier for which we wish to create a value binding, an equal sign, and an expression that gives the value we wish to associate with that identifier.[3]

◇ **Example 3.3.** Here is an example of how the identifier **pi** shown in Fig. 3.1 might have been added to the environment.

```
val pi = 3.14159;
val pi = 3.14159 : real
```

Notice that in response to the val-declaration we typed, ML responds with the value of **pi** rather than with the value of **it**, as was the case in all previous examples.

- In general, responses to val-declarations tell us the identifiers that have been bound to values and what those values are.

We might next define an identifier **radius** as:

```
val radius = 4.0;
val radius = 4.0 : real
```

Now we have some variables, namely **pi** and **radius**, that we can use along with constants to form expressions. For instance, we can write an expression that is the familiar formula for the area of a circle:

```
pi * radius * radius;
val it = 50.26544 : real
```

Similarly, we could introduce another identifier, say **area**, and use a val-declaration to give it a value.

```
val area = pi * radius * radius;
val area = 50.26544 : real
```

Note that in the above example, the expression supplying the value itself involves variables. In previous examples the "expression" was a single constant. □

- Remember to use the keyword **val** to cause a value binding to occur.

---

[3] The val-declaration is actually considerably more general, and in place of a single identifier we can have arbitrary "patterns." The matter is discussed in Chapters 7 and 19.

- It is tempting to think of the equal-sign in a val-declaration as equivalent to := in Pascal or = in C. However, these assignment operators from other languages cause side-effects, namely the change in the value stored in the place named on the left of the assignment operator. In ML, the val-declaration causes a *new* entry in the environment to be created, associating what is to the left of the equal sign with the value to the right of the equal-sign.

A View of ML Programming

We now have a rudimentary view of what ML programs look like. They are sequences of definitions, such as the val-declaration that associates values with identifiers (which are loosely the same as "program variables"). So far, we don't have any really interesting assignments to make; we can only bind values of a basic type (e.g., real or string) to identifiers, and we can ask for the value of an expression involving these identifiers and constants. In Chapter 5 and following, we shall see how to give identifiers values that are functions and how to apply functions to values in order to compute new values. When these functions are recursive, we shall find ourselves programming in a mode that gives us all the power of programs in other programming languages, yet has a distinctive flavor of its own.

It is natural to think of a val-declaration as an assignment, and often we shall not go wrong if we do so. However, there is a subtle but important difference in the way ML views what happens in response to a val-declaration. The next example illustrates some of that difference.

◇ **Example 3.4.** Suppose that after issuing the val-declarations of Example 3.3 we "redefine" radius to be equal to 5.0 by:

```
val radius = 5.0;
```
val radius = 5.0 : real

We might imagine that the entry in the environment for radius has had its value changed from 4.0 to 5.0. However, the proper ML view is suggested in Fig. 3.2. Below the top entry is the environment that existed before radius was "assigned" 5.0. We do not show all the identifiers that ML defines for us (e.g., +), but we concentrate on those we have defined: pi, radius, and area.

The topmost entry in Fig. 3.2 is an addition to the environment that results from the new val-declaration. We have shown in the current environment two entries that are named by the identifier radius, but only the most recent (upper) one is visible. The situation is akin to what happens in a conventional language like Pascal or C, when one procedure P that has a declaration of a variable like radius calls another procedure Q that also has a declaration of radius. While Q is executing, its local definition of radius "intercepts" any references to that variable, and it is not possible to access P's variable named radius.

The difference is that in Pascal, when Q returns, Q's variable named

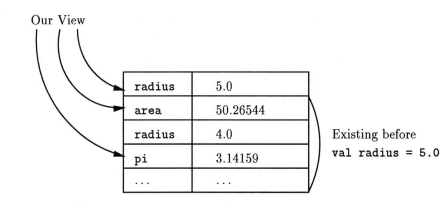

Fig. 3.2. The environment after redefining `radius`.

`radius` disappears, and P's variable with that name becomes accessible again. In Fig. 3.2, it is not possible to make the upper box named `radius` go away, although there are other situations, for example those involving function calls, where ML environments behave more like the model of procedure calls in conventional languages that we just described. □

- Note that when creating an entry with an old name, as we did in Example 3.4, there is no restriction that the new value be of the same type as the old value. We could just as well have defined `radius` to be an integer in Example 3.4, for instance,

      val radius = 5;

  However, we then could not have used this variable `radius` in expressions like `pi * radius * radius` because of the type mismatch.

Exercises

3.1: Tell whether each of the following character strings is (i) an alphanumeric identifier suitable for ordinary values, (ii) a symbolic identifier, (iii) an identifier that must represent a type as a value, or (iv) not an identifier of ML.

a)* `The7Dwarves`
b) `7Dwarves`
c)* `SevenDwarves,The`
d) `'SnowWhite'`
e)* `a<=b`
f) `hurrah!`
g)* `#1`
h) `'123`

3.2: Show the effect on the environment of making the following sequence of val-declarations. Which variables are now accessible?

```
val a = 3;
val b = 98.6;
val a = "three";
val c = a^chr(floor(b));
```

4 Tuples and Lists

So far we have seen only four types that ML values may have: integer, real, string, and Boolean. Technically, unit is a fifth type whose only value is (). Most languages start with a similar collection of types and build more complex types with a set of operators or notations that allow us to define new types from simpler types.

For example, Pascal has, among other type constructors,

1. The `record...end` notation to build record types, whose fields may be of any type,

2. The ^ operator to build a type whose values are pointers to values of some simpler type, and

3. The array constructor that defines an array type from a type for elements and an index type.

ML also has a number of ways to define new types, including datatype constructions discussed in Chapter 12 that go beyond what we find in C, Pascal, or most other languages. However, the simplest and possibly most important ways of constructing types in ML are notations for forming tuples, which are similar to record types in Pascal or C, and for forming lists of elements of a given type. In this chapter we shall learn these notations and also cover the most important operations associated with these types.

Tuples

A *tuple* is formed by taking a list of two or more expressions of any types, separating them by commas, and surrounding them by round parentheses. Thus, a tuple looks something like a record, but the fields are named by their position in the tuple rather than by declared field names.

◇ **Example 4.1.** In the following val-declaration we assign to variable **t** a tuple whose first component is the integer 4, whose second component is the real 5.0, and whose third component is the string **"six"**.

```
val t = (4, 5.0, "six");
val t = (4, 5.0, "six") : int * real * string
```

26

Let's try to understand the ML response. It repeats the fact that the value of t is the one we just gave it, which should be no surprise. However, it uses terminology we have not seen before as it describes the type of t. Recall from Chapter 2 that the type int * real * string is a product type. Its values are tuples that have three components. The first component is an integer, the second is a real, and the third component is a string. The operator * has a different meaning when applied to types than it does when applied to integer or real values. Here * has nothing to do with multiplication, but indicates tuple formation. □

- In general, a product type is formed from two or more types $T_1, T_2, \ldots, T_k$ by putting *'s between them, as $T_1 * T_2 * \cdots * T_k$. Example 4.1 showed a case where $k = 3$, T_1 is int, T_2 is real, and T_3 is string. Values of this type are tuples with k components, the first of which is of type T_1, the second of type T_2, and so on.

◇ **Example 4.2.** Here are some further examples of tuples and their types.

1. (1,2,3,4) is of type int * int * int * int.

2. (1,(2,3.0)) is of type int * (int * real).

3. (1) is of type int. Strictly speaking, it is not a tuple, just a parenthesized integer.

In (2) the tuple has two components, the first of which is an integer. The second component is itself a tuple with two components: an integer and a real. This grouping is reflected in the type. Also observe that the * operator applied to types is not an associative operator; int * (int * real) is not the same type as (int * int) * real. The latter type describes tuples of two components, the first of which is a pair of integers and the second of which is a single real. For example, ((1,2),3.0) is a value of type (int * int) * real. Neither is the same as the type int * int * real, which describes "flat" tuples like (1,2,3.0). □

Accessing Tuples

Given a tuple or a variable whose value is a tuple, we can get any particular component, say the ith, by applying the function #i.

◇ **Example 4.3.** In Example 4.1 identifier t was bound to the tuple value

```
(4, 5.0, "six")
```

Now we can obtain its components. For example:

```
#1(t);
```
val it = 4 : int

```
#3(t);
```
val it = "six" : string

It is an error to apply a function like **#4** that designates a component number higher than the number of components the tuple has. □

Tuples can be likened to records whose field names are the numbers $1, 2, \ldots$. In truth, tuples as we have defined them are a special, simplified case of a more general record-structure construct that does allow the programmer to specify names for fields. However, the tuple is adequate and quite convenient for most purposes. We defer the more general case of record structures to Chapter 18.

Lists

ML provides a simple notation for lists whose elements are of a single type. We take a list of elements, separate them by commas, and surround them with square brackets.

◇ **Example 4.4.** The list of three integers 1, 2, 3 is represented in ML as `[1,2,3]`. The response of ML to an expression that is this constant value is

```
[1,2,3];
```
val it = [1,2,3] : int list

The response to our list expression is informative. In addition to the usual repetition of the value in the expression, it assigns the list the type **int list**, which is ML's way of saying "list of integers."

- In general, "**T list**" is ML's way of saying "a list of elements each of which is of type **T**."

In our second example, the list has a single element that is of type string.

```
["a"];
```
val it = ["a"] : string list

The type attributed to the list expression is **string list**, or "list of strings." The fact that there is only one string in the list is irrelevant. The square brackets differentiate the expression **"a"**, which is of type **string**, from the expression **["a"]**, which is a list of strings that happens to have only one string on the list.

Finally, here is an example where we erroneously try to mix the types of elements.

```
["a",3,4];
```
Error: operator and operand don't agree (tycon mismatch)
    *operator domain: string * string list*
    *operand: string * int list*
    in expression
        "a" :: 3 :: 4 :: nil

We shall explain the error message after we have learned some of the notation of lists. Roughly, when looking at the square bracket and the first element "a", ML decided it had a list of strings. When the remainder of the list, ...3,4] was identified correctly as an integer list, ML couldn't put the first element together with the rest of the list, because all elements of a list must be of the same type. □

List Notation and Operators

Empty list

Head and tail

The *empty list*, or list of no elements, is represented in ML by either the name nil or by a pair of brackets, []. Any list besides the empty list is composed of a *head*, which is the first element, and a *tail*, which is the list of all elements but the first, in the same order.

◇ **Example 4.5.** If L is the list [2,3,4], then the head of L is 2, and the tail of L is the list [3,4]. If M is the list [5], then the head of M is 5, and the tail of M is the empty list, or nil. □

- Remember that the types of the head and tail are different. If the type of the head is T, then the type of the tail is "list of T," or T list in ML.

hd and tl

We can get the head or tail of a list by applying the function hd or tl to the list, respectively. The following restates Example 4.5 in a sequence of ML expressions.

◇ **Example 4.6.** Suppose we define lists L and M by the val-declarations

```
val L = [2,3,4];
val L = [2,3,4] : int list
```

```
val M = [5];
val M = [5] : int list
```

Now we can get the head and tail of each of these lists as follows.

```
hd(L);
val it = 2 : int
```

```
tl(L);
val it = [3,4] : int list
```

```
hd(M);
val it = 5 : int
```

```
tl(M);
val it = [] : int list
```

In the last of these expressions, ML describes the type of nil as int list. It is possible for nil to be of any list type. In this case, since it is the tail of an integer list, it is appropriate to assign it this type. □

While **hd** and **tl** take apart lists, there are also two operators that construct lists.

Cons

1. The *cons* operator, represented by a pair of colons (::), takes an element (the head) and a list of elements of the same type as the head, and produces a single list whose first element is the head and whose remaining elements are the elements of the tail. Thus

   ```
   2::[3,4];
   ```
   val it = [2,3,4] : int list

   ```
   2.0::nil;
   ```
   val it = [2.0] : real list

Concatenation

2. The *concatenation* operator for lists **@** takes two lists whose elements are the same type and produces one list consisting of the elements of the first list followed by the elements of the second. Thus

   ```
   [1,2]@[3,4];
   ```
   val it = [1,2,3,4] : int list

There are several common confusions regarding these operators that we should avoid.

- Remember that the first argument of the :: operator is an element of some type **T**, while the second argument is of type **T list**. Both arguments of **@** must be of some type **T list**.

- Do not interchange the ^ operator, which is concatenation of strings, with the **@** operator, which is concatenation of lists.

The precedence of the :: and **@** operators is below that of the additive operators such as +, but above that of the comparison operators like <. Most unusual is that these operators are *right-associative*, meaning that they group from the right instead of the left as do most operators we have seen.

◇ **Example 4.7.** What is especially important about right-associativity of these operators is the interpretation of a cascade of cons operators, like

```
1::2::3::nil
```

This expression is grouped from the right, as 1::(2::(3::nil)). Expression 3::nil represents the list with head 3 and an empty tail, that is, [3]. Next, 2::[3] is the list whose head is 2 and whose tail is the list whose only element is 3; this list is [2,3]. Similarly, the entire expression denotes the list [1,2,3].

Notice that when we have a sequence of cons operators, only the last operand must be a list, such as **nil** in the example above. The other operands must be elements. It would not make sense to group an expression like

```
1::2::3::nil
```

from the left, as `((1::2)::3)::nil`, because `1::2` is a type mismatch. That is, when the cons operator sees the left operand `1`, it expects that the type of the tail will be `int list`. Since the type of `2` is `int`, not `int list`, it is not possible to apply `::` to this pair of operands. □

◇ **Example 4.8.** Let us reprise Example 4.4 and consider the meaning of the error message that we saw there. We repeat the relevant part of Example 4.4 in Fig. 4.1.

```
["a",3,4];
```
Error: operator and operand don't agree (tycon mismatch)
       *operator domain: string * string list*
       *operand: string * int list*
   in expression
       "a" :: 3 :: 4 :: nil

Fig. 4.1. Error message for Example 4.8.

First of all, the operator the message talks about is the cons operator `::`. When ML sees the first element of the list, which is `"a"`, it concludes that it must be seeing a list of strings — something of type `string list`. However, when the tail `[3,4]` is examined, ML correctly identifies it as an integer list or `int list`. Remember that ML regards each operator as applying to a single argument, in this case a pair consisting of the head and tail of the list. Thus, the second line of the error message says that it expects the `::` operator to be applied to a pair consisting of a string and a list of strings, the head and the tail, respectively. But the third line says that it actually found a pair consisting of a string, `"a"`, and an integer list, `[3,4]`. The cons operator cannot be applied to this mismatched pair, and so ML complains.

The last line of the error message indicates the erroneous expression. Observe that the list has been written in the form using cons operators and `nil`, rather than as a bracketed list. □

Converting Between Strings and Lists

Explode and implode

In ML strings and lists are different types. However, there is a great similarity between a string and a list of characters, and it is possible to convert between the two representations using the built-in functions **explode** and **implode**. The first of these takes a string and converts it to the list of strings in which each element is a single character. These elements are the characters of the given string, in order.

◇ **Example 4.9.** Here are two examples of the use of `explode`.

```
explode("abcd");
```
val it = ["a","b","c","d"] : string list

```
explode("");
```
val it = [] : string list

Notice in the second example that `""` is the empty string, and when exploded it yields an empty list. □

The function `implode` takes a list whose elements are strings and concatenates all the elements together in order, to form a single string.

◇ **Example 4.10.** Here are some examples of imploding lists.

```
implode(["a","b","c","d"]);
```
val it = "abcd" : string

```
implode(["ab","cd"]);
```
val it = "abcd" : string

```
implode(nil)
```
val it = "" : string

In the second example we see that `implode` does not require the elements of the list to be strings of length 1. The third example points out that we can implode the empty list and get the empty string. □

Exercises

4.1: What are the values of the following expressions?

a)* `#2(3,4,5)`
b) `hd([3,4,5])`
c)* `tl([3,4,5])`
d) `explode("foo")`
e)* `implode(["foo","bar"])`
f) `"c"::["a","t"]`
g)* `["c","o"]@["b","o","1"]`

4.2: What is wrong with each of the following expressions? If possible, suggest an appropriate correction.

a)* `#4(3,4,5)`
b) `hd([])`
! c)* `#1(1)`
d) `explode(["bar"])`
e)* `implode("a","b")`

f)   ["r"]::["a","t"]
g)* 1@2

4.3: Give the types of the following expressions.

a)* (1.5,("3",[4,5]))
b)   [[1,2],nil,[3]]
c)* [(2,3.5), (4,5.5), (6,7.5)]
d)   (["a","b"],[nil,[1,2,3]])

! **4.4***: Are (1,2) and (1,2,3) the same type? Are [1,2] and [1,2,3] the same type?

4.5: Give examples of values for each of the following types.

a)* int list list list
b)   (int * string) list
c)* (string list * (int * (real * string)) * int)
d)   (((int * int) * (string list) * real) * (real * string))

◇◇◇ 5 It's Easy; It's "fun"

Now we know everything there is to know about ML, except how to program! In this and the next several chapters we shall learn about defining and using functions. All "real" programming in ML is conducted by the definition of functions and the application of these functions to arguments. As we shall see, ML uses functions in places where more traditional languages use iteration (e.g., while-loops).

The simplest form of function declaration is

fun <identifier>(<parameter list>) = <expression>;

That is, the keyword **fun** is followed by the name of the function, a list of the parameters for that function, an equal-sign, and an expression involving the parameters. This expression becomes the value of the function when we give it arguments to correspond to its parameters.

Parameters

Arguments

- In this book we call the variables to which a function is applied in its definition the *parameters*, while the expressions to which the function is applied are *arguments*. In other works, one sometimes sees the terms "formal parameters" and "actual parameters" where we use "parameters" and "arguments."

◇ **Example 5.1.** Let us define a function that converts a lowercase letter to the corresponding uppercase letter. To do so, we need to know that the ASCII code for an uppercase letter is always 32 less than that of the lowercase version. Thus we may write the following function that implements the formula in which

1. A character is converted to an integer,
2. 32 is subtracted, and
3. The result is converted back to a character.

```
fun upper(c) = chr(ord(c)-32);
val upper = fn : string → string
```

For example, we can use this function to convert "a" to "A" as:

```
upper("a");
val it = "A" : string
```

There are a number of observations we should make about the function **upper**. First, it has one parameter **c**. Its value is computed by the expression **chr(ord(c)-32)**. We use the function **upper** as we would in most other languages; we apply it to the desired argument, **"a"** in the above example. ML responds to expression `upper("a")` as it would to any expression, by assigning its value to `it` and telling the value. □

Notice from Example 5.1 how ML represents function types. The response to the definition of function `upper` was

```
val upper = fn : string -> string
```

In general, when a function is defined, ML does not respond with the value of that function, which is hard to express other than by repeating the definition of the function. Rather, it responds with the type of the function. The specification of the function type starts with the keyword `fn` and a colon. Then comes

Domain

the type of the parameter(s), called the *domain type* for the function. This type is `string` in Example 5.1. ML regards each function as having one parameter, but the type of this parameter can be a product type. So in practice there can be any number of parameters for a function.

After the parameter type comes the symbol `->` and the type of the result

Range

of the function, that is, the *range type* for the function. In Example 5.1 the range type is also `string`, but it is common for the domain and range types to differ. ML views each function as returning a single value, but since this value may be a tuple, in effect a function can return several items.

- The response in Example 5.1 uses the keyword `fn`, which should not be confused with `fun`, even though both are short for "function." We use `fun` to introduce a declaration of a particular identifier to be a certain function, while `fn` is used in ML to introduce a value that has a function type.

- The operator `->` is another way to construct types, just like `*` and the word `list`. If T_1 and T_2 are types, then $T_1 \to T_2$ is the type of functions with domain type T_1 and range type T_2, that is, functions which take an argument of type T_1 and return a result of type T_2.

- Operator `->` is right-associative, so $T_1 \to T_2 \to T_3$ is interpreted as

$$T_1 \to (T_2 \to T_3)$$

and is the type of a function whose parameter is of type T_1 and whose result is itself a function; that function has domain type T_2 and range type T_3. The notion of a function producing a function as a value may seem strange, but it is an integral part of ML programming that we shall examine starting in Chapter 11.

Overloading

◇ **Example 5.2.** Sometimes, when we define a function we must give ML some clues as to what types were intended for the arguments. The reason is that some operators, like the arithmetic or comparison operators, are *overloaded*, which means they apply to values of several types. ML cannot proceed unless it can figure out the types of all variables and operators. Our next example is a function that squares reals.

```
fun square(x:real) = x*x;
```
val square = fn : real → real

The function **square** has one parameter, **x**. By following parameter **x** with a colon and the type **real**, we declare to ML that the parameter of function **square** is of type **real**. Recall that the colon symbol is also used in ML responses to connect values with their types.

It is necessary to indicate the type of **x** somewhere. Otherwise, ML cannot disambiguate the * operator, which could represent real multiplication or integer multiplication. We could have attached the :**real** to any or all of the three occurrences of **x** in the definition of Example 5.2. For example

```
fun square(x) = (x:real)*x
```

is a possibility. However, we must adhere to certain conditions.

- We must be careful to parenthesize the colon — for example, **(x:real)** — because the colon has lower precedence than the arithmetic operators.

- In general, ML is parsimonious in its requirement that types be declared, unlike Pascal or C, which require that every variable be declared. ML tries its best to figure out types and only complains when it cannot. □

◇ **Example 5.3.** Some care must be exercised in how we specify the types of variables in a function definition. Here are two examples of surprising errors that can occur, along with the diagnostics.

```
fun square(x) = x:real*x;
```
Error: unbound type constructor: x

```
fun square(x) = x*x;
```
Error: overloaded variable "" cannot be resolved*

In the first case, because * has higher precedence than :, ML has tried to "multiply" **real** by **x**. That is not as strange as it seems. ML knows **real** is a type, and * applied to types forms a product type. That is, ML is trying to form a type consisting of pairs whose first component is of type **real** and whose second component is of type **x**. But it doesn't know about any type named **x**, so it complains. The solution is to parenthesize the **x:real** so ML will group its operators as we intend.

In the second example of an error, we have simply failed to declare the type of **x** anywhere. Since * is overloaded, ML doesn't know which interpretation to put on this *, so it complains. Note that the "variable" referred to in the second error message is the symbolic identifier *. □

Function Application

As an example of the use of the square function, suppose we have defined the variables **pi** and **radius** to have values 3.14159 and 4.0, as in Example 3.3. Then we can write

```
pi*square(radius);
```
val it = 50.26544 : real

In this example, function application looks just like it does in Pascal or most languages; a function is applied to a list of arguments, with parentheses around the argument list. However, formally, the ML syntax for function application is simply a pair of expressions standing next to one another, with no intervening punctuation. That is, $F\ E$ requires the expression F to be evaluated and interpreted as a function. Then, expression E is evaluated and function F is applied to the value of E.

◇ **Example 5.4.** We could have computed the area of a circle by

```
pi * square radius;
```
val it = 50.26544 : real

Function application has higher precedence than any of the arithmetic operators, so the above expression first applies function **square** to argument **radius**, and the result is multiplied by **pi**. □

In principle, it doesn't matter whether or not we put parentheses around the argument; that is, $F\ E$ and $F(E)$ are treated the same by ML. However, we advise using the parentheses. Not only do parentheses make the syntax of function application look more familiar, but sometimes they prevent an error such as failure to put parentheses around an operand and its type that are connected by the : symbol. There is, however, one important reason why we might not want the parentheses around arguments. This concept, called "Currying," is discussed in Chapter 21.

Functions With More Than One Parameter

We can define a function that has any number of parameters. As mentioned, it is permitted to put parentheses around the list of arguments, both in the function definition and use. The effect is to combine the list of arguments into a tuple, which formally is a single argument but which we may treat as if there were several arguments.

```
(1)    fun max3(a:int,b,c) = (* maximum of three integers *)
(2)        if a>b then
(3)            if a>c then a
(4)            else c
(5)        else
(6)            if b>c then b
(7)            else c;
```
*val max3 = fn : int * int * int → int*

Fig. 5.1. Function computing the maximum of its three arguments.

◊ **Example 5.5.** Figure 5.1 is another example of a function; it produces the largest of three integers. It begins by comparing parameters **a** and **b** in line (2). If **a** is larger, it returns as a result the larger of **a** and **c** at lines (3) and (4). If **b** is larger, then in lines (6) and (7) it returns the larger of **b** and **c**. □

- Notice that in Fig. 5.1 ML deduces that **b** and **c** are integers, even though only **a** was declared. One way to make this deduction is to use the fact that the **if** ⋯ **then** ⋯ **else** operator must have the same type in both branches. We shall discuss type deduction at the end of this chapter.

- Also notice that the type of **max3** is a function that takes a triple of integers as its argument and produces an integer. That type is shown in the response as **int * int * int -> int**.

- In type expressions ***** takes precedence over **->**. Thus in the type expression above, the domain type is **int * int * int**, and the range type is **int**.

- One advantage of the ML view that functions have only one parameter is that a variable whose value is of the appropriate product type can be defined and used as the argument of a multiparameter function. For example,

```
val t = (1,2,3);
max3(t);
```

is correct ML and produces the value 3.

Comments

Now that we can write programs of more than one line, we shall have reason to comment our code. The proper way to do so is shown in line (1) of Fig. 5.1. The pair of characters (***** introduce a comment, which continues, even across lines, until the matching sequence of two characters *****) is encountered. This convention is similar to most implementations of Pascal, but in ML it is possible to nest pairs of (*****...*****), just like parentheses are nested.

Recursive Functions

It is possible, and indeed frequently necessary, for functions to be recursive, that is, defined in terms of themselves, either directly or indirectly. However, we must be careful that when a recursive function calls itself, it does so with an argument that is, in some sense, smaller than its own argument. For example, if the argument is an integer i, we could safely call the function with argument $i - 1$. If the argument is a list L, we could call the function on the tail of the list. Often, a recursive function consists of

Basis

1. A *basis*, where for sufficiently small arguments we compute the result without making any recursive call, and

Inductive step

2. An *inductive step*, where for arguments not handled by the basis, we call the function recursively, one or more times, with smaller arguments.

◇ **Example 5.6.** Let us write a function reverse(L) that produces the reverse of the list L.[1] For example, reverse([1,2,3]) produces the list [3,2,1].

List reversal

BASIS. The basis is the empty list; the reverse of the empty list is the empty list.

INDUCTION. For the inductive step, suppose L has at least one element. Let the first or head element of L be h, and let the tail or remaining elements of L be the list T. Then we can construct the reverse of list L by reversing T and following it by the element h.

For instance, if L is [1,2,3], then $h = 1$, T is [2,3], the reverse of T is [3,2], and the reverse of T concatenated with the list containing only h is [3,2]@[1], or [3,2,1].

```
(1)        fun reverse(L) =
(2)                if L = nil then nil
(3)                else reverse(tl(L)) @ [hd(L)];
           val reverse = fn : 'a list → 'a list
```

Fig. 5.2. A recursive function to reverse a list.

In Fig. 5.2 we see the ML definition of **reverse** that follows the basis and inductive step described above. Lines (2) and (3) are the expression that forms the body of the function definition. In line (2) we handle the basis case: the reverse of **nil** is **nil**. Line (3) covers the inductive step, and we should appreciate how succinctly and naturally it does so. The subexpression **reverse(tl(L))** takes the tail of the given list and reverses it, recursively. We then concatenate this new list with the head element, which is obtained by subexpression **hd(L)**.

- In order to concatenate the reversed tail with the head element, we must place square brackets around the head element, as [hd(L)]. Remember that the concatenation operator @ requires two lists as its arguments. If we were to omit the square brackets, we would be concatenating a list and an element, leading to a type mismatch.

---

[1] ML actually has a built-in function **rev** that performs this operation.

The response to the definition of **reverse** in Fig. 5.2 illustrates an interesting point. Unlike our previous examples of functions, ML cannot tell exactly what the type of argument and result is. It can only deduce that these types are both lists of elements of the same type. It calls the element type 'a, and it calls the argument and result types 'a list.[2] The type of **reverse** is then a function from 'a lists to 'a lists. □

Incidentally, the difference between Example 5.6 and previous examples of functions that work on parameters of only one type, is that some functions use an overloaded operator such as + or < that require us to tell ML what type its operands have. In Example 5.6, there is no overloaded operator, and thus, we were able to avoid specifying the types of elements of the list. We shall discuss in Chapter 10 more about when an operator needs to know the type of its operands.

Function Execution

Call-by-value

Whenever a function is called, its arguments are evaluated, and an addition to the environment is created that associates the resulting values with the parameters of the function. This style of argument passing is known as *call-by-value*. It is the same as the manner by which arguments are passed to functions and procedures in C, and the manner in which non-var parameters are handled in Pascal.

When the function is executed, we place on top of the old environment entries that bind the parameters of the function to their associated values. If the function is recursive, new additions are built on top of the old ones for each recursive call. Each addition binds the parameters of the function to the argument values. These bindings intercept any reference to the parameters, thus distinguishing themselves from the entries with the same identifiers in levels below. When a function completes and returns its value, its addition to the environment goes away, but the returned value is available for use in the expression being evaluated.

◇ **Example 5.7.** Suppose we are in the top-level environment that has the definition of the function **reverse** from Example 5.6, along with all the usual identifiers (not shown) of the top-level environment. If we call

```
reverse([1,2,3])
```

then we add to the environment an entry for L and its value. We show this first step above the line in Fig. 5.3.

With this value as argument, the condition of line (2) in Fig. 5.2 is false, that is, L is not **nil**. Thus, we must evaluate the expression on line (3), which

---

[2] Recall that identifiers beginning with a quote are variables whose values are types. Actually, the type variable used by ML in this example is ''a (i.e., two quotes before the a). There is a subtle distinction between 'a and ''a, which we shall discuss in Chapter 10. Before then, we shall use 'a, 'b and so on as type variables.

L	[1,2,3]	added in call to reverse([1,2,3])
reverse	definition of reverse	top level environment

Fig. 5.3. Environment after the initial call to reverse.

requires us to evaluate **reverse(tl(L))** or **reverse([2,3])**. Thus we set up another call to **reverse**, adding to the environment a new binding for L that associates L with the value **[2,3]**.

In a similar manner, the new call to **reverse** causes us to make another call, with L bound to **[3]**, and an addition to the environment is set up with this binding. Again a recursive call to **reverse** is necessary, and in the fourth call L is bound to **nil**. The additions to the environment for all four calls are stacked one above the other as suggested in Fig. 5.4. At this point, the identifier L refers to the top binding, with value **nil**.

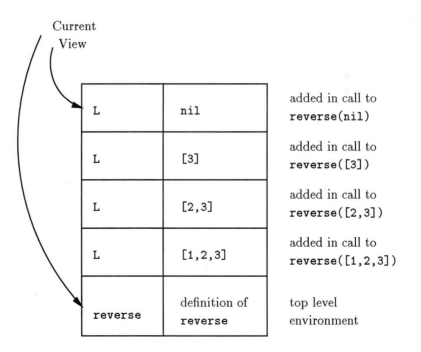

Fig. 5.4. Additions to the environment when four calls to reverse are made.

Now when we evaluate the body of **reverse**, the test of line (2) is satisfied, because L has the value **nil**. The value **nil** is returned and used in place of **reverse(tl(L))** by the call below it — that is, by **reverse([3])** — to produce its own answer on line (3). After the return, the top entry for L in Fig. 5.4 disappears, exposing the appropriate value of L, namely **[3]**. Since **hd([3])** is 3, the result produced by **reverse([3])** is the empty list concatenated with **[3]**, or just **[3]**.

Now, the addition to the environment for **reverse([3])** goes away, and its result is used by the call below it: **reverse([2,3])**. That, in turn, produces **[3,2]** as a result and its addition to the environment goes away, leaving the environment that was originally shown in Fig. 5.3. However, the corresponding call, **reverse([1,2,3])**, now has the value **[3,2]**, returned from above, to use in place of **reverse(tl(L))** in line (3). Thus the original call to **reverse** is able to produce its value, **[3,2,1]**. At this point, all bindings for L have disappeared, leaving only the top-level environment. $\square$

A Nonlinear Recursion

The form of recursion illustrated in Examples 5.5 and 5.6 is relatively simple. Each call either results in one recursive call with a smaller argument, or we reach the basis case and there is no need for a recursion. Now we shall examine a function where the recursion involves more than one recursive call.

n choose m

The function *combinations of* m *things out of* n or "n choose m," usually written $\binom{n}{m}$, is the number of ways we can pick a set of m things out of n distinct things. For example, two aces out of the four aces in a card deck can be picked in six possible ways. That is, we can pick any of the four aces first and any of the three remaining aces second. That looks like 12 ways, but in fact we have picked each set in two different orders. For example, the aces of spades and hearts could be picked spade-then-heart or heart-then-spade.

Factorial

In general, $\binom{n}{m} = n!/((n-m)!m!)$, where $x!$ (x *factorial*) is the product of all the integers from 1 up to x. For instance,

$$\binom{4}{2} = 4!/(2!2!) = 4 \times 3 \times 2 \times 1/(2 \times 1 \times 2 \times 1) = 6$$

Intuitively $n!/(n-m)!$, which equals $n \times (n-1) \times \cdots \times (n-m+1)$, is the number of ways we can select among n things for the first choice, then among the $n-1$ remaining things for the second choice, and so on for m choices. We must divide this number by $m!$ because each set of m elements will have been selected in $m!$ different orders.

There is also a natural recursive way to define $\binom{n}{m}$. Here are the basis and induction rules.

BASIS. There are two parts to the basis. If $m = 0$, then the number of ways to pick 0 things out of n is 1 — don't pick anything. Thus, $\binom{n}{0} = 1$ for any n. Also, if $m = n$, then there is one way to pick all n things out of n — pick them all. Thus, $\binom{n}{n} = 1$ for all n.

INDUCTION. If $0 < m < n$, then $\binom{n}{m} = \binom{n-1}{m} + \binom{n-1}{m-1}$. The reason is that if we must select m things out of n, we can either:

1.   Reject the first thing and then pick m things out of the remaining $n - 1$ things, or

2.   Select the first thing and then pick $m - 1$ things out of the remaining $n - 1$.

Note that $\binom{n}{m}$ makes no sense if $m < 0$ or if $m > n$, so this basis and induction entirely define the function.

◇ **Example 5.8.** We can write a function `comb(n,m)` that computes $\binom{n}{m}$. The code appears in Fig. 5.5. Line (2) handles the basis case, and line (3) implements the inductive step. Note that the program will not behave well if the assumption about n and m in the comment of line (1) is violated. We really should test for violations, and there is an important mechanism, the "exception," that allows us to do so and still adhere to the principle that functions return a value of one particular type invariably. We discuss exceptions in Chapters 8 and 20. □

```
(1)        fun comb(n,m) = (* assumes 0 <= m <= n *)
(2)             if m=0 orelse m=n then 1
(3)             else comb(n-1,m) + comb(n-1,m-1);
       val comb = fn : int * int → int
```

Fig. 5.5. Function to compute n choose m.

The sequence of recursive calls initiated by a single use of function `comb` is rather complex. For example, in the expression

```
comb(4,2);
val it = 6 : int
```

the initial call first calls `comb(3,2)` and later calls `comb(3,1)`. However, before the latter call, `comb(3,2)` calls `comb(2,2)` and `comb(2,1)`, and so on. Figure 5.6 shows the structure of the calls as time progresses from left to right.

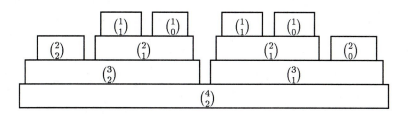

Fig. 5.6. Structure of recursive calls for the `comb` function.

Mutual Recursion

Occasionally, one needs to write two or more functions that are *mutually recursive*, meaning that each calls at least one other function in the group. Most languages, such as Pascal or C, put some obstacles in the way of writing such functions, but ML has a straightforward mechanism. We shall give an example of mutually recursive functions, first showing the problem that arises if we are not careful. Then, we shall show how ML lets us handle the problem.

◇ **Example 5.9.** Suppose we want to write a function that takes a list L as argument and produces a list consisting of alternate elements of L. There are two natural versions of this function. One, which we call `take(L)`, takes the first element of L and alternate elements after that (i.e., the first, third, fifth, and so on). The other, which we call `skip(L)`, skips the first element and takes alternate elements after that (i.e., the second, fourth, sixth, and so on). It is convenient to define these two functions in terms of each other.

BASIS. If L is empty, both functions return the empty list.

INDUCTION. If L is not empty, `take` returns the head element of L followed by the result of applying `skip` to the tail of L. On the other hand, `skip` returns the result of applying `take` to the tail of L.

Erroneous
mutual
recursion

Figure 5.7 shows a failed attempt to define the functions `take` and `skip`. At the third line of `take`, we assemble the result using the cons operator, taking as head the head of L and as tail the result of applying `skip` to the tail of L. The problem is that at the third line, the function `skip` is not defined, even though we intend to define `skip` immediately thereafter. Thus, ML responds with an error message. Defining `skip` first would cause a similar error because `take` is used in the third line of `skip`. □

```
fun take(L) =
        if L = nil then nil
        else hd(L)::skip(tl(L));
Error : unbound variable or constructor skip

fun skip(L) =
        if L = nil then nil
        else take(tl(L));
```

Fig. 5.7. Erroneous attempt to define mutually recursive functions.

We can get ML to wait until it has seen both functions `take` and `skip` before trying to interpret variables, by using the keyword **and** between the function definitions. The general form for defining n mutually recursive functions is

```
fun
     <definition of first function>
and
     <definition of second function>
and
     . . .
and
     <definition of nth function> ;
```

Fig. 5.8. Form of a mutually recursive function definition.

shown in Fig. 5.8. There we see the n definitions connected by **and**'s. There is one use of **fun** at the beginning and one use of the semicolon at the end.

- Do not confuse **and**, which is used to indicate mutual recursions, with **andalso**, which is the logical AND operator in ML.

- It is not necessary to use the **and** construct if there is no mutual recursion. If we define functions $f_1, f_2, \ldots, f_n$, and in the definition of f_i we only use functions that appear earlier on the list — that is, $f_1, \ldots, f_{i-1}$ — then there is no mutual recursion.

◇ **Example 5.10.** The correct definition of the functions **take** and **skip** from Example 5.9 are shown in Fig. 5.9. Notice that the response from ML does not come until after both functions have been seen. Both are identified as functions from lists to lists. The elements of the input and output lists of both functions must be of one type **'a**, but ML cannot identify the type.

```
fun
     take(L) =
          if L = nil then nil
          else hd(L)::skip(tl(L))
and
     skip(L) =
          if L = nil then nil
          else take(tl(L));
val take = fn : 'a list → 'a list
val skip = fn : 'a list → 'a list
```

Fig. 5.9. Correct definition of mutually recursive functions.

Here are two examples of the use of these functions.

```
take([1,2,3,4,5]);
val it = [1,3,5] : int list
```

```
skip(["a","b","c","d","e"]);
```
val it = ["b","d"] : string list

When we use the functions, ML can figure out the type of list elements from the argument. □

How ML Deduces Types

ML is quite good at discovering the types of variables, the types of function parameters, and the types of values returned by functions. The subject of how ML does so is quite complex, but there are a few observations we can make that will cover most of the ways types are discovered. Knowing what ML can do helps us know when we must declare a type and when we can skip type declarations.

1. The types of the operands and result of arithmetic operators must all agree. For example, in the expression `(a+b)*2.0`, we see that the right operand of the `*` is a real constant, so the left operand `(a+b)` must also be real. If the use of `+` produces a real, then both its operands are real. Thus, `a` and `b` are real. They will also have a real value any other place they are used, which can help make further type inferences.

2. When we apply an arithmetic comparison, we can be sure the operands are of the same type, although the result is a Boolean and therefore not necessarily of the same type as the operands. For example, in the expression `a<=10`, we can deduce that `a` is an integer.

3. In a conditional expression, the expression itself and the subexpressions following the **then** and **else** must be of the same type.

4. If a variable or expression used as an argument of the function is of a known type, then the corresponding parameter of the function must be of that type. Similarly, if the function parameter is of known type, then the variable or expression used as the corresponding argument must be of the same type.

5. If the expression defining the function is of a certain type, then the function returns a value of that type.

◇ **Example 5.11.** Consider the function `comb(n,m)` in Fig. 5.5, which we reproduce here for convenience.

```
(1)        fun comb(n,m) = (* assumes 0 <= m <= n *)
(2)            if m=0 orelse m=n then 1
(3)            else comb(n-1,m) + comb(n-1,m-1);
```
*val comb = fn : int * int → int*

In line (2), we see that in the basis case the result returned by the function is the integer 1. Thus, in all cases the function returns an integer. In line (3) we see that the expressions n-1 and m-1 are computed. Since one operand of each subtraction is the integer 1, the other operands, n in one case and m in the other, must also be integers. Thus, both arguments of the function are integers, or strictly speaking, the (one) argument of the function is of type int * int, that is, a pair of integers.

Another way we could have discovered that m and n are integers is to look at line (2). We see m compared with integer 0, so m must be an integer. We also see n compared with m, and since we already know m is an integer, we know the same about n □

References

The fundamental ideas behind the way ML discovers types by equating pairs of types known to be the same were described in R. Milner, "A theory of type polymorphism in programming," *J. Computer and System Sciences* **17**:3 (Dec., 1978), pp. 348–375.

The problem of discovering types in ML appears to require exponential time in the worst case. However, the worst case occurs essentially never, and the algorithm is quite fast in practice. The paper by P. C. Kanellakis, H. G. Mairson, and J. C. Mitchell, "Unification and ML type reconstruction" in *Computational Logic: Essays in Honor of Alan Robinson* (J.-L. Lassez and G. D. Plotkin, eds.), pp. 444–478, MIT Press, 1991 explains the complexity of the type-inference problem.

Exercises

5.1: Write function declarations to compute the following.

a)* The cube of a real number x.

b) The smallest of the three components of a tuple of type int * int * int.

c)* The third element of a list. The function need not behave properly if given an argument that is a list of length 2 or less.

d) The length of a list.[3]

e)* The third character of a character string. *Hint*: Use explode and your function from Exercise 5.1(c).

f) Cycle a list once. That is, given a list $[a_1, a_2, \ldots, a_n]$, produce the list $[a_2, \ldots, a_n, a_1]$.

! **5.2**: Write the following recursive functions.

---

[3] There is a function length in the ML top-level environment that performs this function; the exercise asks you to write the function as if it were not already available.

a)* The factorial function that takes an integer $n \geq 1$ and produces the product of all the integers from 1 up to n. Your function need not work correctly if the argument is less than 1.

b) Given an integer i and a list L, cycle L i times, where "cycle" is as defined in Exercise 5.1(f). That is, if $L = [a_1, a_2, \ldots, a_n]$, then the desired result is

$$[a_{i+1}, \ldots, a_n, a_1, \ldots, a_i]$$

c)* Duplicate each element of a list. That is, given the list $[a_1, a_2, \ldots, a_n]$, produce the list $[a_1, a_1, a_2, a_2, \ldots, a_n, a_n]$.

d) Compute x^i, where x is a real and i is a nonnegative integer. This function takes two parameters, x and i, and need not behave well if $i < 0$.

e)* Compute the largest element of list of reals. Your function need not behave well if the list is empty.

! 5.3*: In the following function definition

```
fun foo(a,b,c,d) =
        if a=b then c+1 else
            if a>b then c else b+d
```

it is possible to deduce that a, b, c, and d are all integers. Explain how ML makes these deductions.

5.4: Consider the factorial function **fact** described in Exercise 5.1(a); if you have not written this function, use the solution given at the end of the book. Describe the changes to the environment that occur as a result of a call to **fact(4)**.

! 5.5: Write functions to do the following.

a)* Round a real number to the nearest integer, returning a real.
b) Round a real number to the nearest tenth.

6 Patterns in Function Definitions

One of the great sources of power in ML is the definition of functions on the basis of the pattern of its parameters. In Chapter 5 the typical form of a function was "if the argument is `nil` then do one thing, else do another." Instead we can show all the patterns that the argument may have and describe what value **Pattern** to produce in each case. Each *pattern* is an expression with variables, and when the pattern matches the argument, these variables are given the values that match. The same variables can then be used in the expression that defines the value of the function.

◇ **Example 6.1.** A common pattern is `x::xs`. Since `::` represents cons, this pattern will match any list that is not empty. In the match, `x` will get the value of the head element and `xs` will get the value of the tail. For instance, if this pattern is matched to list L, whose value is `[1,2,3]`, then `x` gets the value 1, and `xs` gets the value `[2,3]`. We can now use `x` in place of the more complicated expression `hd(L)` and `xs` in place of `tl(L)`. □

- It is conventional to use a pair of identifiers like `x` for the head of a list and `xs` (read "exes") for the tail of the same list.

- But beware `a::as`. Since `as` is a keyword in ML, you will get a strange diagnostic.

- It is not permissible for a variable to appear twice in one pattern. For example, we might like to use the pattern `x::x::xs` to represent a list whose first two elements are the same, but it is illegal to do so. We have to use a pattern like `x::y::zs` and then test if $x = y$.

The general form for a function defined by patterns involves the symbol `|`, which lets us list alternative forms for the arguments of the function as

```
fun <identifier>(<first pattern>)   = <first expression>
 |  <identifier>(<second pattern>)  = <second expression>
 |      ...
 |  <identifier>(<last pattern>)    = <last expression>;
```

The identifiers must all be the same (they are each the name of the function), and the types of the values produced by the expressions on the right of the equal-signs must all be the same. Likewise, the types of the patterns themselves must be the same, but they can differ from the type of the values produced. As with functions in general, the parentheses around the patterns are optional.

49

- However, the juxtaposition of expressions representing application of a function to its arguments has higher precedence than any of the usual operators. Thus it is wise to put parentheses around patterns that are more complex than a single variable. Otherwise, we run the risk that only the first part of the pattern will be treated as the function argument and an error will result.

ML goes through the various patterns in the order that they appear until it finds one that matches its argument. The first match determines the value produced; other patterns are not considered. Thus, there can be overlap among the various patterns.

- It is legal to fail to cover all possible cases with the forms. However, you will get the diagnostic

    Warning: match not exhaustive

You should then be very sure that the function will be used only with arguments that match one of the patterns.

◇ **Example 6.2.** Let us reconsider the function **reverse** from Example 5.6. There are two patterns for the argument L. If L is empty it matches the pattern **nil**. If L is not empty, it will match the pattern **x::xs**. For instance, if the list has a single element, **x** becomes that element and **xs** gets the value **nil**. A nonempty list cannot match **nil**, and **x::xs** does not match the empty list, because there is no head element to give a value to **x**. (It is not possible to give **x**, the value **nil** because x is an element, not a list). Thus, the following definition works.

```
fun reverse(nil) = nil
|   reverse(x::xs) = reverse(xs) @ [x]
val reverse = fn : 'a list → 'a list
```

Compare this definition with the equivalent definition in Fig. 5.2.[1] Here, **x** plays the role of **hd(L)** and **xs** plays the role of **tl(L)**. The above function operates by first checking if its argument is **nil** and returning **nil** if so. If the argument is not **nil**, then we can match **x::xs** to the argument; **x** acquires the value of the head and **xs** acquires the value of the tail.

Figure 6.1 suggests the addition to the environment that occurs when **reverse(L)** is called, where L has the value **[1,2,3]**. Notice at the last call, to **reverse(nil)**, there are no bindings for **x** or **xs** because the pattern **nil** matches the argument, and we never even try to match the second pattern. All these additions to the top-level environment go away when the initial call to **reverse** completes. □

---

[1] There is actually a subtle difference between the two functions we called **reverse**, concerning the types of the elements that may form the lists being reversed. We shall address this distinction in Chapter 10.

		added in call to `reverse(nil)`
xs	nil	added in call to `reverse([3])`
x	3	
xs	[3]	added in call to `reverse([2,3])`
x	2	
xs	[2,3]	added in call to `reverse([1,2,3])`
x	1	
L	[1,2,3]	top-level environment
...	...	

Fig. 6.1. Binding values to the identifiers of a pattern.

Polynomial

◇ **Example 6.3.** Let us use lists of reals to represent polynomials by their coefficients, lowest degree first. For instance, the polynomial $x^3 + 4x - 5$ is represented by the list [~5.0, 4.0, 0.0, 1.0]. In general, the polynomial $\sum_{i=0}^{n} a_i x^i$ is represented by the list of $n + 1$ elements $[a_0, a_1, \ldots, a_n]$. Conventionally, we shall take the empty list to represent the polynomial 0, but this polynomial also has other representations such as [0.0] and [0.0, 0.0].

An important observation is that if L is a list representing polynomial P, and L is of the form `a::M` (that is, L has head a and tail M), and the tail represents polynomial Q, then $P = a+Qx$. That is, multiplication by x in effect shifts the elements of the corresponding list one position right. For instance, if

$$P = x^3 + 4x - 5$$

then we observed that the representing list is [~5.0, 4.0, 0.0, 1.0]. Thus, `a` is ~5.0 and `M` is [4.0, 0.0, 1.0]. `M` represents the polynomial $Q = x^2 + 4$. Note that $P = a + Qx$, that is, $P = -5 + (x^2 + 4)x$.

In Fig. 6.2 we see three functions that perform common operations on polynomials in this representation. The first, `padd(P,Q)`, adds polynomials P and Q. We recursively define the sum of two lists P and Q that represent polynomials by:

Polynomial addition

BASIS. If either P or Q is the empty list, then the sum is the other. Note that if both are empty, the result is the polynomial 0 represented by the empty list.

INDUCTION. For the induction, assume that neither list is empty. Suppose P has head p and a tail representing polynomial R, while Q has head q and a tail representing polynomial S. Then the sum $P + Q$ is the list with head element $p+q$ and tail equal to the result of applying `padd` to the two tails. The correctness of this rule is seen as follows. If $P = p + Rx$ and $Q = q + Sx$, then

$$P + Q = (p + q) + (R + S)x$$

In line (1) of Fig. 6.2 we see one part of the basis. Whenever the second polynomial is the empty list, the result is the first polynomial. Line (2) handles the other part of the basis. If the first polynomial is empty, the result is the second.

If neither of the first two patterns match the arguments, then it must be that both polynomials are nonempty lists. Thus, in line (3) the pattern `p::ps` is sure to match the first argument, and `q::qs` will surely match the second argument. Notice we have attached type `real` to the variable `p` of this pattern. That is enough for ML to figure out the type of all variables and to disambiguate the use of `+` in line (3).

As a result of the match, `p` acquires the value of the first element of the first polynomial, and `q` acquires the value of the first element of the second polynomial. Their sum becomes the first element of the result, and `padd` is applied to the tails to get the tail of the result. □

```
      (* padd(P,Q) produces the polynomial sum P+Q *)
(1)   fun padd(P,nil) = P
(2)    |   padd(nil,Q) = Q
(3)    |   padd((p:real)::ps, q::qs) = (p+q)::padd(ps,qs);

      (* smult(P,q) multiplies polynomial P by scalar q *)
(4)   fun smult(nil,q) = nil
(5)    |   smult((p:real)::ps,q) = (p*q)::smult(ps,q);

      (* pmult(P,Q) produces PQ *)
(6)   fun pmult(P,nil) = nil
(7)    |   pmult(P,q::qs) = padd(smult(P,q), 0.0::pmult(P,qs));
```

Fig. 6.2. Polynomial addition and multiplication.

◇ **Example 6.4.** In lines (4) and (5) of Fig. 6.2 we see the function `smult` that multiplies a polynomial P by a scalar q. That is, each term in the polynomial is multiplied by q. The recursive definition of this operation is:

Scalar multiplication

BASIS. If P is empty, then the product is the empty list representing 0.

INDUCTION. If P has head p, then the head of the result is pq. The tail of the result is found by recursively applying `smult` to the tail of P and the scalar q.

Line (4) handles the basis and line (5) handles the inductive step. The justification for this algorithm is that if $P = p + Rx$, then $Pq = pq + Rqx$. □

Polynomial multiplication

◇ **Example 6.5.** Now let us consider the function `pmult` of lines (6) and (7) of Fig. 6.2. This function multiplies polynomials P and Q using a recursion on the length of the second polynomial.

BASIS. If the second polynomial is empty, then the result is empty.

INDUCTION. If the second polynomial Q can be written as $q + Sx$, then

$$PQ = Pq + PSx$$

The product Pq is a scalar multiplication. PS is a recursive application of the polynomial multiplication with a smaller second argument.

The basis is implemented by line (6). In line (7) we see the inductive step; `smult(P,q)` produces Pq, while `pmult(P,qs)` produces the polynomial product we called PS in the inductive formula above. To multiply this product by x, we "shift" the terms right by inserting an element 0 in front of the list that represents PS. That shift is the purpose of the subexpression `0.0::pmult(P,qs)`. Finally, we use `padd` to add the lists representing Pq and PSx. □

"As" You Like it: Having it Both Ways

It is possible to take a single value and at one time give the value to an identifier and match the value with a pattern. In the match, variables mentioned in the pattern acquire their own values. The form is

<identifier> **as** <pattern>

Merging

◇ **Example 6.6.** Let us write a function `merge(L,M)` that takes two lists of integers, L and M, that are sorted lowest-first, and *merges* them. That is, `merge` produces a single sorted list with all the elements of L and M. The following recursive definition of `merge` works, assuming that the given lists are sorted. Note that because the `<` operator is used to compare elements, ML needs to know the element type.

BASIS. If L is empty, then the merge is M. If M is empty, the merge is L.

INDUCTION. If neither L nor M is empty, compare the heads of L and M. If the head of L, say x, is smaller, then the sorted list is x followed by the merge of the tail of L with all of M. Note that in this case, x is the smallest of all the elements, so x followed by the merge of the other elements will be the proper sorted list.

If instead, the head of M, say y, is at least as small as x, then the merge is y followed by the merge of L and the tail of M. Since y belongs at the head of the result, the complete list will be sorted.

Figure 6.3 defines the function `merge`. Lines (1) and (2) cover the basis cases. Line (3) begins the inductive step. Here each list is nonempty, or the pattern match would have stopped at line (1) or line (3). When we assemble the result, sometimes we want to use the entire list and sometimes only the

```
(1)        fun merge(nil,M) = M
(2)         |   merge(L,nil) = L
(3)         |   merge(L as x::xs, M as y::ys) =
(4)               if (x:int)<y then x::merge(xs,M)
(5)               else y::merge(L,ys);
```

*val merge = fn : int list * int list → int list*

Fig. 6.3. Merging two sorted lists.

tail. We also need to refer to the head of each list, to tell which is the smaller on line (4). Thus, in line (3) we express the first argument both as L and as x::xs. For instance, if we call **merge** with first argument [1,2,3], L gets the value [1,2,3], x gets the value 1, and xs gets the value [2,3]. Similarly, in line (3) we express the second argument both as M and as y::ys.

Then on line (4) we compare the heads. If the head of L is smaller, we assemble the output by taking the head of L and following it by the result of merging the tail of L, expressed by xs, with the entire list M. On line (5) we cover the case where the head of L is not smaller than the head of M. We assemble the result from the head of M — that is, y — followed by the merge of the entire list L and the tail of M. □

Incidentally, the as-construct in Fig. 6.3 is useful but not essential. We could have used x::xs in place of L and y::ys in place of M. Lines (3)–(5) of Fig. 6.3 would then look like:

```
(3)     |   merge(x::xs, y::ys) =
(4)           if (x:int)<y then x::merge(xs,y::ys)
(5)           else y::merge(x::xs,ys);
```

Anonymous Variables

Wildcard

The symbol _ by itself can be used in patterns to stand for an *anonymous* or *wildcard* variable, which is a variable whose name we do not know and do not care about. We can use _ more than once, but each occurrence refers to a distinct variable not equal to any other occurrence of _ .

◇ **Example 6.7.** We might be tempted to rewrite the function comb(n,m) of Fig. 5.5 making use of two patterns to handle the basis cases where $m = 0$ and $m = n$. Our first attempt might be

```
(1)        fun comb(n,0) = 1
(2)         |   comb(n,n) = 1
(3)         |   comb(n,m) = comb(n-1,m) + comb(n-1,m-1);
```

Unfortunately, this code leads to the error message

Error: duplicate variable in pattern(s): n

reminding us that we may not use a variable twice in one pattern as we did in `comb(n,n)` on line (2).

We are forced to combine lines (2) and (3) into one pattern and a conditional expression. However, as we rewrite the function, we observe that in line (1), the variable n in the pattern was not used to define the result of the function for that pattern. We thus do not need to name n, and it is safe to use the anonymous variable _ in its place. In contrast, we could not use `comb(_,_)` in place of `comb(n,m)` in line (3), because the variables n and m are both used in the expression following the equal sign on line (3). It is, however, legal to use _ several times in one pattern, or in different patterns, to stand for different variables at each use.

```
fun comb(_,0) = 1
|   comb(n,m) =
        if m=n then 1
        else comb(n-1,m) + comb(n-1,m-1);
val comb = fn : int * int → int
```

Fig. 6.4. Correct `comb` function.

Figure 6.4 contains a correct version of `comb` that makes use of anonymous variables where it can. Like the original in Fig. 5.5, Fig. 6.4 suffers from the fact that if m does not lie between 0 and n, the behavior is wrong. □

What Is and What Isn't a Pattern?

We have seen the following kinds of patterns so far:

1.   Constants, for example `nil` or 0.

2.   Expressions using the cons operator, such as `x::xs` or `x::y::zs`.

These can appear either as the sole argument of a function, or as one of several arguments of a function, with the tuple of arguments being the entire pattern.

There are actually many other kinds of patterns. For example, instead of a variable as a head element in a pattern, we could have a tuple. We could also have a list as the head element, with this head element expressed in a form such as `nil` or `x::xs`. Patterns are discussed more fully in Chapter 19, and the formal definition of patterns is in Figs. 26.2 and 26.3.

◊ **Example 6.8.** The following function `sumPairs` takes a list of pairs of integers as argument and sums the integers found in either component of the pairs.

```
fun sumPairs(nil) = 0
  |   sumPairs((x,y)::zs) = x + y + sumPairs(zs);
```
*val sumPairs = fn : (int * int) list → int*

Notice that the type of the argument is (int * int) list, that is, a list of pairs of integers. The head element in the pattern on the second line is (x,y), so x acquires as value the first component of the head pair and y acquires the second component of the head pair. □

◇ **Example 6.9.** Another similar function is sumLists shown in Fig. 6.5. It takes as argument a list whose elements are themselves lists of integers. The purpose is to sum the integers found among all the lists. Notice that ML finds the type of the argument to be int list list, that is, a list whose elements are of type int list. For example, the value of

sumLists([[1,2], nil, [3,4,5], [6]])

is 21. Here, the argument is a list with four elements: the lists [1,2], nil, [3,4,5], and [6].

```
(1)        fun sumLists(nil) = 0
(2)          |   sumLists(nil::YS) = sumLists(YS)
(3)          |   sumLists((x::xs)::YS) = x + sumLists(xs::YS);
```
val sumLists = fn : int list list → int

Fig. 6.5. Summing the elements of a list of lists.

Line (1) of Fig. 6.5 covers the case where the list of lists is empty and the sum is 0. Line (2) covers the case where there is a first element on the list, but that element is itself the empty list. In this case, we can dispense with the head and just sum the integers on the lists of the tail. Line (3) covers the case where there is at least one element on the list that is the head of the list of lists. We take x, which is the head of the head, and add to it the result of applying sumLists to the list in which the element x has been removed from the first list, but all other lists are the same. For instance, if the entire list is [[1,2], [3,4]], then the recursive call's argument is [[2], [3,4]]. □

As we learn about constructors and the creation of our own datatypes, we find there are many other ways to construct data structures besides lists (which are constructed by the cons operator ::) and tuples (which are constructed by parentheses and commas). All datatypes make patterns of their own. However, there are some other patterns that make sense but are illegal in ML. For example, we might expect to be able to construct patterns using the concatenation operator @ or arithmetic operators. The next example indicates what happens when we try to do so.

$\diamond$ **Example 6.10.** We might expect to be able to break a list into the last element and the rest of the list. For instance, we might try to compute the length of a list by:[2]

```
fun length(nil) = 0
|    length(xs@[x]) = 1 + length(xs);
```
Error: non-constructor applied to argument in pattern
Error: unbound variable or constructor xs

However, as we can see, the pattern `xs@[x]` is not legal and triggers two error messages. The first message complains that `@` is not a legal pattern constructor. The second message is caused by the fact that, because the pattern is flawed, variable `xs` does not get bound to a value. Therefore, when we encounter it later, in the expression `length(xs)`, ML has no value to use for `xs`.

Incidentally, we get a similar pair of error messages if we try to use an arithmetic operator to construct a pattern. For instance,

```
fun square(0) = 0
|    square(x+1) = 1 + 2*x + square(x);
```

is equally erroneous, even though it is based on a correct inductive definition of x^2. $\square$

How ML Matches Patterns

A pattern, like any expression, can be represented by a tree. The outermost, or highest-level, operator is the root of the tree, and it has one child for each operand. The child for an operand is, in turn, the root of a subtree for that operand. The basis case, an expression or subexpression that is a constant or variable, is represented by a node labeled by that variable.

$\diamond$ **Example 6.11.** Consider the expression (actually a pattern)

```
(x::y::zs, w)
```

This expression has as outermost operator the pair-forming operator, which we shall represent by (,). Its left operand is the subexpression `x::y::zs`, and the right operand is the subexpression `w`. The latter is represented by a single node labeled `w`. The former is grouped `x::(y::zs)` and is represented by a tree with root operator `::`, left child `x` (a single node) and right child the root of a tree representing subexpression `y::zs`. The entire expression tree is shown in Fig. 6.6(a); for the moment, ignore the curved lines connecting it to Fig. 6.6(b).

Similarly, Fig. 6.6(b) represents the expression (`[1,2,3,4]`, 5). The root operator is again the pairing operator (,), and the right child of the root represents constant 5. The left operand is the list `[1,2,3,4]`. We build lists as expressions by using the cons operator. Note that the last tail must be `nil`, not

---

[2] ML does provide a built-in function `length` that gives the length of a list. It may be implemented by expressing a nonempty list as `x::xs` and returning `1+length(xs)`.

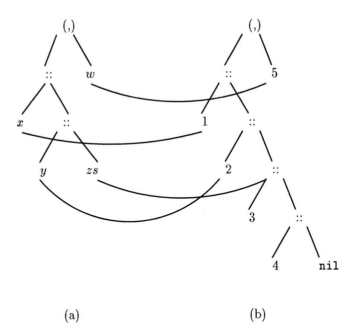

(a)   (b)

Fig. 6.6. Matching a pattern to an expression.

the list consisting of the last element, so there are n uses of the cons operator in a list of length n. □

To match a pattern and an expression, we overlay the pattern's tree and the expression's tree, starting, as a basis step, by matching the roots. For the inductive step, if we have matched nodes N and M of the pattern and expression respectively, then the children of N and M must also be matched in order.

However, sometimes a match will be impossible and the pattern-match fails. This situation occurs when we try to match a pattern node that is labeled by an operator or constant, and the matching node of the expression has a different label.

◇ **Example 6.12.** If we try to match the pattern x::xs with the expression nil, we must match operator :: with constant nil at the respective roots, and we fail. If we try to match pattern x::y::zs with [1] (or as an expression: 1::nil), we match the roots with operators :: successfully. However, at the right children we must match the second :: from the pattern with nil from the expression, and thus we fail. □

If we successfully match the pattern with the expression, then any identifiers at the leaves of the pattern tree match nodes that represent subexpressions.

These subexpressions become the values associated with those identifiers.

◊ **Example 6.13.** Consider again Fig. 6.6. The pattern in Fig. 6.6(a) successfully matches the expression in Fig. 6.6(b); the curved lines indicate the correspondence of the nodes. As a result, the node labeled x in the pattern corresponds to the node labeled 1 in the expression, so x acquires the value 1. The pattern node labeled y corresponds to expression node 2, and pattern node zs corresponds to the expression node representing expression 3::4::nil, or equivalently, the list [3,4]. Finally, the pattern node w corresponds to the expression node 5. □

A Subtle Pattern Bug

Often we wish to use an identifier with a special meaning like nil in our patterns. At this point we have few such special words. But beginning in Chapter 12 we shall see that words of this type, called "data constructors," can be created by the programmer and used in patterns. The misspelling of such a word is an error undetectable by the ML compiler. The reason is that a misspelled word is usually a legal identifier, and such an identifier looks like a pattern that matches anything. At best, we shall get an unexpected warning that there are redundant patterns.

```
(1)      fun reverse(niil) = nil
(2)      |   reverse(x::xs) = reverse(xs) @ [x];
(3)      Warning: redundant patterns in match
(4)            niil ⇒ ...
(5)        →   x :: xs ⇒ ...
(6)      val reverse = fn : 'a list → 'a list

(7)      reverse([1,2,3]);
(8)      val it = [] : int list
```

Fig. 6.7. The reverse function with a misspelling.

◊ **Example 6.14.** In Fig. 6.7 is the reverse function of Example 6.2, in which we have misspelled nil as niil on line (1). We see in lines (3)–(5) that ML has detected the pattern niil will match any argument, and therefore the pattern x::xs on line (2) can never be reached.

Our point that line (1) matches all patterns is reinforced by the example use on line (7). Although reverse is applied to a non-nil list, the pattern of line (1) matches, and the corresponding value, nil, is produced at line (8). □

Exercises

6.1: Write functions for the following polynomial operations, using the representation introduced in Example 6.3.

a)* Compute the difference of two polynomials.

b) Evaluate a polynomial at a given real value a. That is, define a function `eval(P,a)` that takes a list (polynomial) P and a real number a, and computes $P(a)$.

! c)* Given a list of reals $[a_1, a_2, \ldots, a_n]$, find the polynomial whose roots are $a_1, a_2, \ldots, a_n$. *Hint*: Note that this polynomial is the product of $(x - a_i)$ for $i = 1, 2, \ldots, n$.

6.2: Does the pattern of Fig. 6.6(a) match the following expressions? If so, give the value bindings for each of the variables `x`, `y`, `zs`, and `w`.

a)* `(["a","b","c"],["d","e"])`
b) `(["a","b"],4.5)`
c)* `([5],[6,7])`

6.3: Draw trees as in Fig. 6.6 to show how the pattern `[(x,y),zs]` matches the expression `[((1,2),3)]`.

6.4: Rewrite the factorial function of Exercise 5.4 using patterns.

6.5*: There is a recursive definition of the square of a nonnegative integer: $0^2 = 0$ (basis), and $n^2 = (n-1)^2 + 2n - 1$ (inductive step for $n > 0$). Write a recursive function that computes the square of its argument using this inductive formula.

! **6.6**: Write a function that flips alternate elements of a list. That is, given a list $[a_1, a_2, \ldots, a_n]$ as argument, produce $[a_2, a_1, a_4, a_3, a_6, a_5, \ldots]$. If n is odd, a_n remains at the end.

6.7*: Write a function that takes a list of pairs of integers, and orders the elements of each pair such that the smaller number is first. Use the **as** construct to have a way to refer to the pair as a whole when it is not necessary to change it.

6.8: Write a function that takes a list of characters and returns **true** if the first element is a vowel and **false** if not. Use the wildcard symbol _ whenever possible in the patterns.

! **6.9**: The simple rule for translating into "Pig Latin" is to take a word that begins with a vowel and add **"yay"**, while taking any word that begins with one or more consonants and transferring them to the back before appending **"ay"**. For example, **"able"** becomes **"ableyay"** and **"stripe"** becomes **"ipestray"**. Write a function that converts a string of letters into its Pig-Latin translation.

Hint: Use **explode** and the function from Exercise 6.8 that tests for vowels.

6.10: Suppose we represent sets by lists. The members of the set may appear in any order on the list, but we assume that there is never more than one occurrence of the same element on this list. Write functions to perform the following operations on sets.

a)* **member(x,S)** returns true if element x is a member of set S; that is, x appears somewhere on the list representing S.

b) **delete(x,S)** deletes x from S. Remember that you may assume that x appears at most once on the list for S.

c)* **insert(x,S)** puts x on the list for S if it is not already there. Remember that in order to preserve the condition that there are no repeating elements on a list that represents a set, we must check that x does not already appear in S; it is not adequate simply to make x the head of the list.

! **6.11***: Write a function that takes an element a and a list L of lists of elements of the same type as a and inserts a onto the front of each of the lists on the list L. For example, if $a = 1$ and L is **[[2,3],[4,5,6],nil]**, then the result is **[[1,2,3],[1,4,5,6],[1]]**.

Power set

! **6.12***: Suppose sets are represented by lists as in Exercise 6.10. The *power set* of a set S is the set of all subsets of S. A set of sets can be represented in ML by a list whose elements are lists. For example, if S is the set $\{1, 2\}$, then the power set of S is $\{\emptyset, \{1\}, \{2\}, \{1, 2\}\}$, where $\emptyset$ is the empty set. This power set can be represented in ML by the list of lists **[nil,[1],[2],[1,2]]**. Write a function that takes a list as argument, representing some set S, and produces the power set of S. *Hint*: Recursively construct the power set for the tail of the list and use the function from Exercise 6.11 to help construct the power set for the whole list.

! **6.13***: Write a function that, given list of reals $[a_1, \ldots, a_n]$, computes

$$\prod_{i<j}(a_i - a_j)$$

That is, we compute the product of all differences between elements, with the element appearing later on the list subtracted from the element appearing first. If there are no pairs, the "product" is 1.0. *Hint*: Start by writing an auxiliary function that, given a and $[b_1, \ldots, b_n]$, computes $\prod_{i=1}^{n}(a - b_i)$.

6.14*: Write a function to tell whether a list is empty. That is, return **true** if and only if the argument is an empty list.[3]

---

[3] There is a built-in ML function **null** that does this task.

⬥ 7 Local Environments Using "let"

Sometimes we need to create some temporary values — that is, local variables — inside a function. The proper way to do so is with a **let** ⋯ **in** ⋯ **end** expression. A simplified form of this expression, where only val-declarations are used, is shown in Fig. 7.1.

```
let
    val <first variable> = <first expression>;
    val <second variable> = <second expression>;
            ···
    val <last variable> = <last expression>
in
    <expression>
end
```

Fig. 7.1. Simple form of the "let" construct.

That is, following the keyword **let** is a list of one or more val-declarations, just like those introduced in Chapter 3. These are followed by the keyword **in**. Following **in** is an expression that may use the variables defined after **let**, as well as any other variables accessible in the environment that pertained before the **let**. The keyword **end** completes the expression.

- Semicolons following the declarations are optional. We shall adopt Pascal style and follow each but the last by a semicolon.

- Just as for val-declarations in the top-level environment, don't forget to use the keyword **val**.

- We must not omit the keywords **in** and **end**, which are as essential as the **let**.

- In truth, the let-expression is more general than is suggested by Fig. 7.1, and any "declaration" can appear where we have shown val-declarations. So far, we have not seen any other kinds of declarations besides val-declarations and function declarations (with the keyword **fun**). However, there are several others; for example, we shall meet exception declarations in the next chapter. The complete syntax for declarations is in Fig. 26.6.

- As another generalization, a pattern may appear in place of a single identifier in any val-declaration. Also, more than one expression may appear after the **let**, although the utility of an expression list will not become apparent until we study side-effects in Chapter 9.

Common subexpression

◇ **Example 7.1.** One use of the "let" construct is to allow us to use common subexpressions. For example, suppose we wanted to compute the hundredth power of a number x. We could write the expression $x*x* \cdots *x$ if we had the patience, but it is less tedious to use the function in Fig. 7.2.

```
fun hundredthPower(x:real) =
    let
        val four = x*x*x*x;
        val twenty = four*four*four*four*four
    in
        twenty*twenty*twenty*twenty*twenty
    end;
val hundredthPower = fn : real → real

hundredthPower(2.0);
val it = 1.26750600022823E30 : real

hundredthPower(1.01);
val it = 2.70481382942153 : real
```

Fig. 7.2. Raising a number to the 100th power.

In Fig. 7.2 we define two local variables, **four** and **twenty** (no jokes about blackbirds, please). We first define **four** to be x^4, and then define **twenty** to be **four** raised to the fifth power, or x^{20}. Finally, we use **twenty** in the final expression after the keyword **in**, which is **twenty** raised to the fifth power, or x^{100}.

We then see two uses of this function, first computing 2^{100}, which is about 10^{30}, and then computing $(1.01)^{100}$. The latter value is close to $e = 2.718 \cdots$, as it must be because e is the limit as n goes to infinity of $(1 + 1/n)^n$. □

Effect on Environments of "Let"

When we enter a let-expression, an addition to the current environment is created, adding value bindings for all the identifiers defined between the **let** and the **in**.

twenty	1048576.0	added for let-expression
four	16.0	
x	2.0	added on call to hundredthPower
		environment before call to hundredthPower

Fig. 7.3. Additions to environment when hundredthPower is called.

◇ **Example 7.2.** In Fig. 7.3 we see the situation when the function of Fig. 7.2 is called. The first addition is for the function call; it is a binding for the argument **x**. The next additions are for the let-expression and include bindings for the local variables **four** and **twenty**. We have shown **x** assigned the value 2.0 in the call and the local variables assigned their consequent values. As always, when the function call returns, the additions to the environment disappear. However, the returned value is made available as the value of the function in the environment that results after the return. □

```
fun hundredthPower(x:real) =
    let
        val x = x*x*x*x;
        val x = x*x*x*x*x
    in
        x*x*x*x*x
    end;
val hundredthPower = fn : real → real
```

Fig. 7.4. Repeat of Fig. 7.2 with x used for all variables.

◇ **Example 7.3.** We can rewrite Fig. 7.2 to use **x** not only as the argument of the function **hundredthPower**, but also as both local variables. The function then appears as in Fig. 7.4. It behaves exactly like the function of Fig. 7.2. However, the additional bindings in Fig. 7.5 each associate the variable **x** with a value. □

Another important use of let-expressions is when the result of a function has components or parts that we want to separate before we use them. In particular, when the type of the value returned by a function is a tuple, we

x	1048576.0	added for second val-declaration
x	16.0	added for first val-declaration
x	2.0	added on call to `hundredthPower`
		environment before call to `hundredthPower`

Fig. 7.5. Additions to environment corresponding to Fig. 7.4.

Pattern in val-declaration

can get at the components by a more general form of val-declaration than we suggested was possible in Fig. 7.1. Instead of a single identifier following the word **val**, we can have any pattern. For instance, if a function f returns a three-component tuple, we could write

        val (a,b,c) = f(···

and have the three components of the result of f assigned to variables **a**, **b**, and **c** respectively.

- However, we could also write **val x = f(...** and have the entire tuple associated with **x**. Then, the individual components could be extracted by #i operators in subsequent val-declarations.

Split

◇ **Example 7.4.** Let us implement a function **split(L)** that takes a list L and splits it into two lists. One list consists of the first element, third element, fifth element, and so on; the other list consists of the second element, fourth element, sixth element, and so on. This function has an important application. In tandem with the function **merge** of Fig. 6.3, it lets us write a function **mergeSort** that is an efficient sorter of lists. We shall cover **mergeSort** next.

We want the function **split** to produce a pair of lists. The recursion consists of three cases.

BASIS. If L is empty, then produce a pair of empty lists. If L has a single element, the first list of the pair produced has that element and the second list is empty.

INDUCTION. If the given list has two or more elements, let the first two elements be a and b. Recursively split the remaining elements into a pair of lists (M, N). The desired result is the pair of lists $(a :: M, b :: N)$. That is, the first list has head a and tail equal to the first of the returned lists, and the second has head *b* and tail equal to the second of the returned lists.

An ML implementation of `split` is shown in Fig. 7.6. Line (1) implements the first part of the basis: return a pair of empty lists in response to the empty list. Line (2) implements the second part of the basis, where the given list has length 1.

- Note that the way we express "list of length 1" as a pattern is to put square brackets around a single identifier, like `[a]` in line (2). Such a pattern can only match a list with a single element, and variable `a` acquires that element as its value.

- Another way to express "list of length 1" is with the pattern `a::nil`. Again, `a` acquires the lone element as its value.

```
(1)               fun split(nil) = (nil,nil)
(2)                |   split([a]) = ([a],nil)
(3)                |   split(a::b::cs) =
                          let
(4)                           val (M,N) = split(cs)
                          in
(5)                           (a::M, b::N)
                          end;
                   val split = fn: 'a list → 'a list * 'a list

                   split([1,2,3,4,5]);
                   val it = ([1,3,5],[2,4]) : int list * int list
```

Fig. 7.6. Splitting lists.

Lines (3)–(5) handle the inductive case. The pattern `a::b::cs` in line (3) can only match a list with at least two elements; `a` acquires the first element as value, `b` acquires the second, and `cs` acquires the list of the third and subsequent elements as its value. In line (4), we apply `split` recursively to the third and subsequent elements; the result is assigned to the pair `(M,N)`. That is, `M` acquires the first component of the result, which is the elements in positions 3, 5, 7, and so on of the original list. `N` acquires the second component of the return value, which is the elements in positions 4, 6, 8, and so on from the original list.

Finally, in line (5) we construct the return value for the present call to `split`. The first component has head `a` — that is, the first element of the given list — followed by `M`, the list of all the other odd-position components. Thus, the first component is the odd-position elements in order. Similarly, the second component `b::N` is all the even-position elements. □

Mergesort: An Efficient, Recursive Sorter

We can combine the functions `merge` of Fig. 6.3 with `split` of Fig. 7.6 to sort randomly ordered lists of integers. This algorithm is one of the simplest ways to sort n elements in time proportional to $n \log n$ steps. We shall not develop the analysis of this algorithm here, but we shall complete the specification of the algorithm in ML. The idea behind the mergesort algorithm is expressed in the following induction.

BASIS. If the given list L is empty or consists of a single element, then L is surely sorted already, so just return L.

INDUCTION. If L has at least two elements, split L to produce the half-size lists M and N. Recursively mergesort M and N. Then merge the sorted lists M and N to produce the sorted version of L.

◇ **Example 7.5.** The function `mergeSort` is shown in Fig. 7.7. It must be preceded by the functions `merge` and `split` to form the complete implementation of the mergesort algorithm. Incidentally, ML discovers that `mergeSort` works only on integer lists because it uses `merge`, which ML determined worked for only integer lists.

```
(1)   fun mergeSort(nil) = nil
(2)    |    mergeSort([a]) = [a]
(3)    |    mergeSort(L) =
              let
(4)                val (M,N) = split(L);
(5)                val M = mergeSort(M);
(6)                val N = mergeSort(N)
              in
(7)                merge(M,N)
              end;
      val mergeSort = fn : int list → int list
```

Fig. 7.7. Mergesort.

Lines (1) and (2) implement the basis; the remaining lines are for the inductive step. Line (4) splits the given list. Lines (5) and (6) sort the half-sized lists, and the result is produced by merging the sorted lists in line (7). Incidentally, we could also have combined some steps by eliminating lines (5) and (6) and replacing line (7) by `merge(mergeSort(N),mergeSort(M))`. □

Exercises

7.1*: Write a succinct function to compute x^{1000}.

7.2: Rewrite Fig. 7.6 so line (4) does not use a pattern in the val-declaration. That is, replace line (4) by **val x = split(cs)**, and obtain the components of pair **x** as needed.

7.3*: Improve upon the power-set function of Exercise 6.12 by using a let-expression and computing the power set of the tail only once.

7.4: Improve upon the function of Exercise 5.2(e), to compute the maximum of a list of reals, by using a let-expression. *Hint*: Compute the maximum of the tail of the list first.

! **7.5***: Write a function to compute x^{2^i} for real x and nonnegative integer i. *Hint*: Note that we can start with x and apply the squaring operation i times. For example, when $i = 3$, we compute $\left((x^2)^2\right)^2$.

8   Exceptions

Partial function

Many functions are *partial*, meaning that they do not produce a value for some of the possible arguments of the correct type. It is essential that we be able to catch such errors, but the constructs given so far do not really let us do so. The canonical example of an erroneous argument is division by 0. We have claimed that in ML an expression like a/b must invariably produce a value of type real. But what if b has the value 0.0? Will ML in fact produce a real number as a result?

The fact is that, as in other languages, division by 0 produces an error. If we do nothing to handle the error, it will stop the computation with an "uncaught exception" message.

◇ **Example 8.1.** Here are some of the operators we have seen and their response when given operands for which they have no defined value.

```
5 div 0;
```
uncaught exception Div

```
5.0/0.0;
```
uncaught exception Div

```
hd(nil);
```
uncaught exception Hd

```
tl(nil);
```
uncaught exception Tl

```
chr(500);
```
uncaught exception Chr

The first two examples are divisions by zero, and the system raises the exception **Div** in each case. Note that the **Div** exception will be raised and will halt the entire program whenever division by zero occurs. The division might be explicit, as in these examples, or it may be a division by some expression that happens to evaluate to 0. However, as we shall see in Chapter 20, it is possible to replace an exception by an appropriate value. This process is called "handling" exceptions. Handling the exception **Div** keeps the computation going by providing a value for the expression with denominator 0.

Handling exceptions

The third and fourth examples apply the built-in operators hd and tl to get the head and tail, respectively, of the empty list. Since the empty list has neither a head nor a tail, both of these exceptions raise built-in exceptions, **Hd** and **Tl** respectively.

The last example applies the built-in operator **chr** to an integer that is too big to represent a character; **chr** requires an integer in the range 0 to 255. Thus, the exception **Chr** is raised. □

- The built-in exception for improper operands of an operator is often the name of that operator with the first letter capitalized. We have seen **div** and **Div** or **chr** and **Chr**. There are several more examples of this pattern for operators we have not yet introduced.

User-Defined Exceptions

We may also define our own exceptions and "raise" them in code we write when an exceptional condition is discovered. The simplest form of an exception declaration is

>   exception Foo;
>   *exception Foo*

Foo is thus declared to be the name of an exception. In a function definition

Raising exceptions

we can write an expression

>   raise Foo

to make exception **Foo** be the result of the function when we have found an erroneous input or other condition that we associate in our minds with "Foo."

Should this condition actually occur during the running of the program, ML will halt execution and print the message

>   *uncaught exception Foo*

Note that the type of **Foo** is "exception." Values of type exception can be the result of a function no matter what type the function normally returns.

◇ **Example 8.2.** Reconsider the **comb(n,m)** function of Fig. 5.5 that computes $\binom{n}{m}$. This function is

```
(1)    fun comb(n,m) = (* assumes 0 <= m <= n *)
(2)            if m=0 orelse m=n then 1
(3)            else comb(n-1,m) + comb(n-1,m-1);
       val comb = fn : int * int → int
```

We pointed out in Example 5.8 that this function was not designed to work correctly in situations where either n was negative or m was outside the range 0-to-n. One approach to the problem is to define some exceptions and rewrite **comb** to raise them when the input is improper. Figure 8.1 shows this modification.

We begin by defining two exceptions, **BadN** and **BadM**.

```
        exception BadN;
        exception BadN

        exception BadM;
        exception BadM

(1)     fun comb(n,m) =
(2)             if n<0 then raise BadN
(3)             else if m<0 orelse m>n then raise BadM
(4)             else if m=0 orelse m=n then 1
(5)             else comb(n-1,m) + comb(n-1,m-1);
        val comb = fn : int * int → int

        comb(5,2);
        val it = 10 : int

        comb(~1,0);
        uncaught exception BadN

        comb(5,6);
        uncaught exception BadM
```

Fig. 8.1. Using exceptions to catch error conditions in comb.

- It is possible to define several exceptions at one time as

    exception BadN and BadM

    or more generally, any list of exceptions separated by the keyword **and**.

These exceptions are used in lines (2) and (3) of the function comb to check for the erroneous input possibilities. The expressions **raise BadN** and **raise BadM**, when executed, cause the function comb to terminate abnormally.

- Note that this situation violates the principle that a function invariably returns a value of one type (integer for the function comb). However, exceptions are the only violation of this principle in ML.

The rest of the function, in lines (4) and (5), can assume the inputs are in the expected relationship. The first use of the function, comb(5,2), returns an integer, normally. The last two examples of use have improper inputs. Their result is that an exception is raised, and the function comb does not return an integer. Since these exceptions are not caught ("handled"), they result in an error message and termination of the computation. □

Exceptions as Elements of an Environment

Let us trace the effect on the environment of the sequence of declarations in

Fig. 8.1. These effects are shown in Fig. 8.2. Each of the two exception declarations adds to the environment. We show identifiers **BadN** and **BadM** bound to unidentified values. That is, the associated values are internal symbols that are never seen by the user; only identifiers declared to be exceptions are printed when an exception is raised.

m	2	added in response to
n	5	call to `comb(5,2)`
comb	definition of comb	added in response to definition of `comb`
BadM	–	added in response to `exception BadM`
BadN	–	added in response to `exception BadN`
		prior environment

Fig. 8.2. Additions to environments for exceptions.

When we define the function **comb** its binding is a further addition to the environment. Since the definitions of the two exceptions sit below it, **comb** has access to these exceptions for its own code. We then show the further additions that occur when the call to **comb(5,2)** is made. It adds boxes for its parameters as usual; these boxes will disappear when the call returns.

Local Exceptions

It is not necessary to declare exceptions in the top-level environment. We can declare them inside a procedure, so we know they'll make sense any time the procedure is used. Here is an example based on the **comb(n,m)** function.

◇ **Example 8.3.** We could write **comb** as in Fig. 8.3. Here we have used a let-expression with exception declarations instead of the usual val-declarations. The body of the function, between the **in** and **end** keywords, is the same as the function in Fig. 8.1.

When this version of **comb** is called, each call creates two new exceptions whose names are **BadN** and **BadM**. However, these exceptions are technically different from any other exception, even those with the same name. Since it is only the name of an exception that gets printed, not its internal value, the

```
fun comb(n,m) =
    let
        exception BadN;
        exception BadM;
    in
        if n<=0 then raise BadN
        else if m<0 orelse m>n then raise BadM
        else if m=0 orelse m=n then 1
        else comb(n-1,m) + comb(n-1,m-1)
    end;
```
val comb = fn : int * int → int

Fig. 8.3. Function with local exceptions.

user cannot tell the difference. Thus the function of Fig. 8.3 appears to behave exactly like that of Fig. 8.1. □

- There is an unfortunate consequence to the exceptions being local in Fig. 8.3. Should we need to use the exception in a later computation (i.e., by "handling" them as in Chapter 20), they, like any local variable, are not defined outside the function comb. Thus, they cannot be used in any way except to cause termination of the computation.

Exercises

8.1*: Write the factorial function $n! = n \times (n-1) \times \cdots \times 1$, first defining an exception to represent inputs for which the function is not defined, and raising this exception if the input is erroneous. Note that 0! is conventionally defined to be 1, so 0 is not an erroneous input.

8.2: Write a function to return the third element of a list. Define suitable exceptions to tell what is wrong in the cases that the response of the function is not defined. Raise the appropriate exception in response to erroneous inputs.

Pivotal condensation

!! 8.3*: We can represent a matrix of reals by a list of lists. Each list on the "main" list represents one row of the matrix. It is possible to compute the determinant of a matrix by *pivotal condensation*, a technique where we recursively eliminate the first row and the first column.[1] The method can be described as follows.

BASIS. If there is one row and column, then return the one element.

---

[1] This method is not often preferred for computing determinants, since when followed blindly it can result in failure even in cases where the determinant is not infinite (i.e., where the matrix is nonsingular). It can be improved by permuting the rows at each recursive step so the *pivot* (element in the upper left corner) has as large a magnitude as possible.

INDUCTION. If there are more than one row and column,

i.   Normalize the first row by dividing each element by the first element, say a, in the row.

ii.   For each element M_{ij} not in the first row or column, subtract from M_{ij} the product of the first element in row i and the jth element in row 1.

iii.   Recursively compute the determinant of the matrix formed by eliminating the first row and first column. The result is a times this determinant (recall a is the constant from step (i) that was originally in the upper left corner of the matrix.

Write a collection of functions that implement the pivotal condensation algorithm. Define suitable exceptions to catch errors, including

1.   The case where $a = 0$ in step (i) and division by a is therefore impossible in step (ii), and

2.   Cases where the matrix is not originally square. That is, there are not as many rows as columns, or there are unequal-length rows.

Hint: It helps to take this one in easy stages. Start with a function that normalizes a row (list) by dividing each element by a given constant. Also, write a function to subtract a multiple of one row from another. Then, write a function that takes a list of rows and subtracts from the tail of each row the product of the head of the row and a given list. The latter is the heart of the pivotal condensation process. The given row is the normalized tail of the first row. When we multiply it (as a vector) by the head of a row and then subtract the result from the tail of the same row (again, thinking of lists as vectors), we are performing the basic operation required by the pivotal condensation algorithm.

9 Side Effects: Input and Output

While it is more in the spirit of ML programming to produce output by applying functions to some value or list of values, it is possible to do input and output in a fairly conventional way. In particular, ML provides built-in input and output functions that are similar to the way C, Pascal, and other languages perform input/output. These functions have *side-effects*; that is, the changes they make endure after the expressions in which they appear have been evaluated. Side-effects are definitely outside the spirit of functional languages like ML, yet we often find that the use of conventional input/output is essential. For example, we may need to write an ML program that operates on data in a form other than that which ML expects for its own constants.

In this chapter we shall discuss a limited form of input/output — just enough to let us get by. Many details of input/output are deferred to Chapter 22.

The Print Function

Standard output

The `print` function of SML/NJ takes an argument of one of the four basic types: integer, real, Boolean, or string.[1] The expression `print(x)` causes the value of `x` to be printed on the "standard output," which would be the terminal unless you have called SML/NJ with another standard output designated (via the UNIX `>` symbol). The value returned by the `print` function is the unit `()`; `print` does *not* return the value printed as its own value.

◇ **Example 9.1.** In Fig. 9.1 is a function called `testZero`, which tests whether or not its integer argument is 0 and prints one of the strings `"zero"` and `"not zero"` as appropriate. Notice that ML responds by saying that `testZero` is a function from the type integer to the type unit, because the unit is the "value" produced by the `print` function. The fact that a string is produced as a side-effect is not reflected in the type of the function.

We also see in Fig. 9.1 a use of `testZero(2)` and ML's response. We first see the printed response **not zero** on the standard output. Following immediately is the normal response of ML after evaluating a function:

> *val it = () : unit*

---

[1] Function `print` is not defined in standard ML, and so it might not be available in non-SML/NJ implementations.

```
fun testZero(0) = print("zero\n")
  |   testZero(_) = print("not zero\n");
```
val testZero = fn : int → unit

```
testZero(2);
```
not zero
val it = () : unit

Fig. 9.1. A function that uses the print function.

Notice that the value of the expression `testZero(2)` is the unit `()`. That is what `print` returns, and therefore that is what `testZero` returns. □

- Remember from Chapter 1 that in strings we can use the sequence `\n` to represent a newline. Had we omitted printing these characters in the print statements of Fig. 9.1, the output would have run together, as

  not zeroval it = () : unit

- While `print` is one of the few functions that can take arguments of several types, it is essential that ML be able to determine the type of its argument when processing any function declaration that uses `print`. The point is illustrated in the next example.

◇ **Example 9.2.** Consider the function

```
fun printHead(nil) = print("trouble: empty list\n")
  |   printHead(x::_) = print(x);
```
Error: overloaded variable "print" cannot be resolved

This situation is like a use of an overloaded operator such as `+` in a function. ML complains because it cannot figure out whether the integer version of `print`, the real version of `print`, or one of the other two versions is expected.

We can fix the problem as we do for uses of operators like `+`, by declaring a type to tell which we want. For example, consider

```
fun printHead(nil) = print("trouble: empty list\n")
  |   printHead(x::_) = print(x:int);
```
val printHead = fn : int list → unit

By declaring `x` to be an integer on the second line, ML is able to deduce that its argument is a list of integers. Note that the value returned by `printHead` is the unit. Also notice that ML does not object to the fact that sometimes `printHead` prints a string (the "trouble" message) and sometimes it prints an integer: the head of the list L. This situation does not violate ML's strong typing policy because, as mentioned above, the printing of the string or integer is a side-effect, and ML doesn't care about the nature of side effects. The value returned by the function `printHead` is the unit, regardless of whether L is empty or not. □

"Statement" Lists

It is often useful to execute a sequence of two or more "statements" with side-effects, such as `print` expressions.[2] The syntax for doing so in ML is

(<first expression>; $\cdots$;<last expression>)

That is, a list of expressions is separated by semicolons and surrounded by parentheses. The construct is similar to **begin** $\cdots$ **end** in Pascal or { $\cdots$ } in C.

Each expression is evaluated in turn. However, unlike Pascal, C, or most other languages, the list of expressions is itself an expression and produces a value. The value produced by a list of expressions is the value produced by the last of the expressions.

◇ **Example 9.3.** The function `printList` in Fig. 9.2 prints each element of an integer list in order and in a vertical column. Line (1) handles the case where the list is empty. Nothing is printed, and the unit is returned. Note that we do not care what `printList` returns since, unlike most ML functions, `printList` does its job by its side-effects, not by its returned value. However, like all functions, `printList` must return one type of value, unit in this case.

```
(1)    fun printList(nil) = ()
(2)    |   printList(x::xs) =
(3)                  (print(x:int); print("\n"); printList(xs));
       val printList = fn : int list → unit

       printList([1,2,3]);
       1
       2
       3
       val it = () : unit
```

Fig. 9.2. Printing a list as a side-effect.

Lines (2) and (3) handle the case where the list is not empty. In line (3) we see a sequence of three expressions, each of which causes a printing side-effect. The first expression prints the head element of the list and also declares that this element must be an integer. The second expression prints the newline

---

[2] Technically, there is no such thing as a "statement" in ML, only expressions. However, expressions that cause side-effects behave much like statements of ordinary languages. We shall informally refer to them as statements.

character, thus skipping to the next line of output. The third expression is a recursive call to `printList` on the tail of the list. That expression causes the rest of the list to be printed and returns the unit. The unit thus becomes the value of the list of statements and the value returned by the function. The ML response confirms that `printList` is a function that takes an integer list as argument and returns a unit.

In Fig. 9.2 this function is used to print the list `[1,2,3]`. The initial call to `printList([1,2,3])` prints 1, then prints a newline (i.e., it skips to the next output line), and last calls `printList` recursively on the tail `[2,3]`. That call results in the printing of the elements 2 and 3 on separate lines. Finally, since `printList([1,2,3])` is an expression, ML responds with the value of this expression, which is the unit. □

Statement Lists Versus Let-Expressions

You may have noticed a similarity between the list of statements mentioned above and the let-expression from Chapter 7. Each involves a sequence of steps that are evaluated or executed in turn, and the result is the value returned by the last expression. However, different kinds of expressions are allowed between the `let` and `in` keywords from those allowed in statement lists or allowed between the `in` and `end`.

Declaration   Between `let` and `in` we must find *declarations* such as val-declarations, function definitions, exception declarations, and a few more kinds of declarations that we shall learn later (see Fig. 26.6 for a summary of declarations). Intuitively declarations are the kinds of expressions that evoke a response other than *val it = ···* when you type them in the top-level environment. For example, they may result in ML telling the value of some identifier other than `it`, or indicating that a certain identifier represents an exception.

On the other hand, the "ordinary" expressions that can appear in an expression list (or after the `in` of a let-expression) are characterized by an ML response in which the identifier `it` has its value told. See Fig. 26.1 for the complete structure of expressions. Another way to look at the distinction is that let-expressions make significant alterations to the environment through their declarations, while expressions leave the environment unchanged. Note that side-effects such as printing or reading input do not change the environment as far as ML is concerned, although they do change the state of the surrounding file system.

- Although we have not yet seen an example, an expression list can appear between the `in` and `end` in a let-expression, in place of a single expression. The surrounding parentheses are unnecessary in such a list.

Simple Input

In order to read a file, we need to learn some more about file handling in ML. The approach will be familiar if you have used UNIX file reading and writing commands from C or another language. In this chapter we shall learn just enough to allow file reading. There is an analogous way to write files, but we shall defer this and other input/output matters until Chapter 22. The `print` function gives us enough output capability for the examples before that chapter.

open_in

First, we must open the file for reading. The form of this operation is

```
open_in("<file name>")
```

This expression causes the file named by the quoted string to be opened for reading. It returns a "token," or internal value, that must be used to read from the file in the future. This token may be thought of as the file identifier returned by the UNIX call to open a file. For example,

```
val infile = open_in("foo");
val infile = - : instream
```

opnes the file named **foo** in the directory in which the ML program is running. To read from the file subsequently, we refer to it by the identifier **infile**, not **foo**. The expression

```
val infile2 = open_in("/usr/spool/mail/ullman");
val infile2 = - : instream
```

opens the author's mail file for reading. In the future, this file must be referred to by the identifier **infile2**.

- The value returned by **open_in** is of type **instream**. That type, which we have not encountered before, is in effect a file of characters opened for reading. Note that − is shown as the value of any instream, because such values are not knowable by the user.

- In general, the argument of **open_in** can be any string that denotes a UNIX path name relative to the directory in which the ML program is running.

- Don't forget to put quotes around the file name given to **open_in**.

Once we have opened the file, we can read characters from it. We need to know two more of the functions that ML uses in connection with reading and writing of files.

end_of_stream

1. **end_of_stream**(<file>) is a *predicate* (function that returns a Boolean) that tells whether or not the end of the file has been reached. The value of <file> must be an **instream**, that is, a token returned by **open_in**. Function **end_of_stream** remains true after the end of the file has been reached, and the test can be applied many times, if desired.

input

2. **input**(<file>,n) reads the next n characters from the file named <file>. What is read is returned as a string. Again, <file> is an **instream** or internal token used to designate an opened file. If there are fewer than n characters remaining in the file, then only what remains is read, and fewer than n characters are returned. However, if the "file" is actually a source like an input terminal, then **input** will wait until n characters appear or

an explicit end of file is seen. There will be an indefinite wait if these characters never arrive.

◇ **Example 9.4.** Figure 9.3 shows a function `readList` that opens a file, reads it character-by-character, and returns the list whose elements are the characters of the file, in order. Each element is a string of length 1, which is the normal representation of characters in ML.

```
(1)          fun readList(file) =
(2)                  if end_of_stream(file) then nil
(3)                  else input(file,1) :: readList(file);
          val readList = fn : instream → string list

          readList(open_in("test"));
          val it = ["1","2","\n","a","b","\n"] : string list
```

Fig. 9.3. Reading a file and turning it into a list of characters.

Line (2) says that if we have reached the end of the file, then we return the empty list. Line (3) handles the case where the file is not empty. We use the **input** function to read one character from the file, and this character becomes the head of the list being formed. The tail of the list is constructed by a recursive call to the function **readList**. ML deduces that **file** must be of type **instream**, because function **input** requires that type for its first argument.

We also see in Fig. 9.3 the application of **readList** to a file named **test** that holds the six characters

```
          12
          ab
```

Note that two of the characters in the file are newline characters, one after each line.

In the expression **readList(open_in("test"))**, **open_in** opens the file **test** and produces a token of type instream representing this file. We never see the value of this token, but it immediately becomes the argument of **readList**; that is, the parameter **file** of **readList** gets this instream as its value for the call.

Finally, we see the response of ML to this expression; it ascribes to identifier **it** the list of characters of the file **test**. Note that we have, in effect, "dropped the list on the floor." In a more realistic example, we would pass the list as an argument to another function, which would perform some useful computation on the list. □

A More Complex Example

We shall now give a long example that illustrates more about using input in ML and also shows something of how several functions fit together to form a complete program. The problem we shall address is how to read a list of integers from a designated file and compute their sum. The following restrictions are assumed.

1. Integers are positive only.

White space

2. Integers are separated by one or more *white-space* characters: blanks, new-lines, and tabs.

3. The last integer may or may not be followed by one or more white-space characters before the end of the file is reached.

4. Any character in the file except for white space and digits is an error.

Our first job is to write two useful predicates that tell whether a character is a white-space character or is a digit. These are:

```
fun white(c) =
        c=" " orelse c="\n" orelse c="\t";
val white = fn : string → bool

fun digit(c) =
        c >= "0" andalso c <= "9";
val digit = fn : string → bool
```

Function `white` simply checks whether its argument is one of the three white-space characters. Function `digit` checks whether its argument lies between the characters `"0"` and `"9"` in lexicographic order. Note that in the ASCII code, which is effectively the universal code for characters, the digits have consecutive codes.

• If you are like the author, you are tempted to write a predicate like `white` as

```
fun white(c) =
        if c=" " orelse c="\n" orelse c="\t" then true
        else false;
```

This code is correct but "illiterate." Note that when a function returns a Boolean, we can use the test as the return value itself.

Next, we need to declare an exception to warn us if there is a character other than white space or digits. That warning is provided by the following expression:

```
exception BadChar;
```

> **if** there are no more integers on the file **then**
>   return 0
> **else begin**
>   get an integer from the file;
>   recursively sum the rest of the file;
>   return the sum of the first integer and
>   the rest of the file
> **end**

Fig. 9.4. Sketch of integer-summing program.

Now, let us divide the task into some components. Our initial sketch of the program, in a "Pidgin-Pascal" notation, is shown in Fig. 9.4.

Getting the next integer from the file is itself a complex task. First, there may not be any more integers, since only white space may remain on the file. We shall handle this situation by producing the integer -1.[3] Note we can do so here because of the assumption that there are no negative integers. Thus there can be no ambiguity whether -1 is a legitimate integer — it cannot be. However, to make the role of -1 more transparent, we shall use END as a variable defined to have value -1 in this context.

If there is an integer to be found, we can divide the process into two steps:

1. Skipping over white space to find the first digit, and

2. Reading subsequent digits until either white space or the end of file is encountered, computing the value of the integer as we go.

The first of these operations is performed by the function `startInt` shown in Fig. 9.5. Line (1) tests if we have reached the end of the file. If so, we return END, that is, the integer -1. That value will warn other functions calling `startInt` that the end of file has been reached and no integer was found.

If the end of file has not been reached, then in line (2) we read the next character and bind it to the local variable **c**. Line (3) handles the case where a digit has been found. We return the integer value of that digit, which in the ASCII code can be computed by subtracting the code for digit 0 from the code for the digit at hand. Line (4) handles the case where we have found a white-space character. Then, we call `startInt` recursively, expecting eventually to find either the end of the file or a digit. However, if the character read is neither white space nor a digit, we raise the exception `BadChar` on line (5). This exception causes the whole summation to fail. A better approach would be to ignore bad characters, which we suggest as an exercise.

---

[3] Admittedly, this style is fraught with danger and should be avoided. We shall learn two safer ways to represent the end of file. One is in an exercise of Chapter 12, where we consider the use of datatypes, and another is in Chapter 20, where we consider exceptions and their handling.

```
        val END = ~1;
        val END = ~1
```

```
        fun startInt(file) =
(1)             if end_of_stream(file) then END
                else
                    let
(2)                     val c = input(file,1)
                    in
(3)                         if digit(c) then ord(c)-ord("0")
(4)                         else if white(c) then startInt(file)
(5)                         else raise BadChar
                    end;
        val startInt = fn : instream → int
```

Fig. 9.5. Finding the beginning of an integer.

Now, we have a way to find the first digit of an integer and return its value. Next, let us design a function finishInt(i,file) that takes an integer i, which represents the value of digits read so far, and reads as many more consecutive digits as there are in the file named file. Eventually the value of the integer represented by this entire sequence of digits is produced by finishInt. The key arithmetic point to remember is that if i is the value of digits read so far, and we read one more digit, say d, then the value of the integer up to the newly read digit is $10i + d$. The function finishInt is shown in Fig. 9.6.

```
        fun finishInt(i,file) =
(1)             if end_of_stream(file) then i
                else
                    let
(2)                     val c = input(file,1)
                    in
(3)                         if digit(c) then
(4)                             finishInt(10*i+ord(c)-ord("0"), file)
(5)                         else if white(c) then i
(6)                         else raise BadChar
                    end;
        val finishInt = fn : int * instream → int
```

Fig. 9.6. Completing the read of one integer.

At line (1), if we have reached the end of the file, then finishInt returns the integer i found so far.

- It is important to note that if i was produced by **startInt**, and that function encountered the end of the file before any digits, then the value of i will be **END**, or -1. In that case, line (1) of **finishInt** passes the value **END** along to warn that the end of file was encountered and there are no more integers.

If the end of the file has not been reached, then line (2) reads the next character. If that character is a digit, then on line (3), **finishInt** multiplies the integer i by 10, and adds the value of the digit read, to get a new integer, which we may call j. Then, on line (4), **finishInt** calls itself recursively with integer j and the same file.

If, on the other hand, the character read at line (2) is a white-space character, then the integer being read is finished. We return the integer i on line (5), and the call to **finishInt** is completed. The final possibility is that we have an erroneous character in the file, in which case we raise the **BadChar** exception at line (6).

The functions **startInt** and **finishInt** can be combined as follows into one function **getInt** that either reads the next integer from a file or returns **END** if the end-of-file is encountered before any digits.

```
fun getInt(file) =
        finishInt(startInt(file), file)
```
val getInt = fn : instream → int

If there are one or more digits in the file, **startInt** will get the value of the first, and **finishInt** will repeatedly multiply its integer argument by 10 and add in the value of the next digit, eventually returning the value of the entire string of consecutive digits. Should **getInt** be called when there is no integer left on the file, then **startInt** will return **END**; so will **finishInt**, and therefore **getInt** returns **END**.

```
      fun sumInts1(file) =
            let
(1)               val i = getInt(file)
            in
(2)               if i=END then 0
(3)               else i + sumInts1(file)
            end;
```
val sumInts1 = fn : instream → int

```
(4)   fun sumInts(filename) = sumInts1(open_in(filename));
```
val sumInts = fn : string → int

Fig. 9.7. Functions to sum integers.

Finally, we see in Fig. 9.7 the functions that do the summing of integers.

The work is really done by `sumInts1(file)` that at line (1) reads an integer off the file. If the integer is `END` (i.e., −1), then we have reached the end of the file and found no integer, so the sum of integers found is 0. We handle this case in line (2). If a nonnegative integer is found, then on line (3) we recursively call `sumInts1` to sum the rest of the integers on the file, and add the integer found first, to produce the correct sum.

The final touch is the function `sumInts` of line (4). This function takes a string `filename`, which is the name of the file whose integers we must sum, and applies `open_in` to it. The result is an instream representing the file. This instream is passed to `sumInts1` and, through it, to the other functions that read from the file: `getInt`, `startInt`, and `finishInt`. The entire collection of functions is reprised in Fig. 9.8.

Eager Evaluation

One might wonder whether all the complexity of the previous long example is really necessary. For example, we could have converted the file into a list of characters, using the function of Fig. 9.3, and then applied a few functions to make the job simpler. For example, we could collapse strings of white space into a single blank and trim white space from the end of the file.

However, there is a disadvantage to doing so, because of ML's method of parameter passing, which is call-by-value (recall Chapter 5). That is, the first thing that would happen is that the entire file would be turned into a list of characters. If we applied a function that deleted white space from the end, we would produce another list almost as long. Collapsing strings of white space would produce a third long list and so on.

Even more significantly, suppose we had agreed to terminate the list of integers not by the end of the file, but by some special character like `"e"`, which could appear in the middle of the file. In that case, we would not even need to read the part of the file beyond the first `"e"`. However, should we start with the function of Fig. 9.3 to convert the file to a list, we would wind up reading the entire file whether or not we needed it. This style of computing values is called *eager evaluation*. Its opposite, where parts of an argument such as a list are evaluated only as needed, is called *lazy evaluation*.

Eager, lazy evaluation

ML follows the eager evaluation approach because of the call-by-value semantics associated with its function arguments. However, by careful programming, we can have a measure of lazy evaluation.[4] Notice that the program of Fig. 9.8 reads one integer at a time, and it never creates a list of all the integers before it sums them. More to the point, if we had used a marker like `"e"` to indicate the end of the group of integers to be summed, and suitably modified the program of Fig. 9.8 to look for `"e"` instead of the end-of-file, the program would never even read the file beyond the first `"e"`.

---

[4] In truth, it should be pointed out that while ML argument evaluation is "eager," there are other aspects of the language design that are "lazy." For instance, we mentioned that the second argument of `andalso` or `orelse` is evaluated "lazily," that is, only if needed.

```
exception BadChar;

val END = ~1;

fun white(c) = c=" " orelse c="\n" orelse c="\t";

fun digit(c) = c >= "0" andalso c <= "9";

fun startInt(file) = (* get the first digit from file;
  return END if there is no integer *)
      if end_of_stream(file) then END
      else let
              val c = input(file,1)
          in
              if digit(c) then ord(c)-ord("0")
              else if white(c) then startInt(file)
              else raise BadChar
          end;

fun finishInt(i,file) = (* return the integer whose first
  digits have value i and whose remaining digits are found
  on file, up to the end or the first white space *)
      if end_of_stream(file) then i
      else let
              val c = input(file,1)
          in
              if digit(c) then
                  finishInt(10*i+ord(c)-ord("0"), file)
              else if white(c) then i
              else raise BadChar
          end;

fun getInt(file) = (* read an integer from file *)
      finishInt(startInt(file), file);

fun sumInts1(file) = (* sum the integers on file *)
      let
          val i = getInt(file)
      in
          if i=END then 0
          else i + sumInts1(file)
      end;

fun sumInts(filename) = (* sum the integers on file
  "filename" relative to the current UNIX directory *)
      sumInts1(open_in(filename));
```

Fig. 9.8. Complete program to read and sum a file of integers.

Exercises

9.1*: If we were to change line (1) of Fig. 9.2 to

```
fun printList(nil) = 0
```

and left lines (2) and (3) as they are, would there be a type error in the function?

! 9.2: Generalize the program of Fig. 9.8 to:

a) Allow negative integers on the input. We assume that negative integers are preceded by the minus sign (–) rather than the tilde (˜). Note that we not only have to recognize negative integers, but we can no longer use -1 as a convenient value to indicate that the end of file has been reached. *Hint*: Return a pair consisting of an integer and a Boolean that tells whether the end of file has been reached.

b) Ignore all "bad" characters, that is, those that are not digits or white space.

9.3*: Read a file of characters, treating it as a sequence of *words*, which are sequences of consecutive non-white-space characters. Each word is followed by either a single white space character or the end-of-file, so two or more consecutive white spaces indicate there is an empty word between them. Return a list of the words in the file.

9.4: Write the function `comb`, computing $\binom{n}{m}$, in such a way that when we call `comb(n,m)` it prints n and m before printing the result. Print out suitable words so n, m, and $\binom{n}{m}$ are clearly distinguishable from one another.

9.5*: Rewrite the function `white` of Fig. 9.8 using pattern matching instead of a logical expression. That is, write a pattern for each white-space character and end with a pattern to handle all non-white-space characters.

! 9.6: Design the following calendar-printing function. Take as input a month, the day of the first of that month, and the number of days in the month. Months and days are abbreviated by their first three letters. The month, day, and number of days are each separated by a single white-space character. For example, a request to print the calendar for a September in which the first of the month is on a Thursday would be

```
Sep Thu 30
```

Print the calendar as:

1. A row with the month (full name) indented by three tabs.
2. A blank row.
3. A row with the names of the days (three-letter abbreviations) separated by tabs.
4. As many rows as necessary, with the days printed in the proper columns.

September

Sun	Mon	Tue	Wed	Thu	Fri	Sat
				1	2	3
4	5	6	7	8	9	10
11	12	13	14	15	16	17
18	19	20	21	23	24	25
26	27	28	29	30		

Fig. 9.9. Example calendar page.

For example, Fig. 9.9 shows the calendar desired for September when Sept. 1 falls on a Thursday.

PART **2** | *Advanced*
Features
of ML

◊◊
◊

Now we shall discuss some of the innovative aspects
of ML that make it both a powerful programming
language and an incubator for new programming language ideas. These features include polymorphism
and higher-order functions, datatype definitions and
modules. In this second part we shall also cover some
of the features like arrays and references that have
been added to allow the programmer more options
to implement efficient data structures.

10   Polymorphic Functions

We saw in Part 1 that sometimes a function requires arguments of a particular type. Other times, arguments are not restricted to a type, or they are partially restricted. For example, an argument might have type `'a list`, meaning a list of any one type of element is required. The ability of a function to allow arguments of different types is called *polymorphism* ("poly" = "many"; "morph" = "form"), and such a function is called *polymorphic*.

In this chapter, we study what makes a function polymorphic, or conversely, what forces an argument to be restricted to a single type. Before proceeding, it is useful to remember some points about ML types.

- ML is strongly typed, meaning it is possible to determine the type of any variable or the value returned by any function by examining the program, but without running the program. Put another way, an ML program for which it is not possible to determine the types of variables and function return-values is an incorrect program.

- The algorithm whereby ML deduces the types of variables is complex and beyond the scope of this book. In practice, it is usually easy to see what ML is doing to discover types, as we discussed informally at the end of Chapter 5.

- Although we must be able to tell the types of all variables in a complete program, we can define functions whose types are partially or completely flexible; these are the polymorphic functions.

Identity function

◇ **Example 10.1.** The extreme example of a polymorphic function is the *identity* function, which we can define by

```
fun identity(x) = x;
val identity = fn: 'a → 'a
```

This function simply produces its argument as its own result, and the argument can be of any type whatsoever. ML observes that the type of the argument and the result are the same, and so designates the type of the identity function as `'a -> 'a`.

We can use the identity function with anything as an argument. For instance

```
identity(2);
val it = 2 : int
```

Here the type of the result is found to be an integer. We can even give the identity function a function as an argument; it will produce that function as result. For example, we can apply the identity function to itself, as:

```
identity(identity);
val it = fn : 'a → 'a
```

The result is again the identity function. Although ML does not tell us specifically what function is returned, the fact that the result is `identity` is suggested by the description of the type of the result, a function from any type to the same type. □

Operators that Restrict Polymorphism

Most of the operators that we have met prevent polymorphism in functions where they are used. These "polymorphism-destroying" operators include:

1.   Arithmetic operators +, −, *, and ~.

2.   The division and remainder operators /, div, and mod.

3.   The inequality comparison operators <, <=, >=, and >. Note we exclude = (equal-to) and <> (not-equal-to) from this group. They behave differently from the inequality comparisons as far as polymorphism is concerned.

4.   The Boolean operators andalso, orelse, and not.

5.   The string concatenation operator ^.

6.   Type conversion operators ord, chr, real, floor, ceiling, and truncate.

All but groups (1) and (3) force their argument(s) and result to be of one specific type. Groups (1) and (3) include operators that apply to several different types, but ML requires that the type be known from inspection of the program. Thus, operators in groups (1) and (3) not only restrict their arguments and results to one type, they frequently require us to indicate with a colon what that type is.

Operators that Allow Polymorphism

We have seen several operators that allow polymorphism, although they somewhat restrict the types of their results and/or arguments. Three classes of operators in this category are:

1.   Tuple operators, such as the tuple-forming operator, consisting of parentheses and commas, as (, , . . . ,). Also in this group are the component-reading operators, #1, #2, and so on.

2.   The list operators ::, @, hd, and tl, the list constant nil, and brackets used as the list-former [· · ·].

Equality operator

3.   The *equality* operators = and <>.

When we apply a tuple constructor, we get a tuple type of some sort. When we apply a list-building operator, we are restricted to create a list type of some sort. When we apply an equality operator, we restrict the arguments to be of the same "equality type," a concept we shall discuss shortly. However, there are no other constraints forced on the types of operands or results.

List Operators

Let us consider why list operators do not prohibit polymorphism. A similar explanation applies to the tuple-forming operators. First, consider an expression like $x + y$. ML implements the addition operator by computing a new value, the sum of x and y. To compute the sum, ML needs to know whether to add integers or reals.

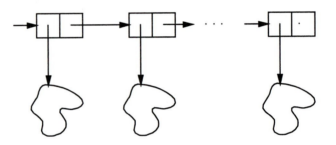

Fig. 10.1. Representing a linked list.

In contrast consider the cons operator : : . ML represents lists internally in the conventional, linked-list fashion suggested in Fig. 10.1. Cells consisting of a pair of pointers, the first to an element and the second to the next cell, represent the list.

To apply the cons operator, we need to create a new cell, put a pointer to the head in the first field of the cell, and put a pointer to the tail in the second field of the cell. The process is suggested in Fig. 10.2. Notice that with this scheme, the operation is performed in exactly the same way regardless of the types of the head and tail. Of course, ML requires that it be able to deduce the types of head and tail before running the program and requires that they be compatible types (i.e., if the head is of type T, then the tail is of type T list). However, the motivation for this strong typing requirement is to make error detection easier. We could construct lists without knowing types if the rules of ML permitted it.

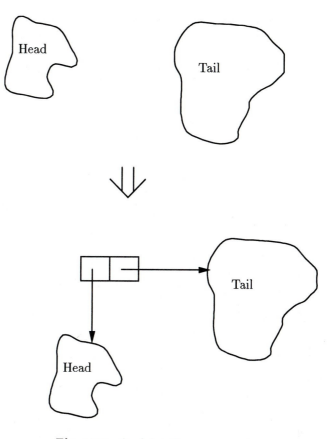

Fig. 10.2. Applying the cons operator.

The Equality Operators

Equality type

Now let us look at the *equality operators* = and <>. ML defines a class of types called *equality types*, which are those that allow equality to be tested among values of that type. The basic types — integer, real, Boolean, and string — are equality types. Two ways to form more equality types are:

1. Forming products of equality types (for tuples).
2. Forming a list whose elements are of an equality type.

Note that rules (1) and (2) can be applied recursively. So, for example,

```
int * int
```

is an equality type, `(int * int) list` is an equality type,

```
real list * string
```

is an equality type, and so on. We shall also see how to define datatypes in Chapter 12, and some of these new types will be equality types.

◇ **Example 10.2.** Let us define two variables to be pairs of integers.

```
val x = (1,2);
val x = (1,2)
```

```
val y = (2,3);
val y = (2,3)
```

Then we can compare these values, for instance:

```
x=y;
val it = false : bool
```

```
x = (1,2);
val it = true : bool
```

Similarly, we could define and compare lists, as:

```
val L = [1,2,3];
val L = [1,2,3]
```

```
val M = [2,3];
val M = [2,3]
```

Then we can compare as follows:

```
L <> M;
val it = true : bool
```

```
L = 1::M;
val it = true : bool
```

Notice in the last example that ML evaluates expressions before testing for equality, so it discovers that the expression `1::M` denotes the same list as is denoted by the variable `L`. □

On the other hand, functions cannot be compared for equality even though we might think it should be possible in some cases. Any type involving a function is not an equality type.

◇ **Example 10.3.** Let us define the identity function again as before:

```
fun identity(x) = x;
val identity = fn : 'a → 'a
```

If we try to compare the identity with itself, we get the error message shown in Fig. 10.3.

Line (1) of Fig. 10.3 says that the operator (the = sign) does not agree with its operand (the pair of identity functions). The problem is that equality

```
               identity = identity;
```

(1)   *Error: operator and operand don't agree (equality type required)*
(2)   *operator domain: "Z * "Z*
(3)   *operand: ('Y → 'Y) * ('X → 'X)*
(4)   *in expression:*
(5)   *= (identity, identity)*

Fig. 10.3. Functions cannot be compared for equality.

or inequality can only be tested among pairs of the same equality type, and no function type is an equality type. Thus, even though the two uses of **identity** as a function name obviously denote the same function, the comparison is not legal in ML.

Line (2) further explains that the operator = requires arguments of the same equality type, here denoted by **''Z**.

- Remember that type variables whose values are restricted to be an equality type are distinguished by having names that begin with two quote marks rather than only one.

Line (3) points out that the actual pair of arguments given is two polymorphic functions. One function is from some type **'X** to the same type, and the second is from some type **'Y** to that same type.

- Note that there is no reason to believe that **'X** and **'Y** are the same type. As with polymorphic functions in general, two uses of the identity function need not apply to the same type.

Finally, lines (4) and (5) indicate that the error was in the expression

```
    identity = identity
```

However, it gives the operator and operands in prefix form, where the operator is applied in the same way a function is applied to its argument. □

◇ **Example 10.4.** To explore further the effect of an = or <> comparison on the set of permissible types, let us reconsider the two versions of the function **reverse** that we developed in Examples 5.5 and 6.2. These are repeated in Fig. 10.4(a) and (b), respectively. However, here we have used the correct type variable name **''a** (with two quotes) that ML uses to describe the type of the function in Fig. 10.4(a). This type name tells us that any type can be used, provided it is an equality type.

In Fig. 10.4(b), we see the ML response telling us that the function can take an argument of any type whatsoever, regardless of whether it is an equality type. If we give each of these programs a list whose elements are from one equality type, both functions produce the same answer. The difference shows up, however, if we apply each function to a list whose elements are chosen from

```
(1)         fun reverse(L) =
(2)                 if L = nil then nil
(3)                 else reverse(tl(L)) @ [hd(L)];
```
val reverse = fn : "a list → "a list

(a) Reversal using an equality comparison.

```
(4)         fun reverse(nil) = nil
(5)         |   reverse(x::xs) = reverse(xs) @ [x]
```
val reverse = fn : 'a list → 'a list

(b) Reversal without using an equality comparison.

Fig. 10.4. Two functions for reversing a list.

one non-equality type. For instance, consider

```
reverse([identity, identity])
```

Here **identity** is the function from Fig. 10.3, so the type of list elements is **fn : 'a -> 'a**.

If **reverse** is the function of Fig. 10.4(b), then the list will be reversed normally, which yields the same list in this example. However, if **reverse** is the function of Fig. 10.4(a), then we get the error message in Fig. 10.5.

```
(1)         Error: operator and operand don't agree (equality type required)
(2)         operator domain: ''Z list
(3)         operand: ('Y → 'Y) list
(4)         in expression:
(5)                 reverse(identity::identity::nil)
```

Fig. 10.5. Error response when **reverse** requires an equality type.

This message is similar to that in Fig. 10.3. Line (2) refers to the operator **reverse**, which takes as an argument a **''Z list**, that is, a list whose elements are from any one equality type. Line (3) says that the argument actually found, which is **[identity, identity]**, is a list of functions from any type **'Y** to the same type. The type **'Y -> 'Y**, being a function type, is not an equality type and therefore is not suitable as the type **''Z**. Lines (4) and (5) indicate the offending expression. Note that lists are represented by **::** and **nil** rather than by square brackets. □

We may well wonder why the function of Fig. 10.4(a) requires an equality type. The reason is found in line (2), where the comparison L=nil occurs. If list L is to be tested for equality to something, then surely L must be of an equality type, which means its elements must be chosen from an equality type.

In contrast, line (4) in Fig. 10.4(b) makes essentially the same test by matching L to the pattern nil. Recalling the discussion at the end of Chapter 6 about how ML matches patterns, we see that here we are not testing for equality of L to nil. Rather we are matching the expression tree for the value L currently has to the one-node tree for the "expression" nil. ML can match trees without testing for equality of anything except constants of the basic types and identifiers.

You may think that there is something wrong with this analysis and observe that in line (2) of Fig. 10.4(a) we don't really need to test equality of elements to compare a list L with nil. That is quite true, although if we had replaced the test of line (2) by a test for equality to any other list but nil, for instance L=[a,b], then L would surely have to be of an equality type. The designers of ML have chosen to infer that an equality type is needed by the presence of an operator = or <>, and they have chosen not to consider equality to nil as a special case. You may regard that choice as either "a bug or a feature" of ML, as you wish.

null
- ML has a built-in function null that tests whether a list is empty without requiring that list to be of an equality type. We could write line (2) of Fig. 10.4(a) as

```
if null(L) then nil
```

and then the function reverse of Fig. 10.4(a) would not require an equality type. Its type would be 'a list -> 'a list, just like Fig. 10.4(b).

Exercises

10.1: Suppose that the function reverse of Fig. 10.4(a) is called rev1 and the function reverse of Fig. 10.4(b) is called rev2. What is the result of the following calls?

a)* rev1([rev1,rev1])

b) rev2([rev2,rev2])

! c)* rev2([rev1,rev2])

! d) rev2([rev1,identity])

10.2: We can restrict polymorphic types (type expressions with variables) by: (*i*) equating type variables, (*ii*) replacing a type variable by a constant type, or (*iii*) replacing a type variable by a nonconstant expression. Give an example of each kind of restriction for the following type expressions.

a)* 'a * 'b * int
b)   ('a list) * ('b list)

! **10.3**: Suppose $f(x, y, z)$ is a function. Give an example of a definition of f that would cause the argument of f to have each of the following types.

a)* 'a * ''b * ('a -> ''b)
b)   'a * 'a * int
c)* 'a list * 'b * 'a
d)   ('a * 'b) * 'a list * 'b list

10.4: Tell whether or not each of the following types is an equality type.

a)* int * real list
b)   (int -> real) * string
c)* int -> real -> unit
d)   real * (string * string) list

10.5: Let L have the value [(1,2), (3,4)], let M have the value (1,2), and let N have the value (3,4). Which of the following equality tests have the value true?

a)* L = M::[N]
b)   M::L = L@[N]
c)* [(1,2)]@[N] = L@nil
d)   N::L = (3,4)::M::N::nil

11   Higher-Order Functions

A typical function has parameters that represent "data." That is, the parameters are of some basic type like real, or they are lists or tuples of basic types, lists or tuples of those, and so on. However, it is also possible for parameters or results of functions to have function types. In the previous chapter, we met some functions that can take arguments of other types, including function types. Examples are the identity function, which can take an argument of any type, or the second version of **reverse**, which was able to reverse a list of functions.

Functions that take functions as arguments and/or produce functions as values are called *higher-order functions*.[1] ML makes it easy to define higher-order functions. In contrast, the mechanisms in conventional languages for defining and using higher-order functions tend to be cumbersome, and there may be some limitations on the power of these mechanisms. For example, it may not be possible to define a function like **identity** that works on values of any type whatsoever.

◇ **Example 11.1.** Let us consider a higher-order function that is often used as an example for conventional programming languages: numerical integration **Trapezoidal rule** by the trapezoidal rule. The idea is to compute the integral of some function $f(x)$ between limits a and b — that is, $\int_a^b f(x)dx$ — by dividing the line from a to b into n equal parts for some n. We then approximate the integral as the sum of the areas of the n trapezoids that are suggested by Fig. 11.1 for the case $n = 3$.

In more detail, let $\delta = (b - a)/n$. Then the ith trapezoid has width δ and runs from $a + (i - 1)\delta$ to $a + i\delta$. The area of the ith trapezoid is δ times the average of the two vertical sides, that is

$$\delta\Big(f\big(a + (i - 1)\delta\big) + f(a + i\delta)\Big)/2$$

Figure 11.2 shows the function **trap(a,b,n,F)** that takes two real numbers, the limits a and b, an integer n (the number of trapezoids to use), and a function F to be integrated. As we cannot easily iterate from 1 to n and thereby sum the areas of all the trapezoids, our ML function will use an equivalent recursive strategy. The function **trap** computes the area of the first trapezoid

---

[1] Technically, the order of a function is defined by the following induction. For the basis, a function is "first-order" if its arguments and result are all "data," that is, not functions. Inductively, a function is of order one more than the largest of the orders of its arguments and result. Note that there are some functions, like the identity function, that do not get an order by this induction, and are therefore of "infinite order."

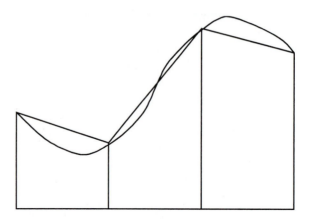

Fig. 11.1. Integration by the trapezoidal rule.

only. It then computes a new lower limit that is one trapezoid's width to the right of the old lower limit a, and decreases n by 1. A recursive call with the new values of a and n sums the areas of the remaining trapezoids.

```
      fun trap(a,b,n,F) =
(1)           if n<=0 orelse b-a<=0.0 then 0.0
              else
                  let
(2)                   val delta = (b-a)/real(n)
                  in
(3)                       delta*(F(a)+F(a+delta))/2.0 +
(4)                           trap(a+delta,b,n-1,F)
                  end;
      val trap = fn : real * real * int * (real → real) → real
```

Fig. 11.2. Function implementing the trapezoidal rule.

- The reader should examine this "trick" carefully, because it is a common way to convert from a loop in an iterative program to a recursive function in a functional program. The general idea is to write a function that, as a basis case, tests if the loop is done. For the induction it does one iteration of the loop and then calls itself recursively to do whatever iterations of the loop remain. The arguments of the function are the loop index and any other variables that are needed in the loop. The hard part in designing the function often is deciding how to express the result of the loop as a value to be returned by the function.

In line (1) of Fig. 11.2 we test for the basis case, where $n = 0$ and $b = a$. Then the value of the integral is 0. However, at the same time we handle data errors, where n or $b - a$ is negative, or where one of n and $b - a$ but not the other is 0. These errors can only occur on the initial call to `trap`, and we really should catch them with exceptions, rather than returning 0 as we do.

If we are not at the basis case, then at line (2) we compute the local variable `delta` to be $1/n$th of the width of the range of integration; that is, `delta` is the width of each trapezoid.[2] Lines (3) and (4) evaluate the integral. In line (3) we compute the area of the first trapezoid, multiplying `delta` by the sum of the heights of the sides — `F(a)` and `F(a+delta)` — and then dividing by 2. Line (4) adds to this area the result of the recursive call on the range that excludes the first trapezoid.

Note the type of the function `trap` as described in the ML response. It is a function that takes a 4-tuple for an argument; the four components (a, b, n, and F) are respectively of types `real`, `real`, `int`, and `real -> real`. The result of the function `trap` is a real.

As an example of a use of the function `trap`, let us define a suitable function F, such as

```
fun square(x:real) = x*x;
val square = fn : real → real
```

Then, we can call, for instance,

```
trap(0.0, 1.0, 8, square);
val it = .3359375 : real
```

This call asks for the integral $\int_0^1 x^2 dx$, whose exact value is 1/3. We divide the range into 8 parts, and the result is high by less than 1%. □

Some Common Higher-Order Functions

We shall now introduce three useful higher-order functions. The first two are actually present as built-in functions of SML/NJ, although they appear in a somewhat different form from that which we shall use to introduce this class of functions.

map

1. The *map* function takes a function F and a list $[a_1, \ldots, a_n]$, and produces the list $[F(a_1), \ldots, F(a_n)]$. That is, it applies F to each element of the list and returns the list of resulting values. This function is known to Lisp users as *mapcar*.

---

[2] `delta` should be the same at each call to `trap`, and we leave it as an exercise to rewrite the function so it evaluates `delta` only once. However, reevaluating `delta` for each trapezoid does have the advantage of preventing the accumulation of roundoff errors in situations where the value of `delta` cannot be represented precisely in the computer.

reduce

2. The *reduce* function takes a function F with two arguments and a list $[a_1, \ldots, a_n]$. The function F normally is assumed to compute some associative operation, such as addition, that is, $F(x, y) = x + y$. The result of **reduce** on F and $[a_1, \ldots, a_n]$ is $F(a_1, F(a_2, F(\cdots, F(a_{n-1}, a_n) \cdots)))$. Thinking of F as an associative binary infix operator, we have the simpler expression $a_1 F a_2 F \cdots F a_n$. For example, if F is the sum function, then $reduce(F, [a_1, \ldots, a_n])$ is $a_1 + a_2 + \cdots + a_n$, the sum of the elements on the list.

filter

3. The function *filter* takes a predicate P, that is, a function whose value is Boolean, and a list $[a_1, \ldots, a_n]$. The result is the list of all those elements on the given list that satisfy the predicate P.

The Map Function

We can define a simple version of the map function as follows.[3]

```
fun map(F,nil) = nil
|   map(F,x::xs) = F(x)::map(F,xs)
val map = fn : ('a → 'b) * 'a list → 'b list
```

In the first line we see that if the list is empty, then there are no elements to apply the function F to, so **map** returns the empty list. The second line covers the inductive case, where we apply F to the head of the list and then recursively apply **map** to the same function F and the tail of the list. The result is assembled by taking $F(x)$, that is, F applied to the head element, and following it by the result of applying F to all the other elements of the list.

Notice the type of **map**. It has two parameters, the first of which is a function F from some type **'a** to a possibly different type **'b**. The second parameter is a list of elements of the type **'a**, which is the type F expects for its argument. The result of **map** is of type **'b list**, that is, a list of elements of the range type of function F. We see that **map** is as polymorphic as it can be; it only requires that the list elements be of the type that the function F expects.

$\Diamond$ **Example 11.2.** Let us define the function **square** to produce the square of an integer, as

```
fun square(x:int) = x*x;
val square = fn : int → int
```

Then we may apply **square** to each element of an integer list by using **map** as follows.

```
map(square, [1,2,3]);
val it = [1,4,9] : int list
```

---

[3] There is a built-in function called **map** that is a different function based on the same idea. We shall introduce the "real" SML/NJ map function shortly.

That is, `map` applies `square` to each of 1, 2, and 3 in turn and produces the list of their squares. □

◇ **Example 11.3.** The function to which `map` is applied need not be something we write; it could be a suitable built-in function. For instance, ~, the unary minus operator, has the form we expect for a function used as an argument of `map`. We can write

```
map(~, [1,2,3]);
val it = [~1, ~2, ~3] : int list
```

This application of `map` has negated each element of the given list. □

Anonymous Functions

If we want to apply `map` to a function that we must define, we need not write the definition of that function separately and give it a name as we did for `square` in Example 11.2. Just as we may write the value of an integer, say 23, without giving it a name, we may express the value of a function anonymously. It is usual to think of the value of a function as "what that function does," and we normally express this value as a program.

In ML, a function-value is introduced by the keyword `fn`. In Chapter 19 we shall give the general form of fn-expressions, that is, expressions for the value of a function. Here we introduce a simplified form only. We can represent a function-value by expression:

```
fn(<parameters>) => <expression>
```

The keyword `fn` introduces the function-value. The position of `fn` makes it appear to substitute for the name of the function. It is followed by the parameter or parameters of the function. As with all ML functions, there is really one parameter, but optional parentheses may be used to group two or more parameters. Next comes the symbol `=>`. Finally, the expression defining the function appears to the right of the `=>`.

- Remember that when defining an anonymous function-value, use the keyword `fn`, not `fun`.

- Also, the operator connecting the parameters and result is `=>`, not `=` or `->`. The latter is used only to connect the types of argument and result in type expressions.

◇ **Example 11.4.** We can apply `square` to each member of a list without actually defining `square` to be the name of the function, as follows.

```
map(fn(x) => x*x, [1,2,3]);
val it = [1,4,9] : int list
```

Notice that in the definition of the squaring function as a value,

```
fn(x) => x*x
```

we did not have to declare x to be an integer. ML was able to figure out that * represents integer multiplication from the fact that the second parameter of `map` is an integer list. □

It is important to appreciate that an expression with `fn` represents the value of a function, just as a string of digits represents the value of an integer. For example, it is legal to use such an fn-expression to bind a function-value to a variable that we wish to be the name of a function. For example, we can write

```
val square = fn(x:int) => x*x;
```
val square = fn : int → int

to give `square` the same value that we gave it in Example 11.2 with the declaration

```
fun square(x:int) = x*x;
```
val square = fn : int → int

In fact, the latter function definition is actually a shorthand for the former val-declaration.

The Function Reduce

Another useful higher-order function is one we shall call **reduce**.[4] Our function **reduce** takes a function F of two arguments and a nonempty list $[a_1, \ldots, a_n]$. A recursive definition of the result of reducing the list by function F is:

BASIS. If $n = 1$, that is, the list is a single element a, then the result is a.

INDUCTION. If $n > 1$, then let b be the result of reducing the tail of the list, which is $[a_2, \ldots, a_n]$, by function F. Then the reduction of the whole list $[a_1, \ldots, a_n]$ by F is $F(a_1, b)$.

◊ **Example 11.5.** Usually the function F defines an associative operator, in which case it does not matter in what order we group the list elements. For instance:

1. The reduction of a list with F equal to the addition function produces the sum of the elements of the list.

2. The reduction by the product function produces the product of the elements of the list.

3. The reduction by the logical AND operator produces the value **true** if all the elements of a Boolean list are **true** and produces **false** otherwise.

---

[4] There is a related function called **fold** available in SML/NJ.

4.   The reduction by the operator **max** produces the largest element on the list. □

```
exception EmptyList;
```
exception EmptyList

(1)   `fun reduce(F,nil) = raise EmptyList`
(2)   `|    reduce(F,[a]) = a`
(3)   `|    reduce(F,x::xs) = F(x, reduce(F,xs));`
       *val reduce = fn : ('a * 'a → 'a) * 'a list → 'a*

Fig. 11.3. The function **reduce**.

A version of the function **reduce** is shown in Fig. 11.3. Since **reduce** does not make sense on the empty list, we create an exception **EmptyList** and raise it at line (1) if the second argument of **reduce** is **nil**. Then, line (2) says that if the list has a single element a, then that element is the value of **reduce** regardless of the function used.

- By intercepting lists of length 1 at line (2), we avoid ever calling **reduce** recursively on an empty list, which would cause an error.

Finally, line (3) implements the inductive step. We reduce the tail of the given list, using the function F, and then apply F to the head and the result of this reduction.

Notice the type of **reduce**. It is a function that takes as first parameter a function F, both of whose parameters are of the same type **'a** and whose result is also of this type. The second parameter of **reduce** is a list of elements of type **'a**, and the result of **reduce** is also of type **'a**.

These equalities of type are inferred by ML as follows. F is used with the result of **reduce** as its second argument in line (3) of **reduce**, so the result of **reduce** and the second parameter of F must be of the same type, say **'a**. In line (2) we see that the elements of the list can be the result of **reduce**, which says that the element type is also **'a**. We see in line (3) that elements of the list can also be the first argument of F, which tells us that the first parameter of F is also of type **'a**. Finally, from line (3) we see that the result types of **reduce** and F are the same, so F produces a value of type **'a** as well.

Variance

◇ **Example 11.6.** The *variance* of a list of reals $[a_1, \ldots, a_n]$ is the average of the squares minus the square of the average. More precisely, one formula for the variance is

$$\left(\sum_{i=1}^{n} a_i^2\right)/n - \left(\left(\sum_{i=1}^{n} a_i\right)/n\right)^2 \tag{11.1}$$

The variance is a measure of the amount by which the elements of a list differ from their average value. In fact, an equivalent formula for the variance is the average of the squares of the differences between each element and the average element. In other words, the variance is $\left(\sum_{i=1}^{n}(a_i - \bar{a})^2\right)/n$, where $\bar{a}$ is the average element, or $\bar{a} = \left(\sum_{i=1}^{n} a_i\right)/n$.

Standard deviation

The square root of the variance, called the *standard deviation*, represents the amount by which a typical element differs from the average. For example, if all the elements are the same then the variance and standard deviation are 0. If half the elements are 10.0 while the other half are 20.0, then each element differs from the average (15.0) by 5.0, so the variance is 25.0 and the standard deviation is 5.0.

We can evaluate Formula (11.1) for the variance using the higher-order functions `map` and `reduce` as follows. Suppose we have function `square` to take the square of a real and function `plus` to sum two reals. We can obtain the sum of the squares of the elements of a list L by the expression `reduce(plus, map(square,L))`. That is, `map(square,L)` produces the list of squares, and `reduce` with first argument `plus` sums these squares. We divide this result by n, the length of the list L, to get the average square. Then we can get the average by `reduce(plus,L)/n`, and we can apply `square` to get the square of the average. The necessary functions, assuming that `reduce` and `map` are as previously defined, are shown in Fig. 11.4.

(1)   `fun square(x:real) = x*x;`
         val square = fn : real → real

(2)   `fun plus(x:real,y) = x+y;`
         *val plus = fn : real * real → real*

(3)   `fun length(nil) = 0.0`
(4)   `|    length(x::xs) = 1.0 + length(xs);`
         val length = fn : 'a list → real

         `fun variance(L) =`
              `let`
(5)   `val n = length(L)`
              `in`
(6)   `reduce(plus,map(square,L))/n -`
(7)   `square(reduce(plus,L)/n)`
              `end;`
         val variance = fn : real list → real

(8)   `variance([1.0, 2.0, 5.0, 8.0]);`
         val it = 7.5 : real

Fig. 11.4. Computing the variance using higher-order functions.

In lines (1) and (2) of Fig. 11.4 we define the functions **square** and **plus**. Lines (3) and (4) define a function **length** that gives the length of a list as a real number.[5] Then we see the definition of function **variance**. At line (5) it computes n, the list length, which is a common subexpression. Lines (6) and (7) are Formula (11.1).

Finally, in line (8) we see a use of the function **variance** on the list of elements $[1, 2, 5, 8]$. Here, $n = 4$. The sum of the squares is $1 + 4 + 25 + 64 = 94$, so the average square is $94/4 = 23.5$. The average element is 4, so the square of the average is 16. Since $23.5 - 16 = 7.5$, the variance is 7.5, as we see in the ML response.

Another way to compute the variance is to take the average of the squares of the differences between the elements and the average. In this case, we would average $(1 - 4)^2$, $(2 - 4)^2$, $(5 - 4)^2$, and $(8 - 4)^2$, or $(9 + 4 + 1 + 16)/4 = 7.5$. □

Op: Converting Infix Operators to Function Names

We might expect that we could use the operator + in place of the function **plus** of Example 11.6. For example, we might expect to be able to write `reduce(+,L)` in line (7) of Fig. 11.4. However, should we do so, we get the error message:

Error: nonfix identifier required

The problem is that ML, like most languages, defines the usual arithmetic operators to be infix. That is, they appear between their operands. However, the function F in the definition of **reduce** is defined, as are all functions, to precede its operands. We can see this requirement explicitly in the way line (3) of Fig. 11.3 is written.

To allow an infix operator to be used as the name of a function, we precede it by the keyword **op**. For example, we may write

```
op + (2,3);
val it = 5 : int
```

In effect, **op** + is the same function as the function **plus** defined in Fig. 11.4, except that the latter is restricted to reals and the former needs to have its parameter type determined. As another example, line (7) of Fig. 11.4 can be written

```
square(reduce(op +, L)/n)
```

with no change in the behavior of the program.

The Function Filter

Another useful higher-order function is **filter**, which we write in Fig. 11.5. This function takes a predicate P and a list L, and produces the list of elements of L that satisfy the predicate P. In line (1) we see the basis case, that if the list

---

[5] ML has a built-in function **length** that produces the length of a list, but as an integer.

L is empty then **filter** produces the empty list regardless of P. Lines (2)–(4) cover the inductive case. We test at line (3) whether $P(x)$ is true for the head element of the list L. If so, the resulting list is x followed by whatever we get by filtering the tail of the list with predicate P. On line (4) we see that if $P(x)$ is false then x is not selected and the result is whatever we get by filtering the tail.

```
(1)        fun filter(P,nil) = nil
(2)        |   filter(P,x::xs) =
(3)                if P(x) then x::filter(P,xs)
(4)                else filter(P,xs);
           val filter = fn : ('a → bool) * 'a list → 'a list

(5)        filter(fn(x) => x>10, [1,10,23,5,16]);
           val it = [23,16] : int list
```

Fig. 11.5. The function filter.

Notice the type of **filter**. It has two parameters, the first of which is of type `'a -> bool`. This type indicates that the argument corresponding to the first parameter can be a predicate with any domain type. The second argument is a list of elements of the type `'a` to which the predicate applies. The result of **filter** is another list of elements of this type.

In line (5) of Fig. 11.5 we see an example of the use of **filter**. The first argument is a description of the Boolean-valued function that is true when its argument is greater than 10. The second argument is a list of integers, and the result is those integers greater than 10, in the order of their occurrence on the list.

Composition of Functions

We shall now study a problem that is of intrinsic importance and that also encourages us to view functions as values disembodied from any arguments to which they might be applied. The composition of functions F and G is that function C such that for any argument x, $C(x) = G(F(x))$.

$\diamond$ **Example 11.7.** Let $F(x) = x + 3$, and let $G(y) = y^2 + 2y$. Then the composition of F and G is $G(F(x))$, which is $(x+3)^2 + 2(x+3)$, or

$$x^2 + 8x + 15$$

We get this formula by substituting $F(x)$ for y in the formula for G and then expanding the formula. $\square$

We can define a higher-order function `comp` that takes two functions as arguments and applies them to a third argument.[6] The ML code is simple:

```
fun comp(F,G,x) = G(F(x));
val comp = fn : ('a → 'b) * ('b → 'c) * 'a → 'c
```

Notice the type of this function. First, recall that `*` takes precedence over `->`, so the type expression is grouped

```
(('a -> 'b) * ('b -> 'c) * 'a) -> 'c
```

Thus, the function has three parameters, the first of which (F) is a function from some type `'a` to some (possibly different) type `'b`. The second parameter, G, takes a value of the type `'b` and produces a value of some (possibly different) type `'c`. The third parameter is of the type `'a` to which F applies, and the result is of the type `'c` that G produces.

◊ **Example 11.8.** We can use `comp` to compute the composition of the two functions from Example 11.7 on a particular value of x, for instance:

```
comp(fn(x) => x+3, fn(y) => y*y+2*y, 10);
val it = 195 : int
```

Here we have defined the first argument of `comp` to be the function $x+3$ and the second to be the function $y^2 + 2y$. The composition of these functions, which we discovered in Example 11.7 was the polynomial $x^2 + 8x + 15$, is then applied to 10, and produces the correct result, $10^2 + 8 \times 10 + 15 = 195$. □

However, Example 11.8 is somehow unsatisfactory. It is true that we can apply the composition of any two functions to an argument, as long as the types match properly. Yet we cannot address the question of Example 11.7, "what function is the composition of functions $x + 3$ and $y^2 + 2y$?" Function `comp` as we defined it is relatively useless. It is a "shorthand" for $F\big(G(x)\big)$, but it fails to save us keystrokes.

What we really want is a function `comp` that takes only the two functions F and G as its arguments and produces the function C that is the composition of F and G. For instance, in the case of Example 11.7, we would like `comp` to return the function $x^2 + 8x + 15$ itself, rather than returning the value of this function for a particular value of x.

The way we do this in ML is a bit tricky. We use a let-expression to define, in terms of a parameter x, what the function that is the composition of F and G does. The expression that follows the keyword `in` is just the defined function. The proper definition appears in Fig. 11.6.

Line (2) defines a function C to have the desired behavior; it is the composition of F and G. In line (3) we see that the value of the function `comp`, which

---

[6] ML actually provides an operator `o` to compose functions (see Chapter 21). The `o` operator differs from `comp` as we define it here by not involving the third argument. In Fig. 11.6 is a revised version of `comp` that is equivalent to the built-in operator `o`.

```
(1)        fun comp(F,G) =
               let
(2)                fun C(x) = G(F(x))
               in
(3)                    C
               end;
           val comp = fn : ('a → 'b) * ('b → 'c) → 'a → 'c

(4)        fun F(x) = x+3;
           val F = fn : int → int

(5)        fun G(y) = y*y+2*y;
           val G = fn : int → int

(6)        val H = comp(F,G);
           val H = fn : int → int

(7)        H(10);
           val it = 195 : int
```

Fig. 11.6. Computing the composition of two functions.

is what we are defining with the let-expression, is the function C itself. The type of comp confirms that we are on the right track. It takes two arguments:

1.   A function F from some type 'a to some type 'b, and

2.   A function G from type 'b to some type 'c.

The result of comp is a function of type 'a -> 'c, that is, a function from type 'a to type 'c.[7] This function is the composition of F and G.

Next, we see in Fig. 11.6 a definition of the function F to be $x+3$ and the function G to be y^2+2y. Then we define the function H to be comp(F,G), that is, the composition of F and G. We now have a name H that we can use to refer to the function that is the composition of F and G, that is, the function whose expression as a polynomial is $x^2+8x+15$. This function can be applied to any integer argument; we show it in Fig. 11.6 applied to argument 10. □

The "Real" Version of Map

The trick used for the function comp is also used in the built-in SML/NJ functions map and fold (the latter is related to our reduce). For example, instead of requiring map to take both the function and the list as arguments, we could define map to take only a function F as argument and produce a function that

---

[7]   To parse this type expression, remember that -> groups from the right. Thus, the proper grouping is (('a -> 'b) * ('b -> 'c)) -> ('a -> 'c).

takes a list of elements as argument and applies F to each element.

Figure 11.7 shows the function `map` that is built into SML/NJ. In line (1), we see that `map` takes one argument, a function F. In a let-expression, we define a function M that takes a list and applies F to each element. Line (2) says that M applied to the empty list is the empty list. Line (3) says that for nonempty list, M applies F to the first element and calls itself recursively on the tail to apply F to the remaining elements. Finally, at line (4) we say that this function M is the result of `map` when it is applied to F.

```
(1)       fun map(F) =
              let
(2)               fun M(nil) = nil
(3)               |   M(x::xs) = F(x)::M(xs)
              in
(4)               M
              end;
          val map = fn : ('a → 'b) → 'a list → 'b list
```

Fig. 11.7. The ML function `map`.

Notice the type of `map` in the ML response. Remembering that `->` groups from the right, this type is `('a -> 'b) -> ('a list -> 'b list)`. That is, `map` is a function that takes as its argument a function (F) from type `'a` to type `'b`. Then, `map` returns a function (M) that takes a list of elements of type `'a` and produces a list of elements of type `'b`.

◇ **Example 11.9.** If `map` is as defined in Fig. 11.7 and `square` is the function that squares integers, then `map(square)` is the function that takes a list of integers and squares each one. We could create this function by

```
val squareList = map(square);
val squareList = fn : int list → int list
```

Then, we can use this function as

```
squareList([1,2,3]);
val it = [1,4,9]
```

to square each element of a particular list. □

We can similarly define a function `filter` to take only a predicate as argument and produce a function that filters elements of a list for satisfaction of that predicate. A version of `reduce` that takes a function F as argument and returns a function that reduces a list by applying F is also possible. We leave the writing of these functions as exercises. However, the function `fold` that is a variation of `reduce` built into SML/NJ is somewhat more complicated. It is deferred to Chapter 21, where we talk about "Currying." In fact, we shall find when we study Chapter 21 that a number of definitions of higher-order functions are made simpler. For example, we can avoid the "trick" used in Figs. 11.6 and 11.7 of defining the desired function in a let-expression.

Exercises

11.1*: Write a function `tabulate` that takes as arguments an initial value a, an increment δ, a number of points n, and a function F from reals to reals. Print a table with columns corresponding to values x and $F(x)$, where $x = a, a + \delta, a + 2\delta, \ldots, a + (n-1)\delta$.

Simpson's rule

11.2: *Simpson's rule* is a more accurate way to integrate functions numerically. If we evaluate a function F at $2n + 1$ evenly spaced points,

$$a, a + \delta, a + 2\delta, \ldots, a + 2n\delta$$

then we may estimate the integral $\int_a^{a+2n\delta} F(x)dx$ by

$$\delta\Big(F(a) + 4F(a + \delta) + 2F(a + 2\delta) + 4F(a + 3\delta) + 2F(a + 4\delta) + \cdots$$
$$+2F(a + (2n - 2)\delta) + 4F(a + (2n - 1)\delta) + F(a + 2n\delta)\Big)/3$$

That is, the even-position terms all have a coefficient of 4, while the odd position terms have coefficient 2, except for the first and last, which have coefficient 1. Write a function `simpson` that takes starting and ending points a and b, an integer n (such that the evaluation is to use $2n + 1$ points as above), and a function F to integrate by Simpson's rule. Try out your function on polynomials x^2, x^3, and so on. What is the smallest integer i such that Simpson's rule fails to get the exact integral of x^i, even with $n = 1$?

11.3: When implementing either the trapezoidal rule or Simpson's rule, it is possible to compute δ once and for all, rather than at each recursive call (although as explained in the text, this strategy may cause roundoff errors to accumulate). Reimplement

a)* The function `trap` of Fig. 11.2
b) Your function `simpson` from Exercise 11.2

in such a way that δ is computed once.

11.4: Improve the function `trap` of Fig. 11.2 by printing an appropriate error message and then raising an exception when the input is bad (as detected by line 1 of Fig. 11.2).

11.5: Use the function `map(F,L)` in the two-parameter form found at the beginning of this chapter to perform the following operations on a list L.

a)* Replace every negative element of a list of reals by 0, leaving nonnegative elements as they are.

b) Add 1 to every element of an integer list.

c)* Change every lowercase letter in a list of characters to the corresponding uppercase letter. Do not assume that only lowercase letters appear in the list.

! d) Truncate each string in a list of strings so it is no more than 5 characters long. That is, delete the sixth and subsequent characters while leaving shorter strings alone.

11.6: Use the function **reduce** to perform the following operations on a list L.

a)* Find the maximum of a list of reals.
b) Find the minimum of a list of reals.
c)* Concatenate a list of strings (i.e., the function **implode**).
d) Find the logical OR of a list of Booleans.

11.7: Use the function **filter** to perform the following operations on a list L.

a)* Find those elements of a list of reals that are greater than 0.
b) Find those elements of a list of reals that are between 1 and 2.
c)* Find the elements of a list of strings that begin with the character **"a"**.
d) Find the elements of a list of strings that are at most 3 characters long.

! 11.8: What is the effect on a list L of **reduce(op -, L)**?

! 11.9*: Write a function **lreduce** that takes a two-parameter function F and a list $[a_1, a_2, \ldots, a_n]$ and produces

$$F\Big(\cdots F\big(F(a_1, a_2), a_3\big) \cdots, a_n\Big)$$

That is, this function is like **reduce**, but it groups the elements of the list from the beginning of the list instead of the end.

11.10: What is the effect of **lreduce(op -, L)**?

11.11*: Another version of **reduce** takes a basis constant g of some type **'b**, a function F of type **'a * 'b -> 'b**, and a list of elements of type **'a**. The result applied to a list $[a_1, \ldots, a_n]$ is

$$F\Big(a_1 \cdots F\big(a_{n-1}, F(a_n, g)\big) \cdots\Big)$$

Write a function **reduceB** that performs this operation.

11.12*: Use the function **reduceB** from Exercise 11.11 to

! a) Compute the length of a list.

!! b) Compute the list of suffixes of a list. For example, given the list **[1,2,3]**, produce **[[1,2,3], [2,3], [3], nil]**.

! 11.13: Write a function like `filter`, but in the style of Fig. 11.7. That is, your function should take a predicate P as argument and return a function that takes a list L and produces those elements of L that satisfy P.

! 11.14: Combine the ideas of Exercises 11.9 and 11.12. That is, your function should take a constant g, a function F, and a list $[a_1, \ldots, a_n]$. The desired result is what we get by starting with g and applying F repeatedly, grouping from the left:

$$F\Big(\cdots F\big(F(g, a_1), a_2\big) \cdots, a_n \Big)$$

11.15: Use your function from Exercise 11.14 to

a) Compute the length of a list.
b) Compute the list of prefixes of a list.

Late binding

! 11.16*: Another use of polymorphic functions is to allow *late binding* of overloaded symbols such as `+` or `*`. That is, instead of using these symbols in a function f, we invent names for them such as `plus` and `times`, and we let these names be parameters of the function f. Then, we can call f with appropriate definitions for the parameters, thus binding the names to the correct meanings as late as possible. As an exercise:

a) Write a function `eval` that takes as parameters functions representing scalar addition and multiplication, as well as taking a polynomial (represented as a list in the manner of Example 6.3) and a value at which to evaluate the polynomial.

b) Show how to call your function from (a) to evaluate the integer polynomial $4x^3 + 3x^2 + 2x + 1$ at the point $x = 5$.

12   Defining New Types

Type system

As in Pascal or C, it is possible to define new types in ML. However, ML has a more powerful *type system* (rules for defining types) than these languages. In ML, types can be polymorphic, taking one or more type-valued variables as parameters. It is also possible in ML to create types whose values are built in more complex ways than is possible in the type systems of most languages.

Before proceeding, let us review what we know about the type system of ML. Types in ML are defined recursively, with a basis of primitive types and rules for constructing more complex types from these.

BASIS. The basic types we have met are `int`, `real`, `string`, `bool`, `unit`, `exn` (exception), and `instream`. We have yet to meet `outstream`. In addition, a type variable such as `'a` or `''a` can serve in place of a constant type such as `int`. These variables appear in the polymorphic types we discussed in the previous chapter and represent values of any type or any equality type respectively.

INDUCTION. We can build new types from old types T_1 and T_2, as follows.

1. $T_1 * T_2$ is a "product" type, whose values are pairs. The first component of the pair is of type T_1 and the second is of type T_2.

2. $T_1 \rightarrow T_2$ is a "function" type, whose values are functions with domain type T_1 and range type T_2.

Type constructor

3.   We may create new types by following a type such as T_1 by certain identifiers that act as *type constructors*. So far, we have met `list` as a type constructor; that is, for every type T_1, there is another type T_1 `list`. We shall meet type constructors, `array` and `ref` in later chapters. In this chapter we learn that the user can define any identifier to be a type constructor by making the appropriate type declaration.

Type expression

The expressions defined inductively as above are called *type expressions*.

New Names for Old Types

To begin, we shall learn the use of the keyword `type`, which defines a new type in a simple way — as an abbreviation for other types. The simplest form of an abbreviation is

   type <identifier> = <type expression>

That is, the keyword `type` is followed by the name we choose for the new type, an equal sign, and an expression involving existing types.

◇ **Example 12.1.** We might define the type **vector** to be a list of reals by

```
type vector = real list;
```
type vector = real list

We can then give a value of the appropriate form this new type as

```
val v = [1.0, 2.0] : vector;
```
val v = [1.0, 2.0] : vector

- Notice that following a value by a colon and a type name declares the value to be of the given type.

The type **vector** is nothing more than an abbreviation. For instance, we can define

```
val w = [1.0, 2.0];
```
val w = [1.0, 2.0] : real list

Here, ML is given a real list and is not told to regard it as of type **vector**. However, if we compare v and w as in

```
v=w;
```
val it = true : bool

ML recognizes that v and w have the same value and does not complain that one is a **vector** while the other is a **real list**. Rather, it recognizes that these are two designations for the same type. □

Polymorphic Type Definitions

More generally, we can define a collection of types with one or more type variables (identifiers beginning with a quote mark) as parameters. The syntax is

type (<list of type parameters>) <identifier> = <type expression>

That is, following the keyword **type** is a list of type variables serving as parameters. If there is only one type variable, the parentheses are optional. The parameters are followed by an identifier, which is the type constructor for the type. Finally comes an equal sign and a type expression, which may involve the parameters.

Types in the defined family are described by providing type expressions corresponding to the type parameters and following the type expressions by the identifier that is the type constructor. An example should help to make these ideas clear.

Mapping

◇ **Example 12.2.** A useful data structure for remembering and retrieving an association between data of two types is the *mapping* (not to be confused with the "map" function of the previous chapter). In ML, we can think of this structure as a list of pairs. The first component of each pair is of some type '**d**,

Domain type

called the *domain type*, and the second component is of some type '**r**, called

Range type

the *range type*.[1] In a mapping we do not expect to see two pairs with the same domain element, although there is nothing in the type definition that requires uniqueness of domain elements.

For instance, we might wish to store a count of words in a document as a list of pairs of the type `(string * int)`. The first component is a word, and the second component is the number of times the word occurs. The counts for the first paragraph of this chapter would include such pairs as

```
[("in",6), ("a",1), ("as",2), ("types",4), ("ML", 4),...]
```

We can see such a set of pairs as assigning an integer value to each domain element (a word) that is mentioned. Mathematicians would say that domain elements are thereby "mapped" to integers.

Here is a definition of the polymorphic type constructor `mapping`.

> `type ('d, 'r) mapping = ('d * 'r) list;`
> *type ('d, 'r) mapping = ('d * 'r) list*

- Note that the list of type parameters `'d` and `'r` is separated by commas after the keyword `type`, as if they were parameters of a function. However, in the type expression `('d * 'r) list`, we represent the type of a pair whose components are respectively of types `'d` and `'r` by separating the types by the product-type operator `*`.

We can now stipulate that a certain value is of a particular mapping type. For example, the "assignment"

> `val words = [("in",6), ("a",1)] : (string, int) mapping;`
> *val words = [("in",6), ("a",1)] : (string, int) mapping*

declares identifier `words` to have a particular value of the type

> `(string * int) mapping`

That type is an instance of the polymorphic type `mapping` formed by choosing the appropriate types for the type parameters `'d` and `'r` in the definition of `mapping`. □

Datatype Declarations and Data Constructors

Since `type` declaration is limited to definitions of "abbreviations," it is of limited power. Often, we want to create datatypes with new structures. For instance, with the types learned so far we cannot express the notion of a tree. For this task, we need *data constructors*, which are identifiers used as operators to build values belonging to a new datatype. The concept of a data constructor

Data constructor

---

[1] Note that the terms "domain" and "range" are used in connection with both mappings and functions. There is no coincidence; the mapping and function describe similar mathematical objects. A mapping associates pairs of values by listing the pairs, and a function is a program that computes the second component of a pair from the first component.

generalizes such ideas as enumerated types in Pascal and union types in Pascal or C, but it goes beyond these. Thus, we shall take the concept in easy stages. In our first example we see a rather simple use of datatype definition corresponding to an enumerated type in Pascal.

◇ **Example 12.3.** Let us define the datatype with type constructor **fruit** to consist of the three values **Apple**, **Pear**, and **Grape**.[2] A suitable declaration appears in Fig. 12.1. The names **Apple**, **Pear**, and **Grape** are the data constructors for the datatype **fruit**, as indicated by the last three lines of the ML response in Fig. 12.1.[3] In this case the "constructors" are quite simple, and they behave like the elements of a Pascal enumerated type.

```
datatype fruit = Apple | Pear | Grape;
```
datatype fruit
con Apple : fruit
con Grape : fruit
con Pear : fruit

Fig. 12.1. Datatype **fruit** is like a Pascal enumerated type.

We can use the new type in a function or other expression. For instance, we can write
```
fun isApple(x) = (x=Apple);
```
val isApple = fn : fruit → bool

The function **isApple** returns true if its argument is **Apple** and false for any other fruit. Since the argument type of **isApple** is **fruit**, it is an error to pass as an argument anything that is not one of the data constructors for the datatype **fruit**. Thus, **isApple** makes the following responses.

```
isApple(Pear);
```
val it = false : bool

```
isApple(Apple);
```
val it = true : bool

```
isApple(Banana);
```
Error: unbound variable: Banana

---

[2] We shall generally adopt the convention that data constructors begin with a capital letter. Note that exceptions also conventionally start with a capital, and as we shall see in Chapter 20, there is a significant similarity between data constructors and exception names, which are often called "exception constructors." Some ML programmers do not start any variable or function name with a capital. We shall not be so strict, since it is often convenient to remind the reader of a variable's type by a capital.

[3] Note that SML/NJ alphabetizes lists of data constructors; they do not necessarily appear in the order in which they were declared.

The last response indicates that `Banana` is not an acceptable argument for the function `isApple`. □

We may observe from Example 12.3 something about the form of datatype definitions that serve as enumerated types. The keyword `datatype` is followed by the name of the type, an equal sign, and a list of the data constructors separated by vertical bars.

- Remember that type abbreviations are introduced by the keyword `type`, but datatypes with data constructors require the keyword `datatype`.

- Notice that `datatype` definitions, even in the simple case of Fig. 12.1, define a new type that is not an abbreviation for any other type.

- For each type there is a set of values. We know, for instance, that the values for the type `int` are the integers. Data constructors are used to build the expressions that are the values for user-defined datatypes. In the simple example above, the data constructors *are* the values. More generally, we shall see that data constructors may be combined in powerful ways to build the set of possible values for a type.

Now we take up a more general form of datatype definition, where

1. Type variables can be used to parameterize the datatype, just as they can for type definitions.

2. The data constructors can take arguments.

This form of a datatype declaration is

```
datatype  (<list of type parameters>) <identifier> =
              <first constructor expression>        |
              <second constructor expression>       |
                          . . .                     |
              <last constructor expression>
```

That is, we use the keyword `datatype` followed by a list of zero or more type variables used as parameters in the type expressions that follow. Parentheses are optional if there is one parameter, and illegal if there are zero parameters as in Fig. 12.1. These are followed by an identifier, which is the type constructor for the datatype. Finally come the equal sign and one or more constructor expressions separated by vertical bars.

Constructor expression

A *constructor expression* consists of a constructor name, the keyword `of`, and a type expression. A simple example is

```
Foo of int
```

This constructor expression says that values of the datatype being defined can have the form `Foo(23)`, or in general, `Foo(`i`)` for any integer i.

- Notice that the data constructor is used to "wrap" the data with (optional) parentheses. In an expression like `Foo(23)`, we not only get a value, 23, but we are told by the data constructor `Foo` something about the form, meaning, or origin of this value.

- Thus, data constructors are "applied" to data as if they were functions, but they are not functions. Rather, we use constructors to form symbolic expressions whose appearance is similar to that of an expression involving function application.

- Do not confuse data constructors with type constructors. Data constructors are used to build expressions that are values for the type. Type constructors are used in expressions that name the types themselves.

Union type

◇ **Example 12.4.** The next example is one in which the datatype capability of ML is used in a manner similar to the union types found in Pascal or C, among other languages. The idea is to manufacture a type whose elements are formed from either of two previously defined types. We use two data constructors, each of which wraps elements of one of the two types, and thus tells us which of the two types is found inside the wrapping parentheses.

We want to deal with "elements" that may be *pairs* or *singles*. The first component of each element will be of some one type `'a`, and the second component, if it exists, will be of some type `'b`. We shall call the datatype `element`. It will have two data constructors, P, which forms a pair, and S, which forms a single. In effect, the first type of the union is `'a` and the second type is `'a * 'b`. The declaration and ML response are shown in Fig. 12.2.

```
(1)            datatype ('a, 'b) element =
(2)                P of 'a * 'b |
(3)                S of 'a;
(4)            datatype ('a, 'b) element
(5)            con P : 'a * 'b → ('a, 'b) element
(6)            con S : 'a → ('a, 'b) element
```

Fig. 12.2. Datatype that is the union of singles and pairs.

In line (1) of Fig. 12.2 we see that a datatype is being declared; it has two type variables as parameters, `'a` and `'b`. The name of the datatype is "`('a, 'b) element`." The identifier `element` becomes a binary type constructor, that is, a type constructor that applies to a pair of types. Line (2) tells us about the data constructor P, which takes as data a pair consisting of an `'a` value and a `'b` value and "wraps" them in the symbol P. Similarly, line (3) tells us about the data constructor S, which takes an `'a` value and wraps it with an S. Note that the type produced is an `('a, 'b) element` even though the data does not involve a value of type `'b` in this case.

Lines (4)–(6) are ML's response. Line (4) echoes the name of the datatype. Line (5) indicates that P is a data constructor that applies to a pair consisting of a 'a-value and a 'b-value, while line (6) tells us that S is a data constructor that applies to a value of type 'a. An ('a, 'b) element is produced by each constructor even though the S data constructor does not take a value of type 'b as part of its argument.

Now let us see how the element datatype can be used. We can let the type parameters 'a and 'b be anything we choose, but for an example let 'a be string and 'b be int. To get concrete, we might wish to extend the word-count problem of Example 12.2 to allow the list to include some words that are not present (represented by "singles"), while pairs represent a word that is present, along with its count of occurrences. For instance, a list of elements representing the first paragraph of this chapter might include

```
[P("in",6), S("function"), P("as",2),...]
```

Suppose we want to take a list of (string, int) element's and sum the integers in the second components of those elements that have second components. The function sumElList given below does this task.

```
(1)        fun sumElList(nil) = 0
(2)        |   sumElList(S(x)::L) = sumElList(L)
(3)        |   sumElList(P(x,y)::L) = y + sumElList(L);
           val sumElList = fn : ('a * int) element list → int
```

Line (1) handles the basis case; when the list is empty the sum is 0. Line (2) handles the case where the first element is a single. Then, there is no contribution to the sum from the head element, so the result is obtained by a recursive application of sumElList to the tail. Line (3) handles the case where the head element is a pair. We recursively apply the function to the tail and then add to the resulting sum the second component of the pair.

- The function sumElList does not constrain the type for first components of pairs. However, line (1) tells us the result of sumElList is an integer. Thus the addition on line (3) is integer addition, so the second components of pairs are integers. Thus, the domain type for the function sumElList is ('a * int) element list.

- In lines (2) and (3), we use the data constructors P and S as part of the pattern to distinguish the two cases of elements. This style is very common when we program with datatypes. We use one pattern for each data constructor, so each kind of value belonging to the datatype is handled appropriately.

Finally, we can apply function sumElList to a particular list as

```
sumElList([P("in",6), S("function"), P("as",2)]);
val it = 8 : int
```

When we apply the function `sumElList` to this particular list, we deduce that the type `'a` for this list is `string`. □

Recursively Defined Datatypes

The datatype `element` of Example 12.4 did not involve nesting of constructors to build values. Rather, we only applied each constructor to appropriate values to form the values of the new type. In many interesting and important examples, values are built by applying the data constructors recursively to build arbitrarily large expressions.

Binary tree

◇ **Example 12.5.** A (*labeled*) *binary tree* is defined recursively as follows.

Empty tree

BASIS. The *empty tree* is a binary tree.

INDUCTION. If T_1 and T_2 are binary trees and a is a label, then we may form another binary tree T by creating a *node* with label a, *left subtree* T_1, and *right subtree* T_2. The new node is the *root* of T.

Left, right subtrees, root

We represent the empty tree by the absence of any mark. A node is represented by its label, a line to the lower left running to the root of its left subtree, and a line to its lower right running to the root of its right subtree. If either subtree is empty, we omit the line to that subtree. Figure 12.3 shows an example binary tree with strings as labels.

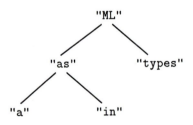

Fig. 12.3. An example of a binary tree labeled by strings.

Figure 12.4 is a datatype declaration for a binary tree with a type parameter `'label` representing the type of labels in the tree. The type constructor for this datatype is "`btree`." In any use, the variable `'label` would be replaced by the actual type. For instance, the binary tree of Fig. 12.3, having string labels, is a value of type `string btree`.

Line (1) of Fig. 12.4 declares the name of the datatype, `btree`, and its type parameter `'label`. Line (2) gives `Empty` as a data constructor. This constructor takes no argument and will appear only as an identifier, just as the fruit names used as data constructors in Example 12.3 appear by themselves. Line (3) introduces the data constructor `Node`, which is applied to a triple of values.

```
(1)        datatype 'label btree =
(2)            Empty |
(3)            Node of 'label * 'label btree * 'label btree;
```
> *datatype 'label btree*
> *con Empty : 'label btree*
> *con Node : 'label * 'label btree * 'label btree → 'label btree*

Fig. 12.4. Datatype definition for binary trees.

The first is of type `'label` and the second two are of type `'label btree`; that is, they are of the same type as the type being defined. The response of ML repeats these points.

The values of type `label btree` are defined recursively as follows.

BASIS. The constructor `Empty` is a value.

INDUCTION. An expression of the form $Node(a, L, R)$ is a value, if a is of the `'label` type and L and R are `'label btree`'s.

- In general, the values for a datatype are those that are constructed by applying the data constructors to values of the appropriate types, as many times as we wish.

For instance, consider the tree of Fig. 12.3. First, we note that the labels are strings, so `'label` must have the value `string`, and this tree is a `string btree`. The leaves (nodes with two empty subtrees) are represented by an expression of the form $Node(a, Empty, Empty)$, where a is the label of the node. For instance, the node labeled `"types"` is represented by the expression `Node("types", Empty, Empty)`.

Then we can work up the tree, constructing the expression for a node after the expressions for its two subtrees have been constructed. Thus, after handling all three leaves, we can work on the node labeled `"as"`. This node has the expression

> `Node("as", Node("a",Empty,Empty), Node("in",Empty,Empty))`

That is, the first component is the label, `"as"`. The second component is the expression for the left subtree, which consists of the leaf labeled `"a"`; this tree has the expression `Node("a", Empty, Empty)`. The third component is a similar expression for the leaf labeled `"in"`.

Finally, the expression for the root uses the expression for the node labeled `"as"` for its left subtree and the expression for the leaf labeled `"types"` as its right subtree. When combined with the label at the root, we find

```
Node("ML",
    Node("as",
        Node("a",Empty,Empty),
        Node("in",Empty,Empty)
    ),
    Node("types",Empty,Empty)
)
```

to be the expression for the entire tree. □

Mutually Recursive Datatypes

Occasionally we need to define two or more datatypes in a mutually recursive way. We can do so by connecting the definitions with the keyword **and**. Type, as opposed to datatype, definitions may also be connected with **and**, but there is less need to do so.

◇ **Example 12.6.** We can define an *even tree* to be a binary tree in which each path from the root to a node with one or two empty subtrees has an even number of nodes. As a special case, the empty tree, whose paths we may regard as having length 0, is an even tree. Similarly, an *odd tree* is a binary tree all of whose paths from the root to a leaf or to a node with one empty subtree have an odd number of nodes. The tree of Fig. 12.3 is neither even nor odd, because there is an even-length path from the root to leaf **"types"** and there are odd-length paths from the root to the other two leaves.

Even, odd trees

There is a simple, mutually recursive definition of the datatypes **evenTree** and **oddTree**.

BASIS. The empty tree is an even tree.

INDUCTION. A node with a label of type **'label** and two subtrees that are odd trees is the root of an even tree. A node with a label of type **'label** and two subtrees that are even trees is the root of an odd tree.

Lines (1)–(4) of Fig. 12.5 show this mutually recursive definition in ML. Line (1) makes **Empty** a constructor for even trees, and line (2) makes **Enode** be a constructor that takes a label and two odd trees to construct an even tree. Similarly, line (4) makes **Onode** the only constructor of odd trees, taking a label and two even trees.

Then, in lines (5) and (6) we define two functions that build even and odd trees respectively, by applying the appropriate constructor to a label x and two trees of the opposite type. Lines (7)–(11) use these functions to build some odd and even trees. Line (7) creates an odd tree consisting of a single node labeled 1. Note that ML now deduces that for this tree the type **'label** is integer. Line (8) similarly creates a node labeled 2. It, like all single-node trees, is an odd tree.

Line (9) uses the two odd trees from the previous two lines to create an even tree whose root has label 3, whose left subtree is the single node labeled 1, and

```
      datatype
(1)       'label evenTree = Empty |
(2)           Enode of 'label * 'label oddTree * 'label oddTree
      and
(3)       'label oddTree =
(4)           Onode of 'label * 'label evenTree * 'label evenTree;
```
datatype 'label evenTree
con Empty : 'label evenTree
*con Enode : 'label * 'label oddTree * 'label oddTree → 'label evenTree*
datatype 'label oddTree
*con Onode : 'label * 'label evenTree * 'label evenTree → 'label oddTree*

```
(5)   fun buildEven(x,T1,T2) = Enode(x,T1,T2);
```
*val buildEven = fn : 'label * 'label oddTree * 'label oddTree →*
    'label evenTree

```
(6)   fun buildOdd(x,T1,T2) = Onode(x,T1,T2);
```
*val buildOdd = fn : 'label * 'label evenTree * 'label evenTree →*
    'label oddTree

```
(7)   val t1 = buildOdd(1,Empty,Empty);
```
val t1 = Onode(1,Empty,Empty) : int oddTree

```
(8)   val t2 = buildOdd(2,Empty,Empty);
```
val t2 = Onode(2,Empty,Empty) : int oddTree

```
(9)   val t3 = buildEven(3,t1,t2);
```
val t3 = Enode(3, Onode(1,Empty,Empty), Onode(2,Empty,Empty)) :
    int evenTree

```
(10)  val t4 = buildOdd(4,t3,Empty);
```
val t4 = Onode(4, Enode(3, Onode #, Onode #), Empty) : int oddTree

```
(11)  val t5 = buildEven(5,t4,t4);
```
val t5 = Enode(5, Onode(4, Enode #, Empty),
    Onode(4, Enode #, Empty)) : int evenTree

Fig. 12.5. Mutually recursive datatype definitions.

whose right subtree is the single node labeled 2. Notice ML's response, which gives the expression for this tree and identifies its type as an **int evenTree**.

Line (10) builds another odd tree by taking a root node with label 4, the even tree *t*3 from line (9), and an empty even tree as left and right subtrees.

• Notice in the response that SML/NJ only shows complicated expressions for a fixed number of levels and elides deeper structure with the # sign.

Here the first # stands for the tree t1, or Onode(1,Empty,Empty), and the
second # stands for t2, or Onode(2,Empty,Empty).

```
Enode(5,
    Onode(4,
        Enode(3,
            Onode(1,Empty,Empty),
            Onode(2,Empty,Empty)),
        Empty
    ),
    Onode(4,
        Enode(3,
            Onode(1,Empty,Empty),
            Onode(2,Empty,Empty)),
        Empty
    )
)
```

(a) Nested expression for tree t5.

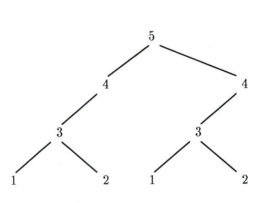

(b) Picture of tree t5.

Fig. 12.6. Representations of the tree t5 from Fig. 12.5.

Finally, line (11) takes a root node labeled 5 and two copies of the odd tree
t4 from line (10) and creates another even tree. Each # in the response to line
(11) represents the tree t3. Figure 12.6(a) shows the complete expression for
t5 expanded out, while Fig. 12.6(b) is a picture of this even tree. Note that
each root-to-leaf path has an even number of nodes. □

The reader familiar with a language like Pascal or C that uses pointers as a type constructor may have seen trees constructed by pointers in records that represent nodes. Notice that the ML approach is somewhat different. The value of the tree is represented in ML programs by an expression built from data constructors applied to arguments. For example, the value of t3 printed after line (9) of Fig. 12.5 does not involve any pointers to the values of t1 or t2.

The distinction is seen if identifiers such as t1 or t2 are redefined. Then, the value of t3 does not change. However, had a tree like t3 been constructed with pointers to t1 and t2, the value of t3 would change as a side-effect of the change to t1 or t2.

Exercises

12.1: Give type definitions (abbreviations) for the following types.

a)* A set of sets, where the type of elements is unspecified and sets are represented by lists.

b) A list of triples, the first two components of which have the same type and the third component of which is of some (possibly) different type.

12.2: Give examples of values of the following types.

a)* A value of type int btree, where btree is the datatype defined in Example 12.5. Your tree should have 3 nodes.

b) A value of type (real * real) mapping, where mapping is the type defined in Example 12.2. Your value should have 3 pairs.

! **12.3***: Define a type mapTree that is a specialization of the btree datatype to have a label type that is a set of domain-range pairs. Then, define a tree t1 that has a single node with the pair ("a",1) at the root.

12.4: Write a function that takes a btree as its argument and returns a pair consisting of the left and right subtrees. Define an exception for the erroneous case where the tree is empty.

! **12.5***: In Fig. 9.8 we wrote a program to read and sum integers, using the awkward convention that -1 represented the situation where the end of file had been reached and no integer was available. A better approach is to define a datatype intOrEof that has one data constructor Eof to represent the absence of an integer and another data constructor Int that wraps an integer. Rewrite Fig. 9.8 to use this strategy and avoid the use of -1, which was represented there by the identifier END.

! **12.6**: Tell whether a type or a datatype declaration would be more suitable for the following. Give the appropriate declaration.

a)* A type whose values are the suits of a card deck.

b)   A type whose elements are either lists of (only) integers or lists of (only) reals.

c)* A type whose values are "things," where a "thing" is either an integer or a list of "things."

d)   A (polymorphic) type whose values are pairs whose components can be of any type, as long as they are of the same type.

! 12.7: Define mutually recursive datatypes `zeroTree`, `oneTree`, and `twoTree` to be those binary trees whose every path from the root to a node with at least one empty subtree has length whose remainder when divided by 3 is 0, 1, or 2 respectively.

$\Diamond\Diamond\Diamond$ **13   Programming with Datatypes**

In this chapter, we shall try to solidify our familiarity with datatypes by writing a number of functions on binary trees. We shall then introduce a datatype representing arbitrary rooted trees, that is, trees in which nodes can have any number of children. Some instructive examples of functions for this datatype will also be presented.

Binary Search Trees

Binary search trees are binary trees whose labels obey a particular property called the *binary search tree property*, or *BST property*, described below. The BST property only makes sense if there is an ordering relation, often referred to as $<$, that allows us to compare values of the label type. For example, the types **int**, **real**, and **string** have this ordering. To be more general, we shall only assume that there is a predicate **lt(x,y)** obeying the important properties of $<$ on integers, reals, or strings. These properties are:

Transitivity

1. *Transitivity.* That is, $lt(x,y)$ and $lt(y,z)$ imply $lt(x,z)$, just as $x < y$ and $y < z$ tell us that $x < z$.

Comparability

2. *Comparability.* If $x \neq y$, then exactly one of $lt(x,y)$ and $lt(y,x)$ is true.

Irreflexivity

3. *Irreflexivity.* $lt(x,x)$ is never true for any x.

Note that, like transitivity, (2) and (3) are obeyed by the conventional $<$. We never have $x < x$, and if $x \neq y$, then either $x < y$ or $y < x$ will be true, but never both.

Now we can state the BST property with regard to a given comparison operator $<$.

BST property

• *BST property*: If x is the label of any node n in a binary search tree, then for every label y in the left subtree of n we have $y < x$, and for every label y in the right subtree of n we have $x < y$.

$\Diamond$ **Example 13.1.** The tree of Fig. 12.3 is a binary search tree if we take the ordering to be the usual lexicographic order on strings but first convert capital letters to lowercase.[1] Thus the desired **lt** function requires first converting capitals to lowercase, and then doing the standard comparison. Here is a function

---

[1] Remember that in ASCII, a capital letter has a code 32 less than its corresponding lowercase letter, and therefore precedes all lowercase letters according to the $<$ relationship defined for ML strings.

129

lower that converts a list of characters by replacing the uppercase letters by the corresponding lowercase letters.

```
fun lower(nil) = nil
|    lower(c::cs) = if c>="A" andalso c<="Z" then
        chr(ord(c)+32)::lower(cs) else c::lower(cs);
val lower = fn : string list → string list
```

Here we test to see if the first character c is a capital letter by determining if it lies between **"A"** and **"Z"**. If so, we convert it to lower case by adding 32 to its code, relying on the character code being ASCII. If c is not a capital, we pass it to the result unchanged.

Now we can use **lower** to define a suitable function **lt**. This function explodes its two argument strings, converts each to lowercase, and compares the results using the built-in **<** comparison operator for strings.

```
fun lt(x:string,y) =
        implode(lower(explode(x))) <
            implode(lower(explode(y)));
val lt = fn : string * string → bool
```

Consider the root, whose label is **"ML"**. The three words in the left subtree — **"a"**, **"as"**, and **"in"** — each precede **"ML"** in the order defined by function **lt** above. The one word **"types"** in the right subtree follows **"ML"**. These observations tell us the BST property is satisfied at the root.

In order to verify the BST property for the tree as a whole, we must consider all the nodes. For the node labeled **"as"**, we find only **"a"** in the left subtree and **"in"** in the right subtree. Since **lt("a","as")** and **lt("as","in")** are both true, the BST property holds at this node. The other three nodes have only empty subtrees, so they cannot violate the BST property. We conclude that Fig. 12.3 satisfies the BST property. □

Lookup in Binary Search Trees

Binary search trees are useful because they let us search for elements at the nodes, insert new elements, and delete elements in time that is usually much less than the number of nodes in the tree. In particular, we only have to follow one path in the tree, starting at the root and heading down the tree. The BST property helps us find a particular label x if it exists somewhere in a binary search tree. We start at the root and progress down the tree in the only direction that could hold x, until we either find x or come to an empty tree.

The following recursive algorithm assumes we have some tree T to search and directs us in the proper way. In practice, we look for an element x by starting our search at the root of the entire binary search tree, although as we proceed, T could be any of the subtrees encountered during our search.

BASIS. If we are at an empty tree, then fail; x is not in the tree. If we are at a tree with root n and the label of n is x, then our search for x succeeds.

INDUCTION. If we are at the root of some nonempty tree, the label of the root is y, and $x \neq y$, then

1. If $lt(x, y)$, then recursively search only the left subtree.
2. Otherwise (i.e., $lt(y, x)$), search only the right subtree.

In Fig. 13.1 is the ML function `lookup` that performs this algorithm on a binary search tree. This function makes use of another function `lt`, which must obey the properties outlined above. We might, for example, suppose that the label type is `string` and that `lt` is defined as in Example 13.1. We suppose this definition of `lt` and the definition of the datatype `btree` from Fig. 12.4 are available when ML processes the definition in Fig. 13.1, which explains how the type of the function `lookup` is determined.

```
         (* lookup(x,T) tells whether element x is in tree T *)
(1)      fun lookup(x,Empty) = false
(2)      |   lookup(x,Node(y,left,right)) =
(3)              if x=y then true
(4)              else if lt(x,y) then lookup(x,left)
(5)              else (* lt(y,x) *) lookup(x,right);
```
*val lookup = fn : string * string btree → bool*

Fig. 13.1. Lookup in a binary search tree.

Line (1) of Fig. 13.1 handles one of the basis cases, where the tree is empty. Line (2) provides the pattern that matches all other cases. Variable **x** matches the value being searched for, and **Node(y,left,right)** matches the expression for any binary tree except the empty tree. In the match, **y** acquires the value of the label, **left** gets the value of the left subtree, and **right** gets the value of the right subtree.

Then, line (3) handles the other basis case, where the desired label has been found. Line (4) handles the case where the desired label is less than the label at the root; we must then search only the left subtree. Line (5) handles the only remaining case, which is that the desired label is greater than the label at the root and we must search the right subtree.

For instance, if we call **lookup** with first argument **"function"** and second argument the tree of Fig. 12.3, we first compare **"function"** with **"ML"**, and at line (4) go to the left subtree, rooted at **"as"**. There we find **"function"** follows **"as"**, so we go to the right, the tree rooted at **"in"**. Next, we find **"function"** precedes **"in"**, so we go to the left subtree. This tree is empty, so at the next call the pattern of line (1) applies and we return **false**. The desired label **"function"** is not in the tree.

- Notice how pattern matching is used in the function **lookup** to determine which data constructor is used at the outermost layer of the expression representing the binary tree.

- Pattern matching is also used to pick apart the structure of the tree and allow us to attack pieces of the expression recursively.

Insertion into Binary Search Trees

Next, let us look at a similar function **insert** to insert an element into a binary search tree in the appropriate place. The function **insert(x,T)** returns the tree that results when x is inserted into tree T. The fact that the modified tree is returned is an essential point in understanding how **insert** works. The recursive algorithm can be described as follows.

BASIS. To insert x into the empty tree, return the tree with one node, labeled x. To insert x into a tree whose root is labeled x, return the given tree. In the latter case, no modification is necessary.

INDUCTION. To insert x into a tree with root labeled y, where $x \neq y$, recursively insert x into the left subtree if $x < y$ and into the right subtree otherwise. Return the tree with its left or right subtree modified respectively.

Figure 13.2 is ML code to execute this algorithm. We again assume that **lt** is written for string arguments as in Example 13.1.

```
          (* insert(x,T) returns tree T with x inserted *)
(1)    fun insert(x,Empty) = Node(x,Empty,Empty)
(2)    |    insert(x, T as Node(y,left,right)) =
(3)            if x=y then T (* do nothing; x was already there *)
(4)            else if lt(x,y) then Node(y,insert(x,left),right)
(5)            else (* lt(y,x) *) Node(y,left,insert(x,right));
        val insert = fn : string * string btree → string btree
```

Fig. 13.2. Insertion into a binary search tree.

Line (1) handles the case of insertion into an empty tree, where a one-node tree is returned. Line (2), like the same line in Fig. 13.1, matches any nonempty tree and breaks it into its important components. However, the whole tree is also matched to the identifier **T** at line (2).

In line (3) we return the same tree T if x is at the root. In line (4), we are directed to insert into the left subtree. We return a tree whose root label is the same as it was: y. The right subtree is also the same as it was, but the left subtree is modified to be whatever the recursive call to **insert(x,left)** produces. That will be the left subtree, modified to include a node labeled x at the appropriate place. Finally, line (5) does the symmetric thing when x must be inserted into the right subtree.

For instance, if we call **insert** with first argument **function** and second argument the tree of Fig. 12.3, we eventually find our way to the empty tree that is the left subtree of the node labeled **"in"**. That empty subtree is replaced by a tree with one node labeled **"function"**. The resulting two-node tree replaces the one-node tree whose node is labeled **"in"**, yielding a four-node tree to replace the three-node tree whose root is labeled **"as"**. Figure 13.3 shows the resulting tree after insertion.

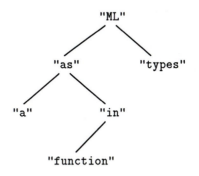

Fig. 13.3. Binary search tree after insertion of "function".

Deletion from Binary Search Trees

We can delete a specified element x from a binary search tree, but the strategy is a bit more complicated than lookup or insertion. The idea is expressed by the following recursive algorithm.

BASIS. Nothing needs to be done to delete x from an empty tree; x is not there anyway. To delete x from a tree whose root has label x, modify the tree to remove x and maintain the BST property as follows.

1. If the root has at least one empty subtree, replace the tree by the other subtree.

2. If the root has two nonempty subtrees:
    a) Find the least element in the right subtree,
    b) Delete it from the right subtree (which is always an example of case (1) above, since the least element in a binary search tree must have an empty left subtree), and
    c) Make the least label be the label of the root, replacing x.

INDUCTION. To delete x from a tree whose root has label y, where $x \neq y$, recursively delete x from the left subtree if $x < y$ and from the right subtree if $y < x$.

```
(1)    exception EmptyTree;
       exception EmptyTree

       (* deletemin(T) returns a pair consisting of the least
               element y in tree T and the tree that results
               from deleting y from T. It is an error if T
               is empty *)
(2)    fun deletemin(Empty) = raise EmptyTree
(3)    |   deletemin(Node(y,Empty,right)) = (y,right) (* This
               is the critical case. If the left subtree is empty,
               then the element at the current node is the min. *)
(4)    |   deletemin(Node(w,left,right)) =
               let
(5)                  val (y,L) = deletemin(left)
               in
(6)                  (y, Node(w,L,right))
               end;
       val deletemin = fn : string btree → string * string btree

       (* delete(x,T) returns tree T with element x deleted *)
(7)    fun delete(x,Empty) = Empty
(8)    |   delete(x,Node(y,left,right)) =
(9)            if lt(x,y) then Node(y,delete(x,left),right)
(10)           else if lt(y,x) then Node(y,left,delete(x,right))
               else (* x=y *)
(11)               if left = Empty then right
(12)               else if right = Empty then left
                   else let
(13)                   val (z,R) = deletemin(right)
                   in
(14)                   Node(z,left,R)
                   end;
       val delete = fn : string * string btree → string btree
```

Fig. 13.4. Deletion from a binary search tree.

Figure 13.4 gives the necessary code to implement this algorithm. To understand it, start with the function **delete** of lines (7)–(14). Line (7) handles the first part of the basis, where we try to delete x from the empty tree and simply return the empty tree. In line (8) we handle all other cases, where the tree is nonempty and we need to dissect it into its important components as we did for **lookup** and **insert**.

Lines (9) and (10) cover the inductive cases, where we must delete from the left or right subtree. For instance, in line (9) we must delete from the left.

To do so, we assemble the result by taking the original label y, the original right subtree, and the left subtree that we get by deleting x from the original left subtree.

Lines (11)–(14) handle the hard basis case where x has been found at the root and we must rearrange the tree. Lines (11) and (12) are for the case where one of the subtrees is empty and we return the other.

If neither subtree is empty, then we call the function **deletemin** (to be described next) on the right subtree. This function returns a pair:

1. z, the smallest label in the right subtree, and
2. R, the tree that results from deleting z from the original right subtree.

In line (14) we assemble the result, which has z in place of x at the root, the original left subtree, and the revised right subtree R. Note that because z is the least label of the right subtree, the BST property is satisfied with z at the root. It surely precedes anything in R, and because $x < z$, it must be that anything in the left subtree precedes z as well as x.

Now let us consider the function **deletemin**. This function is only called on nonempty trees, so we use the exception **EmptyList** in line (1) and raise it in line (2) if somehow the function is called on an empty tree.

The least label in a binary search tree is found by following left branches until we reach a node that has an empty left subtree. The situation is suggested in Fig. 13.5. Thus line (3) handles the case where we are at a tree with an empty left subtree. We return the pair consisting of:

1. The label of this node, which must be the least element, and
2. The right subtree, which is what is left when we delete the node with the least element.

Notice that this deletion is an easy basis case, where one of the subtrees is empty.

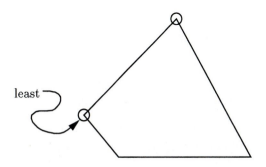

Fig. 13.5. Locating the least label in a tree.

Lines (4)–(6) handle the case where the left subtree is not empty and we must search further. In line (5) we recursively apply **deletemin** to the left subtree, obtaining a pair (y, L) consisting of the least label y and what remains of the left subtree after deleting y. In line (6) we assemble the desired result, a pair with y as the first component. For the second component we construct a tree with the original label w, the new left subtree L, and the original right subtree.

Some Comments About Running Time

We mentioned that the operations of lookup, insert, and delete on binary search trees take time proportional to the length of the path followed. This path in a "typical" binary search tree will have length that is logarithmic in the number of nodes in the tree. So, binary search trees are a very efficient way to represent large sets if we only want to perform these three operations. We shall not try to prove the contention that the typical path is logarithmic in length; the reader may rely on this observation if he or she is unfamiliar with the lore surrounding binary trees.

However, it is useful to verify the fact that the time taken by these algorithms is proportional to the length of the path traversed. Function **lookup** in Fig. 13.1 is the easiest to analyze. Line (1) takes a constant amount of time, independent of the size of the tree, to test whether the second argument is **Empty** and return **false** if so. Line (2) takes a constant amount of time to examine the root node of the tree and match variables **x**, **y**, **left**, and **right** in the pattern. Line (3) takes constant time to test if $x = y$ and return **true** if so.

Line (4) requires constant time to apply function **lt**.[2] We also have to consider the time that is consumed in line (4) or (5) by the recursive call to **lookup**. However, whether we call **lookup(x,left)** or **lookup(x,right)**, we have moved one node down the tree. Thus as we follow our path down the tree, we spend only a constant amount of time at each node and then move down. Hence the total amount of time spent is proportional to the length of the path followed.

The argument about **insert** in Fig. 13.2 is similar. The only difference is that after making the recursive call to **insert** at line (4) or (5), we have to assemble a new tree, for example by evaluating the expression

```
Node(y,insert(x,left),right)
```

in line (4). Is it possible that we have to copy the tree produced by

```
insert(x,left)
```

in this situation?

Fortunately, it is not. ML is implemented in such a way that this value-construction is done by pointers, just as it is typically done by programmers using conventional languages. In ML, these pointers are "behind the scenes," and

---

[2]   Technically, **lt** could be any function that returns a Boolean, but it does not get the tree as an argument, and so its running time could not depend on the size of the tree.

the user may imagine that the trees themselves are manipulated. In practice, the construction of a tree from given trees — or in general, any fixed number of steps of value-construction using data constructors — takes a constant amount of time, independent of the size of the values being manipulated.

Interestingly, we avoid copying values even in situations where it appears to be necessary. For example, consider line (11) of Fig. 12.5, where we construct the value of t5 from two copies of the value of t4. In ML implementations, the value of t5 can have two pointers, each to the value of t4. Because values of variables do not change in ML, we can rely on the value of t4 remaining the same should we ever need the value of t5. In other languages, we normally could not take this risk.

Visiting All the Nodes of a Binary Tree

The previous examples each have the property that we follow one path down a binary tree from the root to a leaf. There is another class of functions that operate on a tree by visiting each node in a systematic order. We shall give two simple examples.

◇ **Example 13.2.** Let us write a function sum(T) that takes a binary tree, defined by the datatype of Fig. 12.4, and sums the labels of all the nodes, which we shall assume are integers. The datatype definition from Fig. 12.4 is:

```
datatype 'label btree =
    Empty |
    Node of 'label * 'label btree * 'label btree;
```

The function sum is written below:

```
fun sum(Empty) = 0
|   sum(Node(a,left,right)) = a + sum(left) + sum(right);
val sum = fn : int * int btree → int
```

That is, the sum over an empty tree is 0, and the sum over any other tree is the label plus the sums over the left and right subtrees. As we see from the ML response, the label type is forced to be integer because of the 0 on the first line. □

Preorder Traversals

A *preorder traversal* of a tree is a listing of the node labels by the following recursive algorithm.

1. List the label of the root.

2. In order from the left, list all the nodes of each subtree in preorder.

◇ **Example 13.3.** Consider the tree of Fig. 12.3. To list its labels in preorder, we first list the label at the root, **"ML"**. Then we work on the 3-node subtree rooted at **"as"**. We list **"as"**, next work on the left subtree **"a"** and finally work on the right subtree **"in"**. Any 1-node tree is listed in preorder by listing the label alone, so we follow **"as"** by **"a"** and then **"in"**.

Last, we return to the root, having listed its left subtree but not its right subtree. The right subtree, being a 1-node tree, is listed by listing its label **"types"**. Thus

> ["ML", "as", "a", "in", "types"]

is the complete preorder listing. □

Here is a function `preOrder(T)` that lists a binary tree in preorder.

```
fun preOrder(Empty) = nil
|   preOrder(Node(a,left,right)) =
        [a] @ preOrder(left) @ preOrder(right);
val preOrder = fn : 'a btree → 'a list
```

This function follows the definition of preorder in a straightforward way. An empty tree yields nothing, while any other tree yields the label of its root, followed by the preorder listings of its left and right subtrees. Note that if either or both of those subtrees are empty, they will not produce any contribution to the preorder listing.

General Rooted Trees

There is a common notion of a (rooted) tree that is in a sense a generalization of a binary tree. In the datatype **tree**, nodes are allowed to have any number of subtrees from 0 up. We can represent such trees with a single data constructor that we shall call **Node**. The datatype definition appears in Fig. 13.6, where we see that a node consists of a label and a list of trees of the same type. That is, type **'label tree list** is a list of elements, each of which is a tree with labels of type **'label**.

```
datatype ('label) tree =
    Node of 'label * 'label tree list
datatype 'label tree
con Node : 'label * 'label tree list → 'label tree
```

Fig. 13.6. Datatype for a general rooted tree.

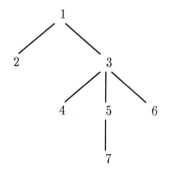

Fig. 13.7. An example tree.

◇ **Example 13.4.** In Fig. 13.7 is a tree with seven nodes and integer labels from 1 to 7 to identify the nodes. A node is drawn with lines downward to its *children*, which are the roots of its subtrees. Notice that node 3 has three children.

Children

Let us represent the tree of Fig. 13.7 as a value of datatype **tree**. First, note that any leaf with label *a* is represented by the expression **Node(a,nil)**. That is, the list of the subtrees of a leaf is empty. Thus the expression for the node labeled 2, for example, is **Node(2,nil)**.

Now we can work up the tree to build expressions for nodes that have children. First, node 5 has one subtree, the tree with only node 7, so the expression for the tree rooted at node 5 is **Node(5, [Node(7,nil)])**. Then, we can construct the expression for node 3. It has a list of three subtrees, so its expression has a second component that is a list of length three, as follows:

```
Node(3, [
    Node(4,nil),
    Node(5, [Node(7,nil)]),
    Node(6,nil)
])
```

Finally, we can construct the expression for the entire tree rooted at 1. The expression is shown in Fig. 13.8. □

There are several differences between binary trees and (general) trees, as we have defined them.

- Unlike nodes of a binary tree, a node with two children, like node 1 of Fig. 13.7, does not identify the first as a "left" child and the second as a "right" child. Rather, node 1 simply has two children and its list of children from the left is [2, 3].

- There is no way to represent the empty tree — that is, the tree with no nodes — in the datatype **tree** as we have defined it.

```
Node(1, [
    Node(2,nil),
    Node(3, [
        Node(4,nil),
        Node(5, [
            Node(7,nil)
        ]),
        Node(6,nil)
    ])
])
```

Fig. 13.8. Expression for tree of Fig. 13.7.

Summing the Labels of a General Tree

Let us write a function **sum** like that of Example 13.2 but for general trees. The strategy is surprisingly tricky. We create new trees that are not subtrees of the original but are constructed from it by lopping off subtrees, one at a time. The function is shown in Fig. 13.9.

```
(1)        fun sum(Node(a:int,nil)) = a
(2)        |   sum(Node(a,t::ts)) =
(3)                sum(t) + sum(Node(a,ts));
           val sum = fn : int tree → int
```

Fig. 13.9. The function **sum** for general trees.

Line (1) handles the case where the tree has only one node. We can identify such a tree by the fact that its second component, the list of subtrees, is empty. In this case, we return the label of the root node.

Lines (2) and (3) handle the case where there is at least one subtree. We break the list of subtrees into its head, the first subtree **t**, and the tail, consisting of the other subtrees, if any. In line (3) we see that we apply **sum** to the first subtree and then construct a new tree, represented by the expression **Node(a,ts)**. This tree has the same root with its same label, *a*. It also has as its list of subtrees all the subtrees of the original, except for the first subtree.

When we apply **sum** to this new tree, we eventually get the sums of all the subtrees. Finally, after eliminating all the subtrees in recursive calls to **sum**, we are left with a tree that has root label *a* and no subtrees. At this point, the basis case of line (1) holds, and we add in the label at the root to the resulting sum.

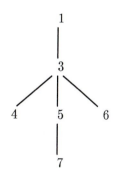

Fig. 13.10. New tree for recursive application of function `sum`.

◇ **Example 13.5.** Consider applying `sum` to the tree of Fig. 13.7. The case of lines (2) and (3) applies. Here `t` represents only the node 2, so the new tree is that of Fig. 13.10. This tree is Fig. 13.7 with node 2 deleted. In general, all nodes descended from 2 would also be deleted.

The value of `sum(t)` in line (3) is clearly 2. We must now evaluate `sum` applied to the tree of Fig. 13.10; this sum is the second term in line (3). When we apply `sum` recursively to Fig. 13.10, we find that `t`, the head of the list of subtrees, is the 5-node tree rooted at 3, and the list of remaining subtrees is empty.

When we compute `sum(t)` this time, we get $3 + 4 + 5 + 6 + 7 = 25$ by a series of recursive calls that we do not show. To this sum we must add the result of `sum` applied to the tree of Fig. 13.10 with the first (and only) subtree of 1 deleted. This tree is the single node 1, and its sum is 1. Thus the call to `sum` on the tree of Fig. 13.10 returns $25 + 1 = 26$.

Finally, we return to the original call of `sum`. We noted that the call `sum(t)` returned 2, and we just deduced that the call `sum(Node(a,ts))` returns 26. Thus the correct answer, 28, is returned. □

Exercises

13.1: Suppose we define the type `mapTree` as in Exercise 12.3 (see the solutions at the back of the book). This type is a binary tree whose labels are pairs, which we may think of as the domain and range values of a pair in some mapping. We may use a `mapTree` as a sort of binary search tree, if we use a $<$ ordering on the domain (first) component of each pair only. We shall assume, for convenience, that we never store two pairs with the same first component. Also assume that the domain type is `int` so we may use the usual $<$ on integers as the function `lt`.

a)* Write a function `lookup(a,T)` that searches for a pair (a, b) for some b and returns b. If there is no such pair, then raise the exception `Missing`.

b) Write a function `assign(a,b,T)` that looks for a pair (a, c) and, if found, replaces c by b. If no such pair is found, insert the pair (a, b) in the tree in a position that preserves the BST property.

13.2: Write a function to list the labels of a general tree in preorder. Next, use the higher-order function `reduce` of Fig. 11.3 to produce the sum of the labels of the tree, assuming these labels are integers.

Graph

! **13.3***: We can define a graph with nodes of some type `'node` as a list of pairs. Each pair consists of a node of type `'node` and a list of its successor nodes.

a) Write this type definition.

b) Write a function `succ(a,G)` that produces the set of successors of node a in graph G. If a is not a node of G, then raise the exception `NotANode`.

!! c) Write a function `search(a,G)` that finds the set of nodes reachable from node a in graph G, including a itself. *Hint*: It helps to write an auxiliary function `search1(L,R,G)` that finds all the nodes that are reachable from one or more of the nodes on list L in graph G, without going through a node of R. Function `search1` then returns all the nodes it has reached plus all the nodes on R. We may use parameter R of `search1` to keep track of nodes we have already reached in our search. We thus avoid getting trapped in infinite loops, even if the graph G has cycles.

Propositional logic

! **13.4**: In propositional logic, statements are represented by *propositional variables*, which we may think of as identifiers. Logical expressions can be built from propositional variables by applying a number of logical operators. In our exercise, we shall define logical expressions and their truth values in a simple but useful form as follows.

BASIS. A propositional variable is a logical expression. Its truth value may be assigned to be either true or false.

INDUCTION. If E_1 and E_2 are logical expressions, then

1. `AND` (E_1, E_2) is a logical expression, and its value is true if and only if both E_1 and E_2 have the value true.

2. `OR` (E_1, E_2) is a logical expression, and its value is true if either E_1 or E_2 or both have the value true.

3. `NOT` (E_1) is a logical expression whose value is true if and only if the value of E_1 is false.

An example of a propositional expression is `AND` $\big($`OR` (p, q), `NOT` $(p)\big)$. Do the following:

a)   Devise a datatype whose values represent logical expressions as described above. You may assume that propositional variables are represented by strings.

b)   Write a function `eval(E,L)` that takes a logical expression E and a list of true propositional variables L, and determines the truth value of E on the assumption that the propositional variables on L are true and all other propositional variables are false.

! **13.5***: The function in Fig. 13.9 to sum the labels of a tree is succinct but tricky. Another approach to the problem is to write two mutually recursive functions, one to sum the labels of a tree and the other to sum the labels of a list of trees. Write these functions.

!! **13.6**: There is a subtle problem with the function `preOrder` defined after Example 13.3. Since concatenation is implemented in ML by copying the lists involved, a call to `preOrder` on a given node takes time proportional to the length of the preorder listing of all the nodes in the subtree of which it is the root, plus the time to compute the preorder listings of its subtrees. Thus in the worst case (a tree with a long path), this function can take time proportional to the square of the number of nodes in the tree. In conventional languages, a typical implementation of preorder traversal will take time that is linear in the number of nodes.

a)* Write a function `preOrder` that takes time proportional to the number of nodes. *Hint*: The trick is to write an auxiliary function `preOrder1(T,L)` that produces the preorder listing of a tree T followed by the arbitrary list L. We define `preOrder(T)` to call `preOrder(T,nil)`, but `preOrder1` calls itself recursively and gradually builds up the preorder listing in the second component. By so doing, we can avoid using @ and can build our listing only using the cons operator ::. Incidentally, this technique, carrying along a list of things that have already been done as an argument of a function, is called *difference lists*. It originated with Lisp programmers, but it is useful in a number of other programming languages, including ML on occasion.

Difference list

b)   The solution given in the back of the book for Exercise 13.5 suffers from the same defect; it is not as efficient as it could be because it uses concatenation instead of cons. Rewrite this function to use only :: in place of @.

c)   Repeat part (b) for the function `search1` given in Fig. S13 in the solution section at the back of the book.

! **13.7**: Rewrite the functions

a)* `lookup` of Fig. 13.1,
b)   `insert` of Fig. 13.2, and
c)   `delete` of Fig. 13.4

so they take a function `lt` as parameter.

! 13.8: Rewrite the functions

a)* `lookup` of Fig. 13.1,
b)   `insert` of Fig. 13.2, and
c)   `delete` of Fig. 13.4

so they avoid requiring an equality type as labels of the trees. Note, however, that whatever type is used for labels, we must assume for values a and b of this type that $a = b$ exactly when neither $lt(a, b)$ or $lt(b, a)$ is true.

◇◇◇ 14   The ML Module System

Encapsulation

One of the great themes of modern programming language design is facilitating the *encapsulation* of information, that is, the grouping of concepts such as types and functions on those types in a cluster that can be used only in limited ways. The limitation on use is not intended to make programming difficult, but rather:

1. To prevent data from being used in unexpected ways that result in hard-to-discover bugs.

Code reuse

2. To encourage reuse of code by allowing the definitions supporting a common idea to be packaged with a simple and precisely defined interface to other pieces of code.

Modules

A *module* is a separately compilable unit, typically a file. The ability to create modules that encapsulate clusters of related ideas is highly useful for the reasons just mentioned. The ML *module system* has three major building blocks.

Structure

1. *Structures* are collections of types, datatypes, functions, exceptions, and other elements that we wish to encapsulate. The definitions of these elements appear in the structure.

Signature

2. *Signatures* are collections of information describing the types and other specifications for some of the elements of a structure.

Functor

3. *Functors* are operations that take one or more structures and produce another structure that combines them in some way.

In effect, a signature is a "type" for a structure, and the syntax of ML reflects this view. That is, we can attach a signature to a structure with a colon, just as we attach a type to an identifier with a colon.

Information Hiding

One important capability of the module system in ML and other languages is *information hiding*. We hide information by arranging that certain definitions within a cluster are not usable outside the cluster. Those terms that are not hidden, and thus are available outside the cluster, are said to be *exported* by

Exported information

the module. The structure is one important kind of cluster we may use to hide information. We shall also take up in Chapter 15 the "abstract type," which is another way to hide information.

145

◇ **Example 14.1.** In the previous chapter we defined a datatype `btree` and gave three useful functions for implementing binary search trees: `lookup`, `insert`, and `delete`. We also defined an exception `EmptyTree` and an auxiliary function `deletemin` that helps with the implementation of `delete` in Fig. 13.4. The binary search tree is a common concept that might be packaged in a cluster and used in many programs.

In a binary-search-tree cluster, we might want to hide `deletemin` because it is not an operation we typically need with binary search trees. Hiding this function has the advantage that we can be sure no one will use it other than through a call to `delete`. Recall that `deletemin` fails when given the empty tree as an argument, but in `delete`, we were very careful to call `deletemin` only on nonempty trees. A user of `deletemin` might not know of the problem and might not be so careful. Moreover, if we hide `deletemin` we can also hide the exception `EmptyTree`, since there is no way for the user to cause the corresponding error.

We might even want to hide the data constructors `Empty` and `Node` for binary search trees. The motivation is similar. If we make the constructors available outside the cluster, an unknowing programmer might use them to build binary trees that did not obey the BST property. On the other hand, if we limit the construction of binary search trees to the `insert` and `delete` functions, we can be sure that the BST property will be preserved. We do, however, need to add another function `create` that takes no argument and returns the empty tree, or else we would never be able to get started building binary search trees outside the cluster. Figure 14.1 suggests what the binary-search-tree cluster would look like from the outside if we hid the constructors, the exception, and the function `deletemin`. We shall return to this example and to the subject of information hiding in Chapter 15. □

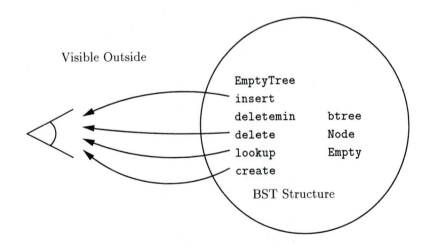

Fig. 14.1. Exporting only the essentials of the binary-search-tree.

Structures

A structure definition has the following form:

> **structure** <identifier> =
>   **struct** <elements of the structure> **end**

The elements of the structure optionally may be ended by semicolons. We shall adopt the same "Pascal-style" convention that we use for elements of a let-expression and follow each but the last by a semicolon.

◇ **Example 14.2.** Let us reconsider the mapping datatype introduced in Example 12.2. The mapping is a list of pairs of the type (`'d`,`'r`), where `'d` is the domain type and `'r` the range type. We make the tacit assumption that for any domain value, there is at most one pair on a list with that value as the first component of a pair. There are three functions we need to use a mapping:

1. **create** to produce the empty list and get us started.

2. **lookup** to find the range value associated with a given domain value.

3. **insert** to take a domain and range element, d and r, and make r the unique range value associated with d.

Figure 14.2 shows the definition of a suitable structure for a mapping, along with the ML response. Line (1) begins the structure declaration for a structure named **Mapping**. The first element of the structure is an exception, declared on line (2). Then, line (3) introduces the identifier **create**. The name **create** is provided by the structure to produce the empty mapping (represented by the empty list). We may view **create** as a function with zero parameters that returns the empty mapping when you "call" it, but it is, in fact, an ordinary variable.

- There is no such thing as a zero-parameter function in ML. However, sometimes, we see a function such as **foo()**, which is really a function named **foo** whose argument type is **unit**.

Lines (4)–(7) define the function **lookup(d,M)**, which finds the value r paired with d in the mapping M. We shall not go into the details of how it works. Similarly, lines (8)–(11) define a function **insert(d,r,M)**, which makes r the unique value paired with d in the mapping M.

After the **end** keyword comes the ML response, which gives the "signature" of this structure. A signature names the elements of the structure and their types. We shall have more to say about signatures shortly, but let us notice what ML has deduced about the types of the structure elements. It sees that **create** is a list of some type, expressed in line (14) by the type `'a list`. For **insert** and **lookup**, ML notes that the domain type in each case must be an equality type, which it represents as `''a`. Recall that type variables starting with two quote marks take equality types as values. The reason an equality

```
(1)        structure Mapping = struct

(2)            exception NotFound;

               (* create the empty mapping *)
(3)            val create = nil;

               (* lookup(d,M) finds the range value r such that
                   (d,r) is a pair in mapping M *)
(4)            fun lookup(d,nil) = raise NotFound
(5)            |    lookup(d,(e,r)::es) =
(6)                if d=e then r
(7)                else lookup(d,es);

               (* insert(d,r,M) puts (d,r) in mapping M and removes
                   any other pair (d,s) that was present in M *)
(8)            fun insert(d,r,nil) = [(d,r)]
(9)            |    insert(d,r,(e,s)::es) =
(10)               if d=e then (d,r)::es
(11)               else (e,s)::insert(d,r,es)
           end;
```

(12)   *structure Mapping :*
           sig
(13)   *exception NotFound*
(14)   *val create : 'a list*
(15)   *val insert : "a * 'b * ("a * 'b) list → ("a * 'b) list*
(16)   *val lookup : "a * ("a * 'b) list → 'b*
           end

Fig. 14.2. The Mapping structure and its signature.

type is needed is that in lines (6) and (10), the equality operator = is applied
to values of the domain type of each function. □

- Note the difference between keywords **structure** and **struct**. The first is a
  declaration word like **fun**; **structure** precedes an identifier being declared
  to be a structure. On the other hand, **struct** is paired with **end** to bracket
  the elements of a structure.

Signatures

An identifier denoting a structure, such as identifier **Mapping** of Example 14.2,
has a signature that serves as the "type" of the structure. As we saw in Example 14.2, the signature gives the types of the structure elements. In analogy with
types and ordinary identifiers, the signature can be used to restrict a structure.

◇ **Example 14.3.** Here is a simple example of how types restrict the value of an identifier. We might define a polymorphic function `foo(x)` to be of type `'a -> 'b`, that is, a function from some type to another type. When we use it, we may wish to or need to restrict the parameter `x` to a particular type, say by using it as `foo(x:int)`. Or, we might wish to restrict it partially by a use such as `foo(x:'c list)`, which restricts the argument to be some kind of list. □

A signature has the form

    sig <specifications> **end**

Some important kinds of specifications are listed below. We shall discuss others later, and the complete syntax for specifications is in Fig. 26.8.

1. **type**, followed by an identifier, possibly parametrized by type variables. Two examples are **type foo** and **type ('a,'b) bar**.

2. **eqtype**, followed as in (1). This keyword declares that the named type must be an equality type. A datatype in a structure can correspond to a type or (if the datatype definition does not involve function types) an eqtype in the signature.

3. **exception**, followed by an exception name.

4. **val**, followed by an identifier, a colon, and a type description. Examples were seen in lines (14)–(16) of Fig. 14.2. The identifier could represent an ordinary variable or a function.

We can bind an identifier to a value that is a signature by

    signature <identifier> =
        sig <specifications> **end**

- Keywords **signature** and **sig** are related like **structure** and **struct**. Word **signature** introduces a signature definition, while **sig**, along with **end**, brackets the specifications in the signature.

- Note in (1) and (2) above that type names do not begin with a quote mark; they are the type constructors. However, any type-valued parameters, such as the parameters **'a** and **'b** in the hypothetical type **bar** of (1) above, *are* represented by type variables and *do* begin with a quote mark.

- As for structures, specifications of a signature may optionally be ended with a semicolon. We shall adopt the Pascal style for semicolon use.

◇ **Example 14.4.** Suppose we want to have a structure that is a mapping, specialized to the case of Example 12.2, where the domain is strings and the range is integers. We shall call this kind of mapping a "string-int mapping." We can define a structure based on the **Mapping** structure from Fig. 14.2 by defining a signature in which the types of the functions are restricted to have

```
signature SIMAPPING = sig
   exception NotFound;
   val create : (string * int) list;
   val insert : string * int * (string * int) list ->
          (string * int) list;
   val lookup : string * (string * int) list -> int
end;
```

Fig. 14.3. A signature for string-int mappings.

string domains and integer ranges. Figure 14.3 shows the definition of a suitable signature SIMAPPING.

We can now use the signature SIMAPPING of Fig. 14.3 to restrict the structure Mapping of Fig. 14.2. We do so by defining another mapping, which we shall call SiMapping, to be equal to Mapping, but with the signature SIMAPPING. The declaration

$$\text{structure SiMapping: SIMAPPING = Mapping} \qquad (14.1)$$

defines the new structure. The functions create, insert, and lookup from the SiMapping structure can only be applied to string-int mappings. □

Structure declaration (14.1) illustrates another useful form of structure definition, where instead of defining a structure explicitly, with struct ··· end, we define one structure equal to another structure. We then attach a signature to the first structure by the typing symbol : to restrict the newly defined structure. Another option is to define a signature in advance and attach it with a colon to the name of the structure as it is being defined. An example is:

```
structure SiMapping: SIMAPPING = struct
   (* same as lines (2)-(11) of Fig. 14.2 *)
end;
```

There are two principal ways that a signature can restrict the structure to which it is attached.

1. The signature can specify a more restrictive type for an identifier than is implicit in the structure definition. Example 14.3 illustrated this capability with the identifiers create, insert, and lookup.

2. The signature can omit certain identifiers, thus hiding them in any structure defined to have this signature. For example, if we did not want a user to be able to modify a mapping, we might eliminate all mention of create and insert, using a signature such as

```
sig
   exception NotFound;
   val lookup : string * (string * int) list -> int
end
```

Accessing Names Defined Within Structures

Executing a structure-statement causes the names defined within the structure to become part of the environment. However, in the environment, these names are qualified by being prefixed by the structure name and a dot.

◇ **Example 14.5.** Suppose we have defined the structure `SiMapping` as in Example 14.4. Having executed the statement

```
structure SiMapping: SIMAPPING = Mapping
```

preceded by the definitions of structure `Mapping` and signature `SIMAPPING`, we can then use string-int mappings. We might, for example, initialize an empty string-int mapping `m` by

```
val m = SiMapping.create;
```
*val m = nil : (string * int) list*

Then, we can insert pairs into `m`. For example:

```
val m = SiMapping.insert("in",6,m);
```
*val m = [("in", 6)] : (string * int) list*

```
val m = SiMapping.insert("a",1,m);
```
*val m = [("in", 6), ("a", 1)] : (string * int) list*

Last, a lookup operation like

```
SiMapping.lookup("in",m);
```
val it = 6

allows us to obtain information from the mapping. □

Opening Structures

Attaching the structure name to the functions and other elements of a structure helps us avoid some mistakes. For example, function names like **insert** and **lookup** were used above as operations on mappings, but in Chapter 13 they were used for different operations on binary search trees. It is possible that structures based on both the mapping and the binary search tree would be useful in one program. By specifying both the operation and the structure, we avoid having one member of a programming team refer to the wrong function, perhaps unaware of the existence of the other.

However, it is cumbersome to repeat the structure name every time we refer to one of its elements. So, ML allows a structure to be *opened* by the declaration

```
open <structure name>;
```

This statement causes all the names exported by the structure to be added to the current environment, where they shield from view any other name with the same identifier. However, identifiers appearing in another structure can still be referenced by prepending the structure name and a dot.

◇ **Example 14.6.** If we execute

```
open SiMapping;
```

then the identifiers `NotFound`, `create`, `insert`, and `lookup` will refer to the exception, variable, and functions belonging to the structure `SiMapping`. We can then replace the statements of Example 14.5 by removing "`SiMapping.`" everywhere it appears. □

- There is a risk in using `open`, because a structure written by someone else may contain declarations you are not aware of, and thereby some variable you use may have its meaning changed accidently. With a little more effort, we can protect ourselves against such an error by defining only the identifiers we know about and need from the structure, for example

```
val create = Simapping.create;
val insert = SiMapping.insert;
```

and so on.

Importing Values into a Structure

Often we want a structure to take some "input," which helps determine some features of the structure. For example, in Chapter 13 we wrote functions to operate on a binary search tree, and we used an unspecified function `lt` to compare elements of the label type of the trees. If we simply define a structure that refers to `lt`, without there being any object in the current environment with that identifier, we shall cause an error. However, as in Chapter 13, we may first write a suitable definition for `lt` and then define a structure using `lt`. While we shall see better ways to handle the problem, this approach does allow us to write one structure definition that, if used in different environments, results in structures with different meanings for the name `lt`. When we use externally **Imported** defined names in a structure, those names are said to be *imported*.
information

- Note that, as with other sorts of definitions, all names in the current environment may be used when a structure or signature is defined. Imported names like `lt` have their values incorporated into the definition of the structure so that, even if an imported name is redefined after the definition, it is still the original value that is used when elements of the structure are invoked.

◇ **Example 14.7.** Let us define a structure `StringBST` that incorporates the definitions and functions of Chapter 13. We shall restrict it to strings as labels by making the definition in an environment that includes a suitable function lt. Figure 14.4 sketches the definition. For succinctness, we do not copy the code for the functions that were defined in Chapter 13.

```
fun lt(x:string,y) = (* definition from Example 13.1 *);
```
*val lt = fn : string * string → bool*

```
structure StringBST = struct
    datatype 'label btree = Empty |
        Node of 'label * 'label btree * 'label btree;
    val create = Empty;
    fun insert(x,T) = (* code of Fig. 13.2 *);
    fun lookup(x,T) = (* code of Fig. 13.1 *);
    exception EmptyTree;
    fun deletemin(T) = (* code of Fig. 13.4 *);
    fun delete(x,T) = (* code of Fig. 13.4 *)
end;
```
structure StringBST :
>   *sig*
>>   *datatype 'a btree*
>>>   *con Empty : 'a btree*
>>>   *con Node : 'a * 'a btree * 'a btree → 'a btree*
>>   *exception EmptyTree*
>>   *val create : 'a btree*
>>   *val delete : string * string btree → string btree*
>>   *val deletemin : 'a btree → 'a * 'a btree*
>>   *val insert : string * string btree → string btree*
>>   *val lookup : string * string btree → bool*
>   *end*

Fig. 14.4. Defining a structure that imports a value for lt.

The definitions of **insert**, **delete**, and **lookup** use the definition of **lt** that appears at the top of Fig. 14.4. Notice that in the response to this structure definition, ML gives it a signature that is as general as possible. It has determined from the use of this **lt** that **insert**, **delete**, and **lookup** involve strings and **string btree**'s, but it has not determined that **create** or **deletemin** require any special type for the labels of their btree's, and in fact they do not. On the other hand, ML will discover that labels are strings as soon as we use the defined functions. Figure 14.5 is an example of how we might create a binary search tree, populate it with two strings, and perform some operations. □

Using Functors to Import Information

There are certain undesirable features of the approach to importation suggested by Example 14.7.

```
open StringBST;

val t1 = create;
```
val t1 = Empty : 'a btree

```
val t2 = insert("foo", t1);
```
val t2 = Node("foo",Empty,Empty) : string btree

```
val t3 = insert("bar", t2);
```
val t3 = Node("foo",Node("bar",Empty,Empty),Empty) : string btree

```
lookup("bar",t3);
```
val it = true : bool

```
val t4 = delete("baz",t3);
```
val t4 = Node("foo",Node("bar",Empty,Empty),Empty) : string btree

Fig. 14.5. Examples of binary search tree operations.

1.   The typing of elements in the structure is rather haphazard, being whatever ML can deduce from the clues given.

2.   We never really created an object that is "a binary search tree that works on any equality type with a less-than function." Rather, we created a structure that in effect is a binary search tree with string labels (although we could execute the same structure definition in another environment to create binary search trees with another label type). It is dangerous to have the meaning of a structure change depending on what code precedes it.

ML provides a way to handle both of these problems through a mechanism called the *functor*. A functor operates on structures to produce other structures. We can define a functor that takes as its argument a structure defining a less-than operation. The result of this functor is a binary-search-tree structure that incorporates the given less-than function to provide versions of **insert**, **delete**, and **lookup**, using the appropriate function **lt**. The idea of "a binary search tree working on any equality type with less-than" is embodied in the functor. This functor may be applied to any number of structures, each of which defines a suitable **lt** function.

The steps we must take to create the functor and the example of binary search trees with string labels is outlined below.

1.   Define a signature, which we shall call **TOTALORDER**, that embodies the restrictions necessary for a suitable label type for binary search trees. That is, a total order is a type with a "less than" predicate.

2.   Define a functor, called **MakeBST**, that takes a structure S with signature **TOTALORDER** as its argument and produces a structure as a result. The resulting structure will provide binary search trees whose labels are of the type described by the structure S.

3. Define a structure `String` that describes character strings with a function `lt` to compare strings. The signature of `String` is `TOTALORDER`.

4. Apply the functor `MakeBST` to the structure `String`, to produce the structure desired `StringBST`.

We shall show how to perform these steps in a sequence of examples.

◇ **Example 14.8.** Here is a suitable definition for the signature `TOTALORDER`.

```
signature TOTALORDER = sig
    eqtype element;
    val lt : element * element -> bool
end;
```

Note that there is an underlying element type, which is defined to be an equality type. The type is not arbitrary since equality tests are used in operations such as `insert`. We expect in later examples that the type `element` will be replaced by `string`. Also, notice that the only operation we need on this type is the function `lt`, which takes two elements and produces true or false as a value. That is all we need to know about `lt` at this point; we do not need to know how it computes its Boolean-valued result. □

To define a functor that transforms one structure into another, we use a definition of the form

```
functor <identifier> ( <structure name> : <signature> )
        = <structure definition>
```

An optional colon and signature describing the result of the functor may appear immediately before the equal-sign. The following example illustrates this form as it applies to the problem of defining binary search trees.

◇ **Example 14.9.** In Fig. 14.6 is the definition of the functor `MakeBST`. In line (1) we see the beginning of the functor definition. The parameter name is `Lt`, and the signature for this parameter is `TOTALORDER`, the signature from Example 14.8.

In lines (2)–(9) we see the definition of a signature for the structure that is to be produced by the functor `MakeBST`. Specifying the signature here is optional, but we include it for instructional value. There are a number of fine points to be made about this signature.

• An open-statement is another kind of element that can appear in a signature or structure definition. In line (2) we open the parameter `Lt` of the functor. That is convenient because we need to refer to the type `element` that is mentioned in the signature `TOTALORDER` associated with the parameter on line (1). It is not essential to use these open-statements. For example, we could have referred to `Lt.element` instead of `element` in lines (5)–(9).

```
(1)          functor MakeBST(Lt: TOTALORDER):
                 sig
(2)                  open Lt;
(3)                  type 'label btree;
(4)                  exception EmptyTree;
(5)                  val create : element btree;
(6)                  val lookup : element * element btree -> bool;
(7)                  val insert : element * element btree ->
                             element btree;
(8)                  val deletemin : element btree ->
                             element * element btree;
(9)                  val delete : element * element btree ->
                             element btree
                 end
             =
             struct
(10)                 open Lt;
(11)                 datatype 'label btree = Empty |
(12)                     Node of 'label * 'label btree * 'label btree;
(13)                 val create = Empty;
(14)                 fun insert(x,T) = (* code of Fig. 13.2 *);
(15)                 fun lookup(x,T) = (* code of Fig. 13.1 *);
(16)                 exception EmptyTree;
(17)                 fun deletemin(T) = (* code of Fig. 13.4 *);
(18)                 fun delete(x,T) = (* code of Fig. 13.4 *)
             end;
             functor MakeBST : <sig>
```

Fig. 14.6. Definition of the functor MakeBST.

- Notice that in the signature, line (3) refers to the datatype **btree** as a "type," not a datatype. The fact that it takes a type parameter, which we call **'label** as usual, is indicated. However, the existence of constructors **Node** and **Empty** is not mentioned. The usual definition of this datatype appears in the structure definition at lines (11) and (12).

Following the signature for the functor's result is the required = sign and the structure definition itself. We open Lt in line (10), so uses of the function **lt** in the unseen code for **insert** and other functions will refer to **lt** in the structure Lt (otherwise, these functions would have to refer to **Lt.lt**). The definitions of the functions and other elements resemble those of Fig. 14.4. Notice the succinct response of ML to this functor definition at the end. □

Next, we need to define a particular structure that can be the argument corresponding to the parameter **Lt** in the functor **MakeBST**.

◇ **Example 14.10.** An appropriate definition is shown in Fig. 14.7. Line (1) says that **String** is a structure, and its signature is **TOTALORDER**. Line (2) says that in structure **String**, the type **element** mentioned in the signature **TOTALORDER** is actually the type **string**. Here the type definition is an ordinary type abbreviation introduced by the keyword **type**. It would also have been possible to replace line (2) by a datatype definition. However the number of type parameters in the signature and structure must agree. So in this case, since **element** was defined in the structure to be a parameterless type, the datatype would likewise have to be parameterless like the datatype **fruit** of Example 12.3.

```
(1)    structure String: TOTALORDER =
           struct
(2)            type element = string;
(3)            fun lt(x:string,y) =
(4)                let
(5)                    fun lower(nil) = nil
(6)                    |   lower(c::cs) = if c>="A" andalso c<="Z"
(7)                        then chr(ord(c)+32)::lower(cs)
(8)                        else c::lower(cs);
(9)                in
(10)                   implode(lower(explode(x))) <
                              implode(lower(explode(y)))
(11)               end;
           end;
```

Fig. 14.7. The structure String.

Finally, lines (3)–(11) give a suitable definition for function **lt**. Notice that we have defined the auxiliary function **lower** to be local to **lt** by using a let-expression. Since the signature defines its type to be

```
element * element -> bool
```

and **element** has been defined to be **string**, the function **lt** is properly written so its type is **string * string -> bool**. □

The last step in our process is to apply the functor **MakeBST** to the structure **String** to produce the structure **StringBST**, which is an appropriate structure representing binary search trees with string labels. The form of this functor application is

```
structure <new structure name> =
    <functor name>(<structure argument>)
```

An optional colon and signature may appear before the equal sign to describe the form of the new structure.

◇ **Example 14.11.** The following functor application:

```
structure StringBST = MakeBST(String);
```

produces the desired structure `StringBST`. □

If we open `StringBST`, operations like `insert` have their desired meaning; they apply only to binary search trees with string labels. Even if we do not open `StringBST`, we can get these operations by names like `StringBST.insert`.

More General Forms for Functor Parameters and Arguments

In the example above, we used a simple form for defining one-parameter functors. The parameter is an identifier standing for a structure, followed only by a colon and a signature describing the structure. An example was given in line (1) of Fig. 14.6. When we apply the functor, we have only to provide an actual structure as argument. For instance, we provided the structure `String` as argument in Example 14.11.

One extension is that we may provide the argument structure explicitly, instead of by name. For example, we could have skipped the definition of `String` in Fig. 14.7 and instead have written the declaration of structure `StringBST` in Example 14.11 as

```
structure StringBST = MakeBST(struct
              <lines (2)-(11) of Fig. 14.7>
     end);
```

That is, the entire structure definition appears as the argument of the functor.

There are more general ways to write the parameters and arguments of functors. We may have more than one parameter, and parameters may be any declarable element such as a value, function, or exception. The entire syntax of functor declarations is in Fig. 26.11, and the syntax of functor use is in Fig. 26.10.

To begin, we can declare structure parameters of a functor using the keyword `structure`. The form is

```
functor <identifier>(structure <structure name> : <signature>)
    = <structure definition>
```

As always, an optional colon and signature may appear before the equal sign to describe the result of the functor. More generally, there can be several structure parameters, each paired with its signature using the syntax

```
functor <identifier>(structure S_1:S_1 and ... and S_n:S_n)
    = <structure definition>
```

where the S's are structures and the $\mathcal{S}$'s are signatures.

We may also have several specifications separated by optional semicolons. A specification may involve one or more structures in the form above. A specification may also tell about a value, function, or in fact be of any of the forms for specifications that may appear in signatures. The complete syntax is in Fig. 26.8.

◇ **Example 14.12.** To illustrate some of the possible forms, let us define two trivial signatures by:

```
signature INT = sig val i: int end;
signature REAL = sig val r: real end;
```

Signature **INT** describes a structure consisting of one integer called **i**, and signature **REAL** describes a structure with a real number **r**. Here are some possible beginnings of functor definitions. In each case we have not continued past the equal sign and thus omit defining the result of the functor.

```
(1)    functor Foo(structure I: INT and R: REAL) =
(2)    functor Foo(structure I: INT; structure R: REAL) =
(3)    functor Foo(structure I: INT and R: REAL; val x : int) =
```

Definition (1) says that functor **Foo** has two arguments, which are structures **I** and **R**, with signatures **INT** and **REAL** respectively. Definition (2) says exactly the same thing but uses separate structure specifications for the two structure parameters. Definition (3) says that functor **Foo** has these two structure parameters but also has a third parameter, which is an integer **x**. □

When we apply a functor that has been defined using structure specifications or other specifications, we must pass its arguments using a similar form. The simple forms used in Examples 14.9 and 14.11 may not be mixed with the specification style of defining parameters. To define the arguments in a use of the functor, we use structure declarations or other declarations to provide values for the parameters of the functor. For example, we can bind a value to a functor parameter by

```
<functor name>(
    structure <functor parameter> = <argument>
)
```

The argument may be a structure name or the explicit definition of a structure, using **struct...end**.

More generally, several structure parameters may be bound to their values following one use of the keyword **structure**, if we separate the parameter-argument pairs with **and**. Several groups of bindings may be separated by optional semicolons. These bindings may also be used to give values to parameters other than structures.

◇ **Example 14.13.** Let us define two structures

```
structure Int = struct val i = 0 end;
structure Real = struct val r = 0.0 end;
```

to match the signatures **INT** and **REAL** of Example 14.12. Here are several ways a signature **Bar** could be defined by applying the functor **Foo** of Example 14.12. Either of the definitions

```
structure Bar = Foo(structure I = Int; structure R = Real);
structure Bar = Foo(structure I = Int and R = Real);
```

can be used with either of the functor declaration forms (1) or (2) of Example 14.12. The following definitions

```
structure Bar =
    Foo(structure I = Int; structure R = Real; val x = 2);
structure Bar =
    Foo(structure I = Int and R = Real; val x = 2);
```

are appropriate with definition (3) of Example 14.12. □

Exercises

14.1*: Define a structure **Tree** with a datatype **tree** representing general trees as in Fig. 13.6 and the following operations:

1. **create(a)** returns a one-node tree with label a.

2. **build(a,L)** returns a tree with a root labeled a and list of subtrees L for the root.

3. **find(i,T)** finds the ith subtree of the root of tree T and raises the exception **Missing** if there is no such subtree.

14.2*: Note that **create(a)** means the same as **build(a,nil)**. We may thus wish to define a new structure **SimpleTree** that has all the elements of structure **Tree** except **create**. Also, we may choose to restrict simple trees to have integer labels. Write a signature **SIMPLE** that makes these restrictions. Then use **SIMPLE** and **Tree** to define structure **SimpleTree**.

14.3*: Use your structure **SimpleTree** from Exercise 14.2 to construct a tree with a root labeled 1 and three children labeled 2, 3, and 4. Apply function **subtree** to obtain the second subtree of the root of your tree.

14.4: Design a structure **Stack** that represents a stack of elements of some arbitrary type. Include the functions: **create** (return an empty stack), **push** (add an element to the top of the stack and return the resulting stack), **pop** (delete the top element and return the resulting stack), **isEmpty** (test whether a given stack is empty), and **top** (return the top element). Also include an exception **EmptyStack** to catch attempts to read or pop the top element of an empty stack.

14.5: Design a suitable signature that will allow us to create from `Stack` of Exercise 14.4 a structure `StringStack` whose stacks have elements that are strings, and that omits the operation `top`.

14.6*: Design a structure `Queue` that represents a queue of elements of some arbitrary type. Include operations: `create` (return an empty queue), `enqueue` (add an element to the end of the queue and return the result), `dequeue` (return a pair consisting of the first element on the queue and the rest of the queue), and `isEmpty` (tell whether the queue is empty). Also include the exception `EmptyQueue` to catch attempts at dequeueing from the empty queue.

14.7: Design a suitable signature that will allow us to create from `Queue` of Exercise 14.6 a structure `PairQueue` whose queues have elements that are pairs consisting of a string and an integer. Do not omit any of the functions.

14.8: In place of the structure `String` of Fig. 14.7, write a structure that defines elements to be tuples of three real numbers. For the `lt` ordering on triples, say that $(a, b, c) < (x, y, z)$ if either

1. $a < x$, or
2. $a = x$ and $b < y$, or
3. $a = x$, $b = y$, and $c < z$.

Then show how to apply the functor of Fig. 14.6 to your new structure and get a structure that stores triples of reals in binary trees.

! **14.9***: A useful class of structures implements a set of elements of some type with a "similarity" relation that is defined by a function that tells whether two elements are "similar." For instance, the set could have strings as elements. Strings could be deemed similar if they where the same after converting uppercase letters to lowercase. Alternatively, strings could be considered similar if they differed in only one position. For another example, elements could be lists of bits indicating whether a document discussed various topics of interest, and "similar" could mean that two documents covered at least two topics in common.

a) Write a signature `SIM` that describes structures that are an element type with a similarity relation on that type.

b) Write a functor `MakeSimSet` that takes as argument a structure `Sim` that includes an element type and a function that decides similarity. The result of your functor should be a structure that implements sets with the given type and notion of similarity. The operations in the result structure should include a function `findSim` that takes an element x and a set S and returns the set of elements in S that are similar to x. It should also include a value `create` to be an empty set, and a function `insert` to return a set with a new element inserted.

c)   Write a structure **Misspell** that defines elements to be strings and defines
two strings to be similar if they are identical or differ in exactly one character. Apply your functor from (a) to produce the structure **MisspellSet**
that implements sets of strings and allows searches for slightly misspelled
words.

14.10: Use the forms with keyword **structure**, as in Examples 14.12 and 14.13,
to define the functor **MakeBST** of Example 14.9 and apply it to the structure
String as in Example 14.11.

15 Software Design Using Modules

The ML module system — structures, signatures, and functors — facilitates the design and reuse of software. We can implement a cluster of definitions, such as datatypes, functions, and exceptions, as a structure and reuse it many times in many different programs. Several programmers can work on structures independently and agree on a shared interface.

ML helps these processes is several ways. Signatures allow us to enforce certain requirements on a structure or functor. For example, signatures may require that functions and other elements be present and that these elements have specified types. Functors make it easy for us to abstract common parts of related structures and produce any of a family of structures without repeating common code. However, there are several other features of ML that also assist in the structuring and validation of large, complex bodies of code. In this chapter we shall discuss:

Information hiding

1. Techniques for *information hiding*, that is, making all or certain parts of a cluster of definitions inaccessible to the user. Information hiding improves the effectiveness of encapsulation, since it limits the ways in which the elements of the cluster can be used. Other auxiliary functions or definitions may exist within a cluster. However, they are not usable from outside the cluster, and the user is therefore prevented from applying these auxiliary elements in ways unanticipated by the designer of the cluster. As a result, we minimize the chance of an error due to misunderstanding between the implementor and user of the encapsulated facilities. There are many ways to hide information. We shall discuss:

   a) Defining a signature that fails to mention the hidden elements.

Abstraction

   b) Using an "abstraction" instead of a structure to hide data constructors and thereby prevent the use of the datatypes defined in this structure in unexpected ways.

Abstract type

   c) Using an "abstract type" in place of a datatype to make its data constructors invisible.

Local definitions

   d) Using "local" definitions within an abstract type or structure to hide certain elements.

Substructures

2. Using *substructures* to further organize clusters of definitions. We can define one structure to be part of another, thus building progressively larger conglomerations of concepts.

Sharing

3. Constraining independent elements with *sharing* specifications in signatures. When we encapsulate definitions within several structures, it is often essential that two or more structures use the same substructures or the same types. If we are to design structures independently and reuse those structures in many programs, we may need to check that the substructures are the same. "Sharing" specifications within a signature cause ML to check that any structure with that signature has the proper internal consistency among its substructures.

Using Signatures to Hide Information

We may define one structure S_2 to be equal to another structure S_1, but with a specific signature S. As was illustrated in Example 14.5, the form of the definition is

$$\text{structure } S_2 \colon \; S \; = \; S_1$$

As we mentioned in the previous chapter, signature S can omit some elements that appear in the structure S_1. These elements will not be available to users of the structure S_2. However, should a function that is exported by S_2 use in its body a function of S_1 that is not exported by S_2, the needed function is available and no error is caused.

◇ **Example 15.1.** Let us revisit Example 14.1, where we spoke of a binary search tree structure that hides the function **deletemin** and the exception **EmptyTree**. Recall that the motivation for doing so is that **deletemin** is a function that is only needed by **delete**. Because **deletemin** does not work on an empty tree, it is best not made available to the user. When we make **deletemin** unavailable, we can also hide the exception, since its sole purpose is to catch erroneous uses of **deletemin**, which now cannot occur.

Figure 14.4 gives a structure called **StringBST**, which has a signature making all its elements available to the user. We can define another signature that is like the one ML suggested for this structure in Fig. 14.4, but with some appropriate modifications. First, we shall restrict the type of labels to be **string** in all elements. Then we shall omit mention of the two elements **deletemin** and **EmptyTree** that we wish to hide. Figure 15.1 shows the signature.

```
signature STRING_BST = sig
    type 'label btree;
    val create : string btree;
    val insert : string * string btree -> string btree;
    val delete : string * string btree -> string btree;
    val lookup : string * string btree -> bool
end;
```

Fig. 15.1. Signature to hide **deletemin** and **EmptyTree**.

Note that in the signature of Fig. 15.1 it is sufficient to refer to `btree` as a "type" rather than a "datatype." We might be tempted in Fig. 15.1 to describe the type `btree` as

```
type string btree
```

However, a concrete type like `string` may never be used as a type parameter for a type or datatype. We must use a type variable, such as the variable `'label` that was used in Fig. 15.1. On the other hand, it would make sense to define a new type `stringBtree` with no parameter and define types of elements in signature `STRING_BST` as

```
val create : stringBtree;
```

and so on.

Now let us create a new structure that has the signature of Fig. 15.1 by the structure definition:

```
structure NewStringBST: STRING_BST = StringBST
```

If we then open the new structure with

```
open NewStringBST;
```

we can use the elements mentioned in the signature `STRING_BST` of Fig. 15.1, as in

```
insert("foo", create);
```
val it = Node("foo",Empty,Empty) : string btree

which creates an empty tree and then inserts the string `"foo"`.

Similarly, a call to `delete` is permitted. This call results in a call to `deletemin`, even though the user is not permitted to call `deletemin` directly. That is, if we try to use `deletemin`, as in

```
deletemin(create);
```
Error: unbound variable or constructor deletemin

we are told that there is no meaning for the identifier `deletemin`. □

Abstractions

The keyword `abstraction` can substitute for the keyword `structure`.[1] The only difference is that data constructors of any types defined in the abstraction are not guaranteed to be available outside. We can define an abstraction explicitly, just as we define a structure. The only difference is that a signature must be specified for an abstraction, while a signature is optional in the definition of a structure.

---

[1] Abstractions may not be available in implementations of ML other than SML/NJ.

◇ **Example 15.2.** In Fig. 14.2 we could have replaced the word `structure` by `abstraction` in line (1). We would then have to follow the name `Mapping` on line (1) by a colon and a signature like the one whose body is in lines (13)–(16) of Fig. 14.2. □

It is also possible to define an abstraction in terms of a structure or another abstraction, as we did in Example 15.1 for the structure `NewStringBST`. However, the signature after the newly defined abstraction, like `STRING_BST` in Example 15.1, is mandatory, not optional as it is for a structure. The following example suggests how we might create an abstraction from a structure.

◇ **Example 15.3.** Suppose we define

```
abstraction NewStringBST: STRING_BST = StringBST
```

If we then open the abstraction, with

```
open NewStringBST;
```

we are still able to access all the identifiers specified in the signature `STRING_BST`. However, data constructors `Empty` and `Node` are not available. For instance, if we type

```
insert("foo",create);
```

we get the ML response

val it = – : string btree

The value of `it`, which is `Node("foo",Empty,Empty)` as we saw in Example 15.1, is hidden from us by the dash. If we try to use the data constructors for datatype `btree` directly, we get an error. The declaration

```
val a = Empty;
```
Error: unbound variable or constructor Empty

illustrates the point. □

Abstract Types

An *abstract type* is essentially a datatype that hides its data constructors. We use the keyword `abstype` to define an abstract type with almost the same syntax as we use to define a datatype. However, for the abstract type we must follow it by the keyword `with` to introduce the only functions, variables, exceptions, and types that have access to the data constructors. The form of an abstract type definition is

```
abstype <datatype definition>
    with
        <declarations using the constructors>
    end
```

```
fun lt(x:string,y) = (* code of Example 13.1 *);
val lt = fn : string * string → bool

abstype 'label btree = Empty |
        Node of 'label * 'label btree * 'label btree
    with
        val create = Empty;
        fun insert(x,T) = (* code of Fig. 13.2 *);
        fun lookup(x,T) = (* code of Fig. 13.1 *);
        exception EmptyTree;
        fun deletemin(T) = (* code of Fig. 13.4 *);
        fun delete(x,T) = (* code of Fig. 13.4 *)
    end;
```
type 'a btree
val create = - : 'a btree
*val insert = fn : string * string btree → string btree*
*val lookup = fn : string * string btree → bool*
exception EmptyTree
*val deletemin = fn : 'a btree → 'a * 'a btree*
*val delete = fn : string * string btree → string btree*

Fig. 15.2. String binary search trees defined as an abstract type.

◇ **Example 15.4.** Figure 15.2 shows an abstract type similar to the structure **StringBST** of Fig. 14.4. As in Fig. 14.4, we have used a previously defined function **lt** to restrict labels to be strings. We could have been less general in our definition of **btree**. Instead of taking a label parameter, we could simply have defined

```
abstype btree = Empty |
    Node of string * btree * btree
```

Having processed the declarations of Fig. 15.2, the elements of the type definition such as **insert** are available, but the data constructors **Empty** and **Node** are not. For instance, we can write

```
insert("foo",create);
```
val it = - : string btree

• Notice ML does not print the value of tree **Node("foo",Empty,Empty)**, because it would reveal the constructors by so doing.

However, should we try to use the constructors as in

```
Node("foo",Empty,Empty);
```
Error: unbound variable or constructor Node

we get an error message. ML would have told us **Empty** was also an unbound identifier, but it found the error involving **Node** first. □

Local Definitions

We can hide some elements in an abstract type definition or a structure definition by using the construct

```
local
    <definitions>
in
    <definitions>
end
```

The second group of definitions can use the definitions in the first group, but only the second group of definitions is exported; the first group is hidden.

- Do not confuse the local-in-end form with the let-in-end form. The former has a list of definitions between the **in** and **end**, while the latter has a list of expressions there. For example, a val-declaration may not follow the keyword **in** in a let-expression, while it may in a local-declaration.

◇ **Example 15.5.** In Fig. 15.3 we see a revision of Fig. 15.2, in which the definitions of **EmptyTree** and **deletemin** are made local to the definition of **delete**. Notice that **EmptyTree** and **deletemin** do not appear in the ML response to this abstract type definition.

We could also make a similar change to the structure definition for the structure **StringBST** in Fig. 14.4. That is, the definitions of **EmptyTree** and **deletemin** could be placed in a local-declaration for the function **delete**. If we did, then the signature in the ML response would omit **EmptyTree** and **deletemin**. □

Sharing

Sharing specification

At the beginning of this chapter we explained how a sharing specification can sometimes be essential to make sure that two or more substructure names or type names in a signature refer to the same thing. Now, let us learn the syntax and meaning of these equivalences. A *sharing specification* is another kind of element that may appear within a signature. This specification can be of the form

```
sharing type <type> = <type> = · · · = <type>
```

or of the form

```
sharing <structure> = <structure> = · · · = <structure>
```

The first form allows us to assert that two or more types mentioned in the signature must actually be the same type. The second allows us to assert that two or more substructures mentioned in the signature are the same.

```
fun lt(x:string,y) = (* code of Example 13.1 *);
val lt = fn : string * string → bool

abstype 'label btree = Empty |
        Node of 'label * 'label btree * 'label btree
    with
        val create = Empty;
        fun insert = (* code of Fig. 13.2 *);
        fun lookup = (* code of Fig. 13.1 *);
        local
            exception EmptyTree;
            fun deletemin = (* code of Fig. 13.4 *)
        in
            fun delete = (* code of Fig. 13.4 *)
        end
    end;
type 'a btree
val create = - : 'a btree
val insert = fn : string * string btree → string btree
val lookup = fn : string * string btree → bool
val delete = fn : string * string btree → string btree
```

Fig. 15.3. Hiding the exception `EmptyTree` and the definition of `deletemin`.

• Remember that the keyword **type** appears after the keyword **sharing** for type sharing, but there is no keyword analogous to **type** for substructure sharing.

Substructures

In order to use sharings, we need another kind of specification, in which we declare a structure to have a substructure. The basic form of this specification within a signature is

> **structure** <identifier> : <signature>

which asserts that the identifier is a structure with the given signature. Optionally, we can assert the existence of several structures, each with a specified signature, if we connect groups of the form <identifier> : <signature> by the keyword **and**.

In addition, structures can declare substructures within themselves. The form of a substructure declaration is

> **structure** <identifier> : <signature> = **struct**
>   <definition of the structure>
> **end**

- The **struct**, the signature definition, and the **end** can be replaced by the name of a previously defined structure.

- The colon and signature are optional in structures, but not in structure specifications that occur in signatures. There is a sound reason for this difference. In a structure, a suitable signature can be deduced from the definition of the substructure itself, but in a signature we have no way of deducing the signature for a substructure.

Sharing of Types

Let us now see how the first kind of sharing, the specification that two types are the same, is accomplished.

◇ **Example 15.6.** Let us examine the top two signatures in Fig. 15.4. First, signature ELEMENT in lines (1) and (2) describes a structure that has a type called **element** and a function **similar** on that type. As two examples from among an unlimited number of possibilities, this function could be equality, or it could be equality of the first components if the type **element** were a pair. In realistic examples, we would expect there to be more functions than one within the signature.

Then in lines (3)–(9) we have another signature BTREE that describes a structure for binary trees. In line (3) we see there is a substructure **Element** whose signature is ELEMENT; that signature is the one we just saw in lines (1) and (2). Then in line (4) we specify a type **elt** that is local to the signature BTREE. We have decided to require that this local type be an equality type, and we so indicate by using the keyword **eqtype** rather than **type**. A possible reason is that we believe the function **lookup** requires an equality test.

However, we also wish to require that the type **element** mentioned in the signature ELEMENT is the same as the local type **elt**. Hence, at line (5) there is a sharing specification that requires these two types to be the same. Should the functions in lines (7)–(9) refer to both the types **Element.element** and **elt**, we can be sure these are the same type in any structure that matches the signature BTREE. An additional effect of the sharing on line (5) is that **Element.element** is forced to be an equality type wherever it is used in lines (7)–(9) because it has been equated to the equality type **elt**. □

Sharing of Substructures

The other kind of sharing specification allows us to require that two substructures be the same.

◇ **Example 15.7.** Continuing with our discussion of Fig. 15.4, we see in lines (10)–(15) another signature TREE. Like BTREE, it uses a substructure with signature ELEMENT, specifies a local equality type called **elt**, equates the local type and the type **element** of the substructure by a type sharing specification, and then specifies a datatype and some functions.

```
       signature ELEMENT = sig
(1)        type element;
(2)        val similar : element * element -> bool;
       end;

       signature BTREE = sig
(3)        structure Element: ELEMENT;
(4)        eqtype elt;
(5)        sharing type elt = Element.element;
(6)        datatype btree = Empty | Node of elt * btree * btree;
(7)        val leaf : elt -> btree;
(8)        val build : elt * btree * btree -> btree;
(9)        val lookup : elt * btree -> bool
       end;

       signature TREE = sig
(10)       structure Element: ELEMENT;
(11)       eqtype elt;
(12)       sharing type elt = Element.element;
(13)       datatype tree = Tree of elt * tree list;
(14)       val build : elt * tree list -> tree;
(15)       val lookup : elt * tree -> bool
       end;

       signature ALLTREES = sig
(16)       structure Btree: BTREE;
(17)       structure Tree: TREE;
(18)       sharing Btree.Element = Tree.Element;
(19)       sharing type Btree.elt = Tree.elt
       end;
```

Fig. 15.4. Signatures that equate types and substructures.

Then in lines (16)–(19) we see a final signature **ALLTREES**. This signature describes a structure that has two substructures. The first, on line (16), is called **Btree** and has **BTREE** for its signature. Line (17) adds a structure **Tree** with signature TREE.

We must find a substructure **Element** within each of these structures, because their respective signatures require that substructure. However, there is no reason to believe that these two substructures are the same. In principle, **element** could refer to different types in each, and/or the function **similar** could be differently defined in each. To prevent a structure with signature **ALLTREES** from using two different substructures called **Element**, the sharing specification on line (18) equates the two substructures **Btree.Element** and **Tree.Element**.

Finally, we note on line (19) an additional type sharing that equates the types `elt` belonging to the two substructures `Tree` and `Btree`. This sharing specification is legal, although it happens to be redundant. The fact that both types are equated to `Element.element` forces them to be equal anyway. □

Exercises

2-3 tree

Separator

!! **15.1***: A *2-3 tree* is a search tree in which each node that is not a leaf has either two or three children. The labels, which for simplicity we shall take to be integers, appear only at the leaves. The subtrees of a node preserve order; that is, the labels in the first subtree are less than those of the second subtree, which are less than the labels of the third subtree if it exists. A node with two subtrees has one *separator*, an integer that is the lowest of the labels of the second subtree. A node with three subtrees has two separators, one giving the lowest label of the second subtree and the other giving the lowest label of the third subtree. Thus, as we search down the tree for a given integer x, the separators tell us which way to go, just as the labels at interior nodes do for a binary search tree. Figure 15.5 suggests the structure of a 2-subtree and a 3-subtree node.

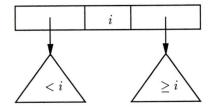

(a) Node with two subtrees.

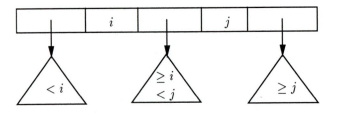

(b) Node with three subtrees.

Fig. 15.5. Nodes of a 2-3 tree.

2-3 trees allow fast insertion, deletion, and lookup, just like binary search trees. However, 2-3 trees remain balanced; that is, all leaves remain the same distance from the root if insertion and deletion are performed properly. That balance guarantees time per operation that is proportional to the logarithm of the number of nodes in the tree, while in the worst case, binary-search-tree operations can be linear per operation. In this exercise, we shall deal only with lookup and insertion.

The insertion algorithm is complex. The idea is that if we are to insert x into the tree T rooted at some node N, there are three cases.

1. If N is a leaf, we return a pair of 2-3 trees; one consists of the leaf N and the other consists of a leaf with label x. We shall call this form of return value a *pair*.

2. If N has two subtrees, use the separator to tell where x should be inserted and recursively insert x into that subtree. The value returned is either a pair of trees or a single tree. If it is a single tree, that tree replaces the subtree into which the insertion was made. If the result is a pair, those trees become subtrees of N, which now is a 3-subtree node. Adjust the separators appropriately. Note that in order to have the proper separators, when a pair of trees is returned a third component must be returned as well to separate the two trees.

3. If N has three subtrees, use the separators to tell into which subtree x must go, and recursively insert x there. If a single tree is returned, substitute it as in case (2). However, if a pair is returned, N now has four subtrees. Split them into two groups of two subtrees, and split N into two nodes that become the roots of two new trees. Then return the pair of trees. The situation is suggested by Fig. 15.6, where we assume the insertion has been in the middle subtree.

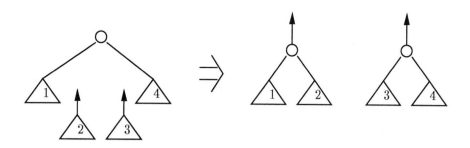

Fig. 15.6. Splitting a 3-subtree node into two 2-subtree nodes.

If at the root a pair is returned, create a new root with these trees as subtrees. For a more detailed explanation of how 2-3 trees work, see A. V. Aho, J. E. Hopcroft, and J. D. Ullman, *Data Structures and Algorithms*, Addison-Wesley, Reading, Mass., 1983.

In this exercise, you are asked to write a structure that supports the operations of **create** (create a tree consisting of one leaf with a given integer label), lookup, and insert on 2-3 trees. We shall not deal with deletion here. Start with a datatype having no parameters and three data constructors, for leaves, 2-subtree nodes, and 3-subtree nodes. Note the labels of leaves are integers, so there is no need for type parameters in this datatype. Next, create a datatype that wraps either a single tree in data constructor S or wraps a pair of trees and an integer separator in the data constructor P. You will need a number of auxiliary functions including, but not limited to, a function we shall call insert1. This function takes an integer x to be inserted and a tree T into which the insertion occurs and returns a wrapped tree (in S) or a wrapped pair of trees (in P). Consult the solutions if you cannot write this code, since it is necessary for the exercises that follow.

15.2: Write a signature that will not allow the functions other than create, lookup, and insert to be available through your 2-3-tree structure of Exercise 15.1. If you have not worked Exercise 15.1, use the solution in Fig. S17 at the end of the book. Then, create a new structure that will offer the user 2-3 trees with only these three functions available.

15.3: Accomplish the same goal as Exercise 15.2 without a new signature by making auxiliary functions local.

15.4: Show how to make the data constructors of the datatypes used in your solution to Exercise 15.1 (or the solution of Fig. S17) unavailable by using an abstraction.

15.5: Show how to achieve the same goal as Exercise 15.4 by using abstract types (abstype's).

15.6*: Give an example of a structure S that can be Element in line (3) of Fig. 15.4 and a structure with signature BTREE (as defined in lines (3)–(9) of that figure) that uses structure S at line (3) and satisfies the type-sharing constraint of line (5). Then, give another example of a structure with signature BTREE that uses the structure S but does *not* satisfy the sharing constraint.

! 15.7: Give examples of structures with signatures BTREE and TREE, as defined in Fig. 15.4, that satisfy the substructure-sharing constraint of line (18) in that figure. Then, give an example of structures that do *not* satisfy that constraint, although they satisfy the type-sharing constraints on lines (5), (12), and (19).

15.8: Show how to move the definition of function lt inside the definition of the abstract types of (a) Fig. 15.2 and (b) Fig. 15.3 without exporting the definition of lt.

◇◇◇ 16 Arrays

We shall now consider a type constructor, the *array*, that is available with SML/NJ, although it is not part of the formal definition of standard ML. While we have seen that programming in a functional style is not hard when one gets used to it, there are certain situations where we need to have a "state" for the data used by a program, or where searching through lists (as in the **Mapping** structure of Chapter 14) is not adequately efficient.

◇ **Example 16.1.** Let us consider the problem of checking that each of the 26 lowercase letters appears in a string. In a language like Pascal we would use a strategy like:

1. Create a Boolean array indexed by the letters. Initialize each entry to **false**.

2. For each character of the string, set the corresponding array entry to **true**.

3. After the entire string has been processed, check that each entry of the array is **true**.

While the above strategy uses iteration in steps (2) and (3), it is possible to substitute a recursion for the iteration in ML. We can use a somewhat different strategy, seen in Fig. 16.1, to get the job done in ML.

The function **member** of lines (1)–(4) tests whether element x is on a list L. Since the ideas should be familiar, we omit a discussion of this function. Lines (5)–(7) are a function **memberAll(ch,L)** that checks whether all the letters between ch and **"z"** are on the list L. That is, line (6) checks if the letter that is the value of variable ch is beyond **"z"**, in which case there is nothing to check and we return **true**. If there is still something to check, line (7) first checks that the letter represented by variable ch is on the list and then calls **memberAll** recursively on the next letter. Notice that the expression **chr(ord(ch)+1)** gives the character with the code one higher than that of ch. Finally, in line (8) we test the code with a call to **memberAll**. The first argument is **"a"**, so it checks all the letters, and the second argument is a list formed by exploding the string of all the letters in keyboard order. □

The solution of Fig. 16.1 works, but it is not a very efficient solution. To see the problem clearly, let us think of the generalization where there are n letters (instead of 26) and the strings to be checked have length at least n. Then **member** on the average must go at least distance $n/2$ down the list to find a given character, and **memberAll** calls **member** n times to get a positive answer.

```
        (* member(x,L) tests if x appears on list L *)
(1)     fun member(x,nil) = false
(2)     |   member(x,y::ys) =
(3)             if x=y then true
(4)             else member(x,ys);
```
*val member = fn : "a * "a list → bool*

```
        (* memberAll(ch,L) checks that character ch and all
            following characters up to "z" are on list L *)
(5)     fun memberAll(ch,L) =
(6)             if ch > "z" then true
(7)             else member(ch,L) andalso
                        memberAll(chr(ord(ch)+1),L);
```
*val memberAll = fn : string * string list → bool*

```
(8)     memberAll("a",explode("qwertyuiopasdfghjklzxcvbnm"));
```
val it = true : bool

Fig. 16.1. Checking that all letters appear: list-based solution.

Thus, a call to **memberAll** that returns **true** takes average time proportional to n^2.

On the other hand, the array-based solution outlined at the beginning of Example 16.1 takes time proportional to n, provided the string is about n characters in length. Step (1) takes time proportional to the length of the array to initialize, and in our generalized scenario we need an array of length n. Step (2) takes time proportional to the length of the string, which we suppose is also about n. Step (3) again takes time proportional to the length of the array, or n. Thus, the whole algorithm takes time proportional to n.

This increase in efficiency is the primary motivation why SML/NJ and many other implementations of ML provide arrays, even though the array violates the functional style of ML. In particular, arrays allow us to change the binding of an array identifier to its value as a side-effect of the **update** function. No other ML construct except the reference to be discussed in the next chapter allows bindings to be changed.

Array Operations

Index set

Arrays have the limited form found in C, where the only permitted index sets are the integers from 0 up to some number. The variety of options for index sets found in Pascal and many other languages is not available in SML/NJ. The most important operations on arrays are the following:

Create array

1.   We can create an array A of n entries (numbered 0 through $n-1$), with each entry initialized to value v by

```
val A = array(n,v);
```

The value v can be of any type, but we must specify the type if it is not obvious from the value (e.g., if v is **nil**). That is, ML does not use its full type-inference power on arrays, for technical reasons we shall not discuss.

Subscript

2. The value of the entry numbered i of array A is produced by the expression `sub(A,i)`.

Assignment in array

3. To store a value v in the entry numbered i of array A, we use the expression `update(A,i,v)`. This function is one of the few in ML that has a side-effect. Notice that the value of an entry of array A is permanently changed by this expression.

Subscript exception

• If `sub` or `update` are given a value of the subscript i that is out of the index set for the array, then the exception `Subscript` is raised.

◊ **Example 16.2.** In Fig. 16.2 we see a program to solve the same problem as that of Fig. 16.1, but it takes only linear time to do so. In line (1) we open the structure **Array**.

• Unlike most other features of ML described in this book, arrays are a structure from the SML/NJ library. They are not made available unless you explicitly open this structure.

Lines (2)–(4) give a function `checkAll` that tells whether array A has only true entries from indices from 0 up to and including i. Line (3) returns **true** if $i < 0$, whereupon there is nothing to check. Line (4) handles the case where something is left to check. We confirm that the entry i of array A is true and, if so, we then check recursively that entries from 0 up to $i - 1$ are also true.

Lines (5)–(8) are the function `fillAndCheck`, which takes an array A and a list L, and for each character on list L sets the appropriate entry of A to **true**. After completing the examination of the list, `fillAndCheck` calls `checkAll` to verify that all entries of array A are **true**. In detail, line (5) handles the case where the list is exhausted, whereupon `checkAll` is called with second argument 25. The number 25 is the highest index for our array, so we are thereby checking that all entries are **true**.

Lines (6)–(8) handle the case where there are elements on the list L. After matching the pattern `x::xs` on line (6), we do a sequence of two steps. First, on line (7) we take the head element `x` and compute the corresponding array index by the expression `ord(x)-ord("a")`. Thus, the entry indexed 0 corresponds to `"a"`, 1 to `"b"`, and so on, up to index 25, which corresponds to `"z"`. Then, the `update` function, as a side-effect, sets the appropriate entry of A to **true**. Second, line (8) calls `fillAndCheck` recursively on the tail of the list L.

Finally, line (9) is a use of function `fillAndCheck`. The first argument is the expression `array(26,false)` whose value is an array with 26 entries, indexed 0 to 25, each of which initially has the value **false**. The second argument is again the string of lowercase letters in keyboard order. □

```
(1)        open Array;
           open Array

           (* checkAll(A,i) checks that array A has only true
               entries from indexes 0 through i *)
(2)        fun checkAll(A,i) =
(3)            if i<0 then true
(4)            else sub(A,i) andalso checkAll(A,i-1);
           val checkAll = fn : bool array * int → bool

           (* fillAndCheck(A,L) sets the entry of array A to true
               for each letter appearing on list L, then checks
               that all entries are true *)
(5)        fun fillAndCheck(A,nil) = checkAll(A,25)
(6)        |   fillAndCheck(A,x::xs) = (
(7)                update(A,ord(x)-ord("a"),true);
(8)                fillAndCheck(A,xs)
           );
           val fillAndCheck = fn : bool array * string list → bool

(9)        fillAndCheck(array(26,false),
               explode("qwertyuiopasdfghjklzxcvbnm"));
           val it = true : bool
```

Fig. 16.2. Checking that all letters appear: array-based solution.

Hash Tables

The hash table is an important data structure that makes it possible to maintain sets by inserting and deleting elements in time per action that does not grow with the size of the set. Arrays are essential if we are to make hash tables work efficiently. Hash tables support structures like the mapping discussed in Chapter 14, but here we shall consider the simpler problem of keeping track of a set of elements while we insert and delete elements. We also allow the operation lookup on the set, to test whether a given element is currently a member of the set. A set with the operations insert, delete, and lookup is sometimes called a **Dictionary** *dictionary*.

We can implement a dictionary as a list. However, if the list grows to length n, then operations will take about $n/2$ steps on the average, since we must go about half way down the list. The hash table does the same operations using an average of a small constant number of steps per operation, independent of the size of the set.

The idea of the hash table is sketched in Fig. 16.3. At the heart is an **Bucket** array called the *bucket headers*. The set being represented is divided into some number b of *buckets*, numbered 0 through $b - 1$. Each bucket is represented by

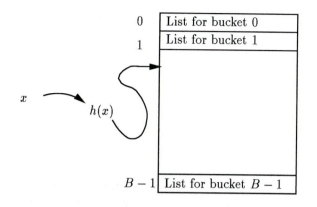

Bucket Headers

Fig. 16.3. A hash table.

a list of the elements in that bucket. If we pick b approximately equal to n, which is the size of the set, then there will be an average of about one element per bucket. However, in rare cases there could be a large number of elements, or even all the elements, in one of the buckets.

Hash function   Which bucket an element x belongs to is determined by a *hash function* $h(x)$ that produces an integer in the range 0 to $b-1$. The hash function can be anything we like, although it is desirable that it "randomize" the buckets so that in any typical set of elements, about an equal number of elements will belong in each bucket.

◇ **Example 16.3.** Suppose elements of the set are strings. A simple hash function sums the codes of the characters, using the **ord** function to get the codes, and then takes the remainder when the sum is divided by b, the number of buckets. The remainder is taken by the **mod** function.

Lines (4) and (5) of Fig. 16.4 show an auxiliary function **h1** that does this calculation for a list of characters. Then, in line (6) is the real function **h** that applies **h1** to an exploded string. □

Figure 16.4 shows a structure definition for a hash table. Prior to defining the structure, we open the **Array** structure at line (1). The structure begins with a number of local declarations. We give a particular value, 10, to the parameter b at line (3). The functions **h** and **h1** discussed in Example 16.3 appear next.

In lines (7)–(15) are three local functions that do insertion, deletion, and lookup on the lists that are array elements. Their workings should be easy to discern and do not depend on arrays at all.

Lines (16)–(18) are the first of the exported functions for the structure.

```
(1)     open Array;
        open Array

(2)     structure Hash = struct
            local
(3)             val b = 10;
(4)             fun h1(nil) = 0
(5)             |   h1(x::xs) = (ord(x)+h1(xs)) mod b;

(6)             fun h(x) = h1(explode(x));

(7)             fun insertList(x,nil) = [x]
(8)             |   insertList(x,y::ys) =
(9)                     if x=y then y::ys else y::insertList(x,ys);
(10)            fun deleteList(x,nil) = nil
(11)            |   deleteList(x,y::ys) =
(12)                    if x=y then ys else y::deleteList(x,ys);
(13)            fun lookupList(x,nil) = false
(14)            |   lookupList(x,y::ys) =
(15)                    if x=y then true else lookupList(x,ys)
            in
(16)            fun insert(x,A) =
                    let
(17)                    val bucket = h(x); val L = sub(A,bucket)
                    in
(18)                    update(A,bucket,insertList(x,L))
                    end;
(19)            fun delete(x,A) =
                    let
(20)                    val bucket = h(x); val L = sub(A,bucket)
                    in
(21)                    update(A,bucket,deleteList(x,L))
                    end;
(22)            fun lookup(x,A) = lookupList(x,sub(A,h(x)));
(23)            fun create () = array(b, nil: string list)
            end
        end;
        structure Hash :
            sig
                val delete : string * string list array → unit
                val insert : string * string list array → unit
                val lookup : string * string list array → bool
                val create : unit → string list array
            end
```

Fig. 16.4. The hash-table structure.

The function `insert(x,A)` inserts string x into its proper bucket in the hash table whose headers are in array A. In line (17) we compute the correct bucket number, using hash function h, and we let L be the current list in the bucket $h(x)$. Finally, line (18) performs the side-effect on the array A that inserts x into the list in the bucket numbered $h(x)$. That is, the first argument A of the `update` expression is the array to be updated. The second argument, `bucket`, is the index of the entry to be updated. The third argument is the new value that we get by inserting string x into the old list L.

- Note that we could have written `insert` without the let-expression by writing the single-expression body:

   ```
   update(A, h(x), insertList(x,sub(A,h(x))))
   ```

   However, this expression repeats the computation of $h(x)$.

Lines (19)–(21) are the function `delete(x,A)` that deletes string x from the hash table whose bucket header array is A. The idea is similar to `insert`; we find the proper index, called `bucket`, and remember L, the old list of that bucket. We then update A in line (21) by storing the list L, with x deleted, in the entry for the proper bucket.

Line (22) is the function `lookup`, which applies function `lookupList` to the bucket whose number is $h(x)$. Finally, in line (23) is a function `create` that takes a unit as argument and returns an array of size 10, each of whose elements is a string list.

- We need to define the type of elements that are used to initialize arrays, even though it seems intuitively that ML should be able to deduce the type when it needs to. Thus, we declared `nil` in line (23) to be of type `string list`. We suggest that a type always be given for the initial value of an array if it is not apparent from the value itself.

- Notice that `create` is not a value; it is a function that takes the unit as argument. Had we defined `create` by

   ```
   val create = array(b, nil: string list);
   ```

   then every time we used `create` we would get the *same* array. By defining `create` to be a function that takes the unit as argument, we instead get a new array every time we use `create`. Compare this situation, where a call to function `array` is necessary to get an array value, with previous uses of `create` such as line (3) of Fig. 14.2, where it was sufficient to define `create` for mappings to be the value `nil`.

The ML response shows the signature of the structure. Only the exported functions are visible.

The structure `Hash` can be used as follows:

```
open Hash
```
open Hash
```
val headers = create ();
```
val headers = prim? : string list array

We first open the structure `Hash`. Then we use `create` to give us a new array named `headers`, with 10 empty buckets. In the response of ML to the declaration, the value of the array is not given. Rather, the abbreviation `prim?` appears to indicate a value that ML is not equipped to represent.

Now we can execute operations on the dictionary represented by array `headers`. Here are three examples of these operations.

```
insert("foo", headers);
```
val it = () : unit

```
lookup("bar", headers);
```
val false : bool

```
delete("baz", headers);
```
val it = () : unit

Note that the operations `insert` and `delete` produce a unit as value, since they do their work by a side-effect and do not otherwise produce a value. □

• This structure definition is not the most general approach and does not represent the best programming practice. A better approach would be to develop a functor like `MakeBST` at the end of Chapter 14. This functor would take as argument a structure that specifies the type of elements, the integer b, and the hash function $h(x)$. We could then apply the functor to create structures that would be hash tables of different sizes with different element types and different hash functions.

Exercises

16.1: Write expressions to perform the following operations.

a)* Create an array `A` of 20 elements, each of which is initially an empty list of reals.

b) Create an array `A` of 100 reals, each of which is initially 0.

c)* Find the 30th entry in an array `A` of 100 reals.

d) Find the 10th entry in an array `A` of 20 integers.

e)* Change the entry with index 10 in array `A` to 43.

f) Change the entry with index 0 in array `A` to [1,2,3].

! **16.2***: Instead of defining a particular hash table with a particular hash function, it would be prudent to design a functor that can produce any sort of hash table, given the number of buckets b, the type of elements, and a suitable hash function that takes elements of the given type and produces an integer between 0 and $b - 1$.

a)   Write a signature that describes hash functions by calling for the specification of the value of b, the type of elements, and the hash function h.

b)   Write a functor that takes as argument a structure whose signature is as given in part (a) and produces a structure that includes:

1.   An array A to serve as the hash table.

2.   Functions **insert(x)**, **delete(x)**, and **lookup(x)** that respectively insert, delete, and look up an element x in the hash table whose bucket array is A.

c)   Write a structure that defines the value $b = 10$, defines elements to be strings, and defines the hash function to be the one used in Fig. 16.4.

d)   Combine the first three parts to produce a structure that has a hash table and functions that perform the same tasks as in Fig. 16.4.

! **16.3**: We can use a hash table to implement mappings if we define the element type to be the product of a domain and range type. The hash function operates only on the first (domain) component of a pair and ignores the second component. As an exercise, implement a hash table that supports string-integer mappings and the operations **insert**, **delete**, and **lookup** on these mappings, as defined in Example 14.4. Note that the **lookup** operation differs from the operation of the same name in Fig. 16.4 or the answer to Exercise 16.2. In particular, for a mapping **lookup** is given only the domain value and must find the associated range value.

! **16.4**: Modify the answer to Exercise 16.2(a) and (b) so it produces hash tables that support mappings from some domain type to some range type. Show how to use it to implement string-integer mappings.

16.5*: How should Fig. 16.4 be modified if the elements are integers instead of strings?

arrayoflist   !! **16.6***: Write a function **arrayoflist** that takes a list of elements of some type, say $[a_0, a_1, \ldots, a_{n-1}]$, and produces an array of length n whose elements are $a_0, a_1, \ldots, a_{n-1}$ in that order.[1] We must assume $n \geq 1$, or else it is not possible to determine the type of the array elements.

---

[1] SML/NJ actually has a function of this name and meaning (see Chapter 25).

◊◊◊ 17 References

Standard ML has a mechanism for assigning new values to names of any type, not just to array elements. This feature, called the *reference*, is another way to violate the functional, side-effect-free style. We advocate its use only in situations where it simplifies the programming.

It is possible to associate with some identifier **x** a value that is a "reference," which we may think of as a box capable of holding any value of a particular type. We add the binding between **x** and this "box" to the environment by:

        val x = ref *v*;

Here, *v* can be a value of any type, say type T, whereupon ML will respond with

        val x = ref v : T ref

- The type of the value *v* must be concrete (no type variables) rather than polymorphic. For example, we could not let *v* be the identity function, whose type is

        fn : 'a -> 'a

The value in the "box" associated with **x** can later be changed to another value of type T by one of several mechanisms we shall describe. In contrast, binding identifier **x** to value *v* rather than to **ref** *v* would not allow the binding to be modified in any way.

◊ **Example 17.1.** The statement

        val i = ref 0;
        val i = ref 0 : int ref

binds identifier **i** to a "box" whose initial value is **ref 0**. Figure 17.1 suggests what the box **i** might look like, with the type constructor **ref** wrapping the current value in the box. Note that it will be possible to change the value in the "box" of Fig. 17.1 without having to create a new binding. □

Obtaining the Value of a Ref-Variable

The operator **!**, applied to a ref-variable, produces the value to which the variable refers. For instance, if **i** is the ref-variable of Example 17.1, which was made to refer to the integer 0, then the value of **!i** is 0. In contrast, the value of the expression **i** is *not* 0 but rather **ref 0**. Function **!** is not defined for

184

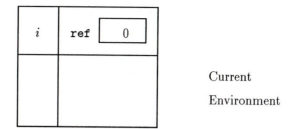

Fig. 17.1. A variable i of type `ref int`.

arguments that are not ref-variables. ML will detect and indicate an error if we write a program that could apply ! to a non-reference.

One way to understand the distinction between the value of a ref variable and the value to which it refers is to imagine there is a datatype **ref** with one data constructor, also called **ref**. This datatype is polymorphic and defined by

```
datatype 'a ref = ref of 'a;
```

That view is consistent with the picture in Fig. 17.1, where the variable i has the value **ref 0** and is of type **int ref**.[1]

In this view, the function ! is defined by

```
fun !(ref(v)) = v;
```

Note ! is not defined for non-reference arguments.

However, there is more to references than a datatype. Only ref-variables can change the value to which they are bound. Other identifier bindings remain the same and can only be overwritten by new additions to the environment that bind the same identifier, as we discussed in Chapter 3.

Modifying Ref-Variables

Assignment

The function denoted by the infix operator := changes the value inside the box that is bound to a ref-variable. For instance, in Example 17.1 the assignment

```
i := 1;
```

Store

replaces by 1 the value in the box that is bound to identifier i. Put another way, the value bound to i changes from **ref 0** to **ref 1**. This assignment changes the current *store*; that is, it changes the value to which some identifier with a ref-value is bound. In contrast, other ML operations that change things, such as var-declarations, act on the environment only, creating new bindings for identifiers and thereby obscuring previously made bindings for the same identifiers, but leaving the store intact.

---

[1] We use **ref 0** rather than **ref(0)** to represent references, although either is correct. Recall that parentheses are optional in function applications and data constructor applications as well.

- Note that := can only be used on a ref-variable that has already been defined. It cannot be used to initialize a ref-variable.

Increment, decrement

There are two other functions that operate only on **int ref** values: increment and decrement.

1. `inc(x)` is equivalent to `x := !x + 1`.

2. `dec(x)` is equivalent to `x := !x - 1`.

◇ **Example 17.2.** If we execute the "statement" `i := 1` and then execute `inc(i)`, the value in the box associated with i becomes 2 and the value of i becomes **ref 2**. If we then execute `dec(i)`, the value of i again becomes **ref 1**. □

Arrays and References

The entries in an array may be thought of as references, although in practice there is a more efficient implementation of arrays in ML as a block of storage, much like the implementations of arrays in other languages. That is, the picture of an array in Fig. 16.3 was not precisely correct. Strictly speaking, the entry for index value 0 should be "**ref**(list for bucket 0)," and similarly for the other entries. Then, the function `sub(A,i)` can be thought of as finding the entry with index i and applying the ! operator to it. We can think of `update(A,i,v)` as performing `e := v`, where e is the entry of the array A having index i.

The While-Do Statement

The expression

        `while <expression> do <expression>`

has the expected meaning in ML:

1. Evaluate the first expression.

2. If the first expression is false, end. If the first expression is true, evaluate the second expression and go to step (1).

Of course, we shall loop indefinitely if the second expression does not change something that affects the value of the first expression. Ref-variables make it easy to have the evaluation of the second expression change the value of the first expression. They thus let us create loops that perform some useful computation and then terminate.

- The value produced by a while-do expression is always the unit, even if the expression after the **do** has a type other than unit.

◊ **Example 17.3.** A simple example of a while-loop is

```
val i = ref 1;
while !i<=10 do (print(!i); print(" "); inc(i))
```

The effect is that the integers from 1 to 10 will be printed on a line. Each time we execute the "body" of the loop (the three statements after the **do**), we increment i by 1 until it exceeds 10. □

- Note that in Example 17.3 we must print the value !i, not i. The value of i is something like **ref 3**, and **print** is not defined on such values.

- Similarly, the termination test is !i<=10, not i<=10; the latter would try to compare a value of type **int ref** with the value 10 of type **int** and cause a type mismatch.

An Example With Matrices

Upper triangular matrix

To gain an appreciation of the way references, arrays, and while-loops can be used productively, let us consider the problem of turning an n-by-n matrix of reals into an *upper-triangular matrix* (a matrix in which all entries below the main diagonal are 0, as suggested by Fig. 17.2). The solution uses row operations in which a multiple of one row is subtracted from another. Upper-triangularization is the key step in the algorithm for solving simultaneous linear equations known as "Gaussian elimination."

- There are cleaner ways to write this code than the reference-based approach we use. For example, Exercise 8.3 discusses a similar problem and solves it using lists of lists. An exercise at the end of this chapter suggests how we could redo this code using arrays but not references. However, the present example illustrates the use of references and also suggests that, when it is really needed, we could write pieces of ML code in a "conventional" style.

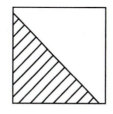

Fig. 17.2. An upper-triangular matrix.

The creation of a matrix M begins in Fig. 17.3. Line (1) opens the **Array** structure, which we need for our program. Line (2) sets n, the dimension of the matrix, to 10. The rest of the code is written with n as the side of the matrix.

The matrix M will be represented by an array of length n, each entry of which is a row. Each row is itself an array of length n, and its entries are

```
(1)    open Array;
       open Array

(2)    val n = 10;
       val n = 10 : int

(3)    val M = array(n,array(n,0.0));
       val M = prim? : real array array

(4)    val i = ref 1;
       val i = ref 1 : int ref

(5)    while !i<n do (
(6)        update(M,!i,array(n,0.0));
(7)        inc(i)
       );
       val it = () : unit

(8)    i := 0;
       val it = () : unit

(9)    val j = ref 0;
       val j = ref 0 : int ref

       (* initialize M to be a particular matrix *)
(10)   while !i<n do (
(11)       while !j<n do (
(12)           update(sub(M,!i),!j,1.0/real(!i + !j + 1));
(13)           inc(j)
           );
(14)       j := 0;
(15)       inc(i)
       );
       val it = () : unit
```

Fig. 17.3. Creating and initializing a matrix.

reals. The matrix element M_{ij}, the entry in row i and column j, is obtained by the expression `sub(sub(M,!i), !j)`, assuming i and j are variables of type `int ref`. Note that we must use the ! operator to get the integer value of such a variable.

Line (3) creates the array M with n entries numbered 0 to $n-1$. Initially, each entry has an array of n reals as value; those reals are all initially 0.

- We might think we are done with the creation of the matrix, but there is a subtle error. The subexpression `array(n,0.0)` has created a single array of n reals, and this one array has become the value of each entry of M.

Thus, in lines (4)–(7) we create a new array for each entry of M except that with index 0.

Line (4) creates a ref-variable i to serve as the iterator. Line (5) begins a while-loop, in which the condition is that the value referred to by i must be less than n. The body of this while-loop does two things. First, line (6) puts a new row-array in the entry of M with index i. Then, line (7) increments i. As a result of this incrementation, the loop terminates after putting a new row-array in the entry of M with index $n - 1$, which is the last row.

Lines (8)–(15) of Fig. 17.3 are a doubly nested loop to initialize the matrix M in a particular way: $M_{ij} = 1/(i + j + 1)$. This particular matrix serves as a good test of the precision of the algorithm, because the rows are almost, but not quite, multiples of one another. However, in reality, a program for upper-triangularization would at this point read in the data rather than creating it.

Lines (8) and (9) initialize i and j, the row and column indices respectively. Notice that i can be initialized with a use of :=, while j, which has not been used before, must be initialized by a val-declaration. Line (10) begins the outer loop.

The inner loop, on j, is lines (11)–(13). The matrix element M_{ij} is given the desired value at line (12), and j is incremented at line (13).

- Note in line (12) that a space is needed between the + and the !. Without it, the substring +! would be interpreted as a symbolic identifier and an error would result.

Lines (14) and (15) complete the outer loop; we reset j to 0 at line (14) and increment i at line (15).

The actual algorithm is shown in Fig. 17.4. In explanation, we use each row i, except the last row (numbered $n - 1$), to put 0's in the column numbered

Main diagonal

i, below the *main diagonal* (the line running from upper left to lower right). Figure 17.5 shows what the matrix looks like when we begin working on row i. All the columns numbered from 0 to $i - 1$ have been given 0's below the main diagonal, as suggested by the shaded area.

The strategy for a given value of i is as follows. We need to subtract a multiple of row i from each row $j = i + 1, i + 2, \ldots, n - 1$. This multiple must be chosen so that M_{ji} becomes 0; thus the appropriate multiplier for i and j is M_{ji}/M_{ii}. We call this multiplier `ratio` in the code of Fig. 17.4. To subtract a multiple of row i from row j under these conditions, we can set M_{ji} to 0, but then must replace each M_{jk} by $M_{jk} - ratio * M_{ik}$, for $k = i+1, i+2, \ldots, n-1$.[2]

Let us now look at the code in Fig. 17.4. Lines (16) and (17) begin the outer loop. Index i will run from 0 to $n - 2$, thus letting us consider each row in

---

[2] This algorithm is not the best way to put a matrix in upper-triangular form. It risks a division by 0 even if the matrix is nonsingular, and it can lead to loss of precision where other approaches could achieve more accuracy. However, it will do as a programming example.

```
(16)    i := 0;
        val i = ref 0 : int ref

(17)    while !i<n-1 do (
(18)        j := !i+1;
(19)        while !j<n do
                let
(20)                val ratio = sub(sub(M,!j),!i)/sub(sub(M,!i),!i);
(21)                val k = ref (!i+1)
                in
(22)                update(sub(M,!j),!i,0.0);
(23)                while !k<n do (
(24)                    update(sub(M,!j),!k,sub(sub(M,!j),!k) -
                            ratio*sub(sub(M,!i),!k));
(25)                    inc(k)
                    );
(26)                inc(j)
                end;
(27)        inc(i)
        );
        val it = () : unit
```

Fig. 17.4. Upper-triangularization of a matrix (continues Fig. 17.3).

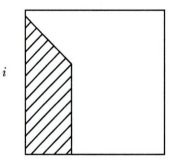

Fig. 17.5. Situation when we begin working on row i.

turn except the last. Lines (18) and (19) similarly begin the second loop, and index j runs from $i+1$ to the last row, $n-1$, to let us zero column i below the main diagonal.

At line (20) we compute the value of `ratio`, which is M_{ji}/M_{ii}. Then line (21) initializes the third index, k, which will range from $i+1$ to $n-1$ and allow us to subtract a multiple of row i from row j. Line (22) sets M_{ji} to 0, and lines (23)–(25) are an inner loop in which we subtract $ratio * M_{ik}$ from M_{jk}, for $k = i + 1, i + 2, \ldots, n - 1$. Finally, lines (26) and (27) complete the middle and outer loop, respectively.

- Note the need for a let-expression in lines (20)–(25). We cannot use a val-declaration inside the while-loop. The **let** allows us to make an addition to the current environment, where we can put the local variables **ratio** and **k**. Without the **let**, there is no place to put additional variables.

References

There is a limitation on the types of ref variables that we have not discussed. Such a limitation is needed to be sure of being able to deduce the type of any variable when the program is compiled. Intuitively, the requirement on polymorphic types involving references is that there is some finite number of times one needs to apply a function to them in order to get to a monomorphic reference type, that is, a reference type not involving type variables. The way SML/NJ decides whether a reference type is allowed is discussed in M. Hoang, J. C. Mitchell, and R. Viswanathan, "Standard ML-NJ weak polymorphism and imperative constructs," *Proceedings of IEEE Symposium on Logic in Computer Science*, pp. 15–25, 1993.

Exercises

17.1: Write expressions that do the following:

a)* Create a ref-variable **i** whose initial value is a reference to 10.
b) Create a ref-variable **word** whose initial value refers to **"foo"**.
c)* Increment the referred value of ref-variable **i** by 1.
d) Decrement the referred value of ref-variable **j** by 1.
e)* Change existing ref-variable **i** to refer to 20.
f) Change existing ref-variable **word** to refer to **"bar"**.

17.2: Write expressions to compute the following functions of the values referred to by ref-variables **x** and **y**, which we shall assume refer to reals.

a)* The square of the sum of the values referred to by **x** and **y**.
b) The average of the values referred to by **x** and **y**.

!! **17.3***: In Exercise 8.3 we discussed the pivotal condensation method of taking the determinant of a matrix, and we gave a list-based solution in Fig. S7 (see the solutions at the end of the book). We can use references and arrays to give a solution that follows more closely the description of the algorithm given informally in Exercise 8.3. Write this function.

!! **17.4***: Is your solution to Exercise 17.3 (or the solution given in Fig. S20) more efficient than the list-based solution given in Fig. S7? Why or why not?

! **17.5***: What happens in response to the ML code

```
val i = 1;
while i<10 do val i = i+1;
```

! 17.6: Add to the triangularization code of Figs. 17.3 and 17.4 to make a complete Gaussian elimination algorithm.

17.7*: Design a structure **Matrix**[3] that implements $n \times m$ matrices of reals and provides the following functions:

1. **matrix(n,m,v)** returns an $n \times m$ matrix with each entry initially v.

2. **sub(M,i,j)** returns the element in row i and column j of the matrix M.

3. **update(M,i,j,v)** changes the element in row i and column j of matrix M to be v.

17.8: Write a functor that takes as argument a structure with type T and produces a structure that implements matrices, as in Exercise 17.7, but with elements of type T instead of reals.

!! 17.9: An improved version of the upper-triangularization algorithm given in this chapter allows rows to be interchanged in order to avoid division by 0 and to minimize roundoff errors. In particular, when it is time to zero column i below the main diagonal, we pick that row among rows i and greater such that the element in the ith column has as large a magnitude as possible. Thus, if any row is nonzero in column i we shall avoid a division by 0 when we compute **ratio** as in line (20) of Fig. 17.4. Also, since **ratio** is as large as possible, we tend to subtract small numbers from the elements of the matrix, thus tending to avoid large roundoff errors. As an exercise, write this improved version of the triangularization algorithm.

For-loop

17.10: Code like that of Fig. 17.3 and 17.4 uses integer references to simulate for-loops in languages like Pascal. We can replace these uses of references if we define a higher-order function

```
fun for(a,b,F) =
        if a>b then ()
        else (F(a); for(a+1,b,F));
```

That is, the function **for** applies function F to each of the integers between a and b. The type of **for** is **int * int * (int -> 'a) -> unit**. Intuitively, F is the body of the for-loop, with the current loop index as an argument.

! a)* Rewrite the while-loop of Example 17.3 that prints the integers from 1 to 10, using **for**.

!! b) Rewrite the code of Figs. 17.3 and 17.4 using **for** to avoid all use of references.

---

[3] There is a similar structure called **Array2** in the SML/NJ library.

PART **3** | *Additional Details and Features*

◇◇◇
◇

In the third part of this book we round out our knowledge of ML by considering some generalizations of ideas introduced in previous chapters. We reconsider tuples, patterns, exceptions, functions, operator precedence, and input/output. The subject of Currying — functions that allow us to build new functions by binding one or more arguments of another function — is also covered here. Finally, we summarize the language ML with enumerations of built-in functions, exceptions, and types, and with a collection of syntax diagrams. The topics covered here are not necessarily less useful or less important than the features of ML mentioned in the first two parts. However, until now, we have been minimalist in our selection of concepts, so the form and flavor of ML programming could be presented quickly. Now, we shall endeavor to fill in the gaps.

◇◆◇ 18 Record Structures

Chapter 4 introduced tuples, which are denoted by round parentheses surrounding a comma-separated list of components. The tuple is actually a simplification of, and a special notation for, a more basic concept: the *record structure*. Records are denoted by curly brackets, { and }, around a comma-separated list

Field

of *fields* of the form

> \<label\> = \<value\>

Label

Labels can be any identifier, including strings of digits; the latter is a very important special case, as we shall see.

The *type* of a record is a comma-separated list of elements of the form

> \<label\> : \<type\>

Record type

The list is surrounded by curly brackets. That is, the notation for record types is the same as for record values, except that instead of equal-signs followed by values, we find colons followed by types. We shall refer to the type of a record as its *record structure*.

◇ **Example 18.1.** Let us design a record structure that can represent information about students. The fields will be

1. An integer `ID`, the "student ID number."

2. A string `name`, the student's name.

3. A `string list` that we call `courses`, indicating the courses in which the student is currently enrolled.

```
val Norm'sRecord = {
        ID=123,
        name="Norm dePlume",
        courses=["CS106X","E40","M43"]
};
val Norm'sRecord = {
        ID=123,
        courses=["CS106X","E40","M43"],
        name="Norm dePlume"
} : {ID:int, courses:string list, name:string}
```

Fig. 18.1. Creating a record.

194

In the val-declaration of Fig. 18.1, the identifier `Norm'sRecord` is assigned a value that is a record with three fields. The first field has label `ID` and value 123. The label of the second field is `name`, and the value of the second field is `"Norm dePlume"`. The third field has label `courses` and a value that is a list of three strings. The response repeats the value of the record and indicates its type.[1] ML has discovered from the values of the fields that `ID` is an integer, `name` a string, and `courses` a list of strings □

- ML reorders the fields in both the value and the type expressions. SML/NJ chooses lexicographic order for the fields.[2]

- In general, record structures are sets of fields, and the order doesn't matter. Thus, the record of Example 18.1 could have been expressed with any of the six possible orders of the three labels, as long as the value associated with each remained the same. For instance,

```
val Norm'sRecord = {name="Norm dePlume",
        courses=["CS106X","E40","M43"], ID=123};
```

  means exactly the same as the val-declaration of Example 18.1.

- Observe that the apostrophe in identifier `Norm'sRecord` has no special significance. It is treated like an ordinary letter when it appears in the middle of an alphanumeric identifier.

Extracting Field Values

The operator `#` takes a label and a record and produces the value associated with that label in the given record. We usually write this operation as

    #<label>(<record>)

The parentheses around the record are not required, and space after the `#` is permissible.

◇ **Example 18.2.** Assume the name `Norm'sRecord` is as defined in Example 18.1. The operation

```
#name(Norm'sRecord);
```
val it = "Norm dePlume" : string

illustrates the use of the field accessing operator. The result is the value of field `name` in the record `Norm'sRecord`. □

---

[1] The response from SML/NJ is not indented in the way we have shown it.

[2] Remember that in the ASCII character code, all uppercase letters precede all lowercase letters, which explains why `ID` appears ahead of `course`.

Tuples as a Special Case of Record Structures

In ML, the record structure is a primitive concept, and the tuple, which we have been using until now, is a special notation for certain record structures. That is, the tuple

$$(<\text{value } 1>, \ldots, <\text{value } n>)$$

is really a shorthand for the record

$$\{1=<\text{value } 1>, \ldots, n=<\text{value } n>\}$$

In this record, the labels are the integers from 1 to n, and they are the names of the n fields, in order. Thus, for example, the tuple (3, "four") is shorthand for the record {1=3, 2="four"}.

Recall from Chapter 4 that we introduced the # operator with an integer and a tuple as arguments, and we learned that #i extracts the ith component from a tuple. Now we see that this convention is an artifact of the definition of tuples as record structures; i is the label for the ith field of a tuple.

- Round and curly brackets are not interchangeable. Round parentheses only denote tuples with the "invisible" labels $1, 2, \ldots$. In contrast, curly brackets only denote records, and the labels are mandatory.

Patterns That Match Records

It is possible to use the record notation to define patterns for such uses as function definitions. A pattern that matches a record will have the expected form. Between curly brackets we find a comma-separated list of fields of the form

$$<\text{label}> = <\text{pattern}>$$

Ellipsis, the wildcard for fields

The pattern can be any pattern expression, built along the lines suggested in Chapter 6. The pattern may also use the *wildcard for fields*, which is the symbol ... (*ellipsis*). Often, there will be many fields in a record structure, and we wish to use only one or a few of them. The ellipsis comes in handy to avoid our having to specify names for the values of all the irrelevant fields. When we match a particular record to a pattern, the ellipsis matches the set of fields that are not mentioned explicitly.

◇ **Example 18.3.** In Fig. 18.2 we see a function getID that takes a string representing a student name and a list of records with the structure given in Example 18.1. Function getID finds the first record with that string as the student name and returns the ID for that student. If there is no such record in the list, the exception NotFound, defined in line (1), is raised.

In line (2) we handle the case where the list of available records is empty. Then the person searched for has not been found, so we raise the exception. In line (3) we consider the case where there is at least one more record, x. Using the keyword as, we express x in the alternative form {name=p,...}.

```
(1)    exception NotFound;
       exception NotFound

(2)    fun getID(person,nil) = raise NotFound
(3)    |   getID(person,(x as {name=p,...})::xs) =
(4)            if p = person then
(5)                #ID(x:{name:string,ID:int,courses:string list})
(6)            else getID(person,xs);
       val getID =
         fn : string * {ID:int, courses:string list, name:string} list → int
```

Fig. 18.2. Finding the ID of a student with a given name.

This expression gives the value of the **name** field of the record x to the pattern variable **p**, and the wildcard . . . is allowed to match the other two fields.

Line (4) checks whether the name of the student in record x, that is, **p**, equals the person searched for, that is, **person**. If so, in line (5) we apply the operator **#ID** to x to return the value of the **ID** field of x. Note that at line (5) we also give the type for x, which is

```
{name:string, ID:int, courses:string list}
```

- Remember that order of fields is irrelevant, so this type will match records such as **Norm'sRecord** of Example 18.1.

Finally, line (6) handles the case where record x does not have a **name** field value that equals **person**. Then we must apply **getID** recursively on the tail of the list. □

Incidentally, in Example 18.3 we could have written line (3) in several other ways. For example, we could avoid the ellipsis and write

```
getID(person, {name=p, ID=i, course=_}::xs) =
```

Then, we could use **i** in place of **#ID(x)** in line (5), and we would not have to specify the type of **x** or the type of the **course** field. Another approach is to let the ellipsis stand for only the **course** field, replacing line (3) by

```
getID(person, {name=p, ID=i,...}::xs) =
```

Again we could use **i** for **#ID(x)** in line (5), but we would still have to declare the record structure somewhere, or ML could not deduce the type of the wildcard symbol . . . , and an error would be indicated.

◇ **Example 18.4.** Suppose we want to take student records as in Example 18.3 and compute the tuition charge. The rules we shall follow are:

1.   A student registered for no courses pays a \$1000 fee.

2.   A student registered for only one course pays \$2000.

3.   A student registered for more than one course pays \$4000 if an undergraduate and \$5000 if a graduate student. Graduate students are given ID's of 100,000 or over, so we can identify which are the graduate students.

```
(1)          fun tuition({name=_, ID=_, courses=nil}) = 1000
(2)          |   tuition({courses=[_],...}) = 2000
(3)          |   tuition({ID=i,...}) =
(4)                  if i>=100000 then 5000
(5)                  else 4000;
```
val tuition = fn : {ID:int, courses='a list, name='b} → *int*

```
(6)          tuition(Norm'sRecord);
```
val it = 4000

```
(7)          tuition({name="Mona Kerr",ID=54321,courses=["CS105"]});
```
val it = 2000

```
(8)          tuition({name="Sue Dunham",ID=200000,
                  courses=["CS105","CS022"]});
```
val it = 5000

```
(9)          tuition({name="Alice O. Nunez",ID=6789,courses=nil});
```
val it = 1000

Fig. 18.3. Computing tuition by matching record patterns.

The function **tuition** is shown in Fig. 18.3. Line (1) implements the first rule above; if the list of courses is empty, the tuition is \$1000. Here, the patterns for the **name** and **ID** fields were chosen to be wildcard variables because we do not need to use their values in the result of the function. The pattern for the **courses** field is the constant **nil**. Note that by specifying all the fields in the record, ML now has a sufficient idea of the record type. However, as we see from the response below line (5), **tuition** is partially polymorphic because ML never learns, nor needs to know, the type of student names or the names of courses.

Line (2) covers the second rule, where the student is taking a single course. The pattern for the list of courses is [_]. Here, the wildcard variable is used, but its position within square brackets creates a pattern that is matched by lists of length one, and only by those lists. We are able to use the ellipsis safely, since ML knows from line (1) what the other fields of the record must be named.

Lines (3)–(5) cover the case where there is more than one course in the course list, because the cases of zero and one course were already intercepted by lines (1) and (2). Now, we need to use the value of the ID field, so we give it a variable name i, while we elide the rest of the record-pattern.

In line (6) we apply **tuition** to the specific record **Norm'sRecord** defined in Fig. 18.1. It identifies the student as an undergraduate taking more than one course and determines the tuition to be $4000. Lines (7)–(9) test the other three possible outcomes. □

Shorthands in Record Patterns

Often a record pattern uses a single variable as the pattern for a field. ML provides a shorthand for this case if we are willing to use the field name itself as the variable. That is, instead of

<label> = <variable>

as a field, we just use <label>.

◇ **Example 18.5.** In line (3) of Fig. 18.3 we used ID = i as a field of the record-pattern, and we then used i as the value of the field in line (4). An equivalent way to write this code is

```
(3)        |    tuition({ID,...}) =
(4)                 if ID>=100000 then 5000
```

Here, just ID appears as the pattern for the field in line (3), and in line (4) we use ID itself as the value of that field. In so doing, there is an increase in clarity. We can see that line (4) is asking if the student ID is at least 100,000. □

Exercises

18.1: Write expressions to do the following.

a)* Define the type **dino** to be an abbreviation for a record structure with fields **name** (a string), **weight** (a real), and **height** (a real).

b) Give a record named **tyranno**, of type **dino**, that represents the facts that Tyrannosaurus weighed 7 tons and was 20 feet tall.

c)* Create a record named **brachio**, of type **dino**, that represents the facts that Brachiosaurus weighed 50 tons and was 40 feet tall.

d) Write an expression that gets from the record **tyranno** the height of a Tyrannosaurus.

e)* Write an expression that gets from the record **brachio** the weight of a Brachiosaurus.

18.2: Suppose we have a list L of items with the record structure introduced in Example 18.1. We can write several functions to search for records with given properties. Write the following functions:

a)* Given a list L and a name n, find all those records with n as the value of its **name** field.

b) Given a list L and an ID i, find the list of courses in the first (and presumably only) record with **ID** field equal to i.

! c)* Given a list L and a course c, find the names of all the students who are taking course c.

!! **18.3**: In Pascal, C, and many other languages, there is a linked-list data structure that we assume is familiar to the reader. There is generally no need to implement this sort of data structure in ML because we have such lists as a primitive, and the implementation of lists in ML is, "behind the scenes," very much like the standard linked list. However, it is an interesting exercise to mimic the linked list using records and references in ML. That is, each cell of a linked list is a record with an **element** field carrying the data and a **next** field that is a reference to the next cell.

Hint: In other languages, a "nil pointer" is a legitimate value of any pointer type, but we do not have the luxury in ML of such a versatile value (although **nil** essentially has that versatility for normal ML lists). Thus, we need to create a datatype with two constructors, **Nil** and **Cell**, to indicate whether a **next** field "points" to another cell or is "nil."

a)* Devise the datatype for "conventional" linked lists.

b) Write a function **pop** that takes a linked list as argument and produces the tail of that linked list. Raise the exception **Tl** (a built-in exception of ML) if the linked list is empty.

c)* Write a function **skip** that takes a cell C as argument and changes the **next** field of C to point to the cell pointed to by the cell C originally points to. Raise the exception **BadCell** if this operation is impossible.

d) Write a function that takes a linked list and produces an ML list of all the elements in all its cells.

◇◇◇
◇ **19   Matches and Patterns**
◇

Patterns and the matching of patterns to expressions play a central role in ML programming. In this chapter we look at some other ways patterns are used.

Match

1.   We use patterns in *matches*, which resemble the sequence of patterns and associated expressions that appear in function declarations using the keyword **fun**. In turn, matches are essential components of

Function expression

a)   *Function expressions.* These allow us to define general functions as values using the keyword **fn**. The idea generalizes the anonymous function expressions that we introduced in Chapter 11.

Case expression

b)   *Case expressions.* These are similar to the case-statements of Pascal or the switch-statements of C. We mentioned case-expressions briefly in Chapter 2, but did not learn their syntax or use.

2.   We use patterns in val-declarations, which we shall find are really much more general than the bindings of values to single variables that we have been using almost exclusively.

Matches

Rule

A *match* consists of one or more *rules*, which are pairs of the form

        <pattern> => <expression>

The rules are separated by vertical bars, so the form of a match is:

        <pattern 1> => <expression 1> |
        <pattern 2> => <expression 2> |
              . . .
        <pattern *n*> => <expression *n*>

Each of the expressions following the =>'s must be of the same type, since any one of them could become the value of the match.

The match is applied to a value v. We compare each pattern of the match with v in order, until we find a pattern that matches v, say the ith pattern. This match of a pattern with v binds values to each of the identifiers in the pattern, in the manner discussed at the end of Chapter 6. Identifiers in the ith expression are then replaced by their associated values, and the resulting value of the ith expression becomes the value of the match.

•   If there exist values that match none of the patterns, then ML will issue a warning:

```
Warning: match not exhaustive
```

when the match is compiled.

- If the match is actually applied to a value that does not match any of the patterns, then the exception `Match` is raised.

Using Matches to Define Functions

If an identifier `f` has a value that is a function, that value is always expressed as a match. An alternative way to define a function `f`, without using the keyword `fun`, is

```
val rec f = fn <match>
```

rec

- The keyword `rec`, short for "recursive," is necessary only if the function f is recursive, that is, if the identifier `f` appears in one or more expressions of the match. This keyword informs ML that any uses of f in the match refers to the function f being defined recursively and is not an undefined or previously defined variable.

◇ **Example 19.1.** Another way to write the definition of the function **reverse** of Example 6.2 is

```
val rec reverse = fn
               nil => nil |
               x::xs => reverse(xs) @ [x];
      val reverse = fn : 'a list → 'a list
```

Here the keyword `rec` is necessary because **reverse** appears in the match itself.

In a function definition like

```
val rec addOne = fn x => x+1;
```

the keyword `rec` is legal. However, it is unnecessary, and possibly confusing, since the match consisting of a single pattern `x` and expression `x+1` does not mention the name `addOne`. □

As a general rule, any function definition using **fun** that has the form

$$\textbf{fun } f(P_1) = E_1 \mid f(P_2) = E_2 \mid \cdots \mid f(P_n) = E_n\,;$$

is a shorthand for the val-declaration

$$\textbf{val rec } f = \textbf{fn } P_1 \Rightarrow E_1 \mid P_2 \Rightarrow E_2 \mid \cdots \mid P_n \Rightarrow E_n\,;$$

The simple form of anonymous function defined in Chapter 11 is a special case of a match, where there is a single pattern.

Case Expressions

The form of a *case expression* is

    case <expression> of <match>

Its value is found by matching each pattern in the match against the value of the expression, in the order of appearance. As soon as a matching pattern is found, the corresponding expression in the match is evaluated and becomes the value of the case-expression. If there is no pattern matching the expression, then the exception `Match` is raised.

◇ **Example 19.2.** In lines (1) and (2) of Fig. 19.1 we see a datatype `card` with thirteen data constructors. This datatype is simple, taking no type parameters, and thus acting like a Pascal enumerated type. Note that the response from ML would list all thirteen constructors in alphabetical order, but we have elided the response.

```
(1)     datatype card = Ace | Deuce | Trey | Four | Five | Six |
(2)             Seven | Eight | Nine | Ten | Jack | Queen | King;
        datatype card
            con Ace ··· (13 data constructors)

(3)     fun value(card) =
(4)         case card of
(5)             Ace => 11 | Deuce => 2 | Trey => 3 |
(6)             Four => 4 | Five => 5 | Six => 6 |
(7)             Seven => 7 | Eight => 8 | Nine => 9 |
(8)             _ => 10;
        val value = fn : card → int

(9)     value(Trey);
        val it = 3

(10)    value(King);
        val it = 10
```

Fig. 19.1. Computing the Blackjack value of cards.

In lines (3)–(8) the function `value` takes a card as argument and produces the value of that card in the game of Blackjack. Line (4) begins a case-expression. The expression to be matched is `card`, which is also the parameter of the function. The match consists of ten patterns, the first nine of which are three-to-a-line on lines (5)–(7). Each of the first nine patterns is for a particular constructor. If they match the card, the appropriate result is produced — the face value of the card or 11 if the card is an ace.

The last pattern is the wildcard variable _. Since it is tried last, it will only match the cards that fail to match one of the earlier cards, namely the ten, jack, queen, and king. These are all the cards that are worth 10 points in Blackjack, so we appropriately return 10 whenever the wildcard variable is the successful match.

In lines (9) and (10) we see two uses of the function **value**. In the first, the pattern **Trey** is the correct match and the value 3 is produced. In the second, the wildcard is the match and 10 is the result. □

- In general, if we are not sure the patterns of our match cover all possible cases, it is a good idea to end with a wildcard pattern. The associated expression could raise an exception if there were no appropriate value.

If-Then-Else Expressions Revisited

The if-then-else expression, which we introduced in Chapter 1, is actually a shorthand for a case-expression. That is,

> if E_1 then E_2 else E_3

stands for

> case E_1 of true => E_2 | false => E_3

- And in turn, a case-expression **case** E **of** M, where M is a match, is equivalent to the function application (**fn** M)(E).

◇ **Example 19.3.** Let us review Example 2.3, where we dealt with the *erroneous* if-then-else expression

```
if 1<2 then 3 else 4.0
```

The above expression is equivalent to the case-expression

```
case 1<2 of
    true => 3 |
    false => 4.0
```

This case-expression in turn can be written as the function application

```
(fn true => 3 | false => 4.0)(1<2)
```

Either way, we see that the rules of the match, **true => 3** and **false => 4.0**, do not produce values of the same type. The first rule tells ML to expect integer results. Thus, when the second rule is encountered, the error message mentioned in Example 2.3:

$$Error: rules\ don't\ agree\ (tycon\ mismatch)$$
$$expected:\ bool \rightarrow int$$
$$found:\ bool \rightarrow real$$
$$rule:$$
$$false \Rightarrow 4.0$$

is produced. □

Patterns in Val-Declarations

We have generally seen the val-declaration as if it were the binding of a value to one variable. In fact, it is a much more powerful kind of declaration. There was an example of this power in line (4) of the function **split** of Fig. 7.6:

(4)   `val (M,N) = split(cs)`

where a recursive call to **split** is made and the pair of lists returned is bound to two variables **M** and **N**.

In general, the val-declaration has the form

`val <pattern> = <expression>`

Its meaning is that the expression is matched to the pattern, and any variables appearing in the pattern are given a value during the match.

◇ **Example 19.4.** Consider the expressions in Fig. 19.2. We start off with a conventional val-declaration defining the variable **Norm'sRecord** exactly as it was defined in the previous chapter. Then we use **Norm'sRecord** as an expression and match it against the pattern `{name=n, courses=x::y::zs,...}`. This pattern will match the record, and variable **n** will acquire **"Norm dePlume"** as its value. The variables **x**, **y**, and **zs** will match respectively the first course (**"CS106X"**), the second course (**"E40"**), and the list of the remaining elements on Norm's course list (the list of one element **["M43"]**).

In the response, we see that ML first warns us that the match is not exhaustive. In particular, it will not match a record where the course list has fewer than 2 elements. Following the warning are the four variables in the pattern and the values to which they are matched. □

Exercises

19.1: Write the following functions as values, using **fn** and a match.

a)* Function **padd** of Fig. 6.3.

b)   Function **sumPairs** of Example 6.8.

c)* Function **printList** of Fig. 9.2.

d)   The function **map** of Chapter 11.

```
val Norm'sRecord = {ID=123, name="Norm dePlume",
            courses=["CS106X","E40","M43"]};
```
val Norm'sRecord =
        {ID=123,
        courses=["CS106X","E40","M43"],
        name="Norm dePlume"} :
    {ID:int,courses:string list,name:string}

```
val {name=n, courses=x::y::zs,...} = Norm'sRecord;
```
Warning: binding not exhaustive
        {courses=x :: y :: zs, name=n,...} = ...
val x = "CS106X" : string
val y = "E40" : string
val zs = ["M43"] : string list
val n = "Norm dePlume" : string

Fig. 19.2. Patterns in val-declarations.

19.2: Define a datatype that enumerates the twelve months. Then write a case expression that produces the number of days of a given month. Assume February always has 28 days. You may use suitable abbreviations for the months, such as **Jan**.

! 19.3*: A year is a leap year if and only if it is divisible by 4, but not by 100, unless it is also divisible by 400. Write a case expression that tells whether year **y** is a leap year.

◇◇◇ 20　More About Exceptions

In this chapter we shall see two extensions of the exception concept in ML:

1. Exceptions may have arguments that are produced with the exception when it is raised.

2. Exceptions may be "handled" to produce a value of the normal type for the expression in which they are raised.

Expressions With Parameters

When we declare an exception, we can give it an associated type. The form of the declaration is:

> **exception** <identifier> **of** <type>

Exception constructor

The identifier is an *exception constructor*, essentially the name of an exception. An exception constructor behaves like a data constructor that has a parameter of the given type. When we raise the exception, it takes an argument of this type.

- Notice that what follows the keyword **exception** — an identifier, the keyword **of**, and a type — is exactly what constitutes the definition of one of the data constructors of a datatype.

◇ **Example 20.1.** Let us define an exception constructor **Foo** that takes an argument of type **string**. The declaration is:

> **exception Foo of string;**
> *exception Foo of string*

When we raise exception **Foo**, it must take a string as argument. For instance, we can say:

> **raise Foo("bar");**
> *uncaught exception Foo*

Now, let us see what happens if we do not provide the string argument.

> **raise Foo;**
> *Error: argument of raise is not an exception*
>   *raised: string → exn*
>   *in expression:*
>   *raise Foo*

In its response, ML indicates that it does not even regard `Foo` by itself as an exception. In the second line of the response it notes that the type of `Foo` is `string -> exn`, that is, a function from strings to exceptions. □

- Note that `exn` is the type of exceptions; this type is a primitive type of ML, like `int`.

Handling Exceptions

Raising an uncaught exception always stops computation. Instead, we may prefer that when an exception is raised, there is an attempt to produce an appropriate value and continue the computation. We can use an expression of the form

<expression> `handle` <match>

to help in this process. Here, the expression E before the `handle` keyword is one in which we fear that one or more exceptions may be raised. The match takes exceptions as patterns and associates them with expressions of the same type as E.

If E produces an ordinary value v, not an exception, then the match is not applied to v, and v is the result of the handle-expression. However, if E raises an exception, perhaps with arguments, then the match is applied. The first pattern that matches the exception causes its associated expression to be evaluated, and this value becomes the value of the handle-expression. If none of the patterns match, then the exception is uncaught at this point. The exception may be handled by another, surrounding handle-expression, or it may remain uncaught, percolate up to the top level, and stop the computation.

◊ **Example 20.2.** Let us reconsider the function `comb` of Fig. 8.1, where we attempted to compute $\binom{n}{m}$ and catch situations where $n \leq 0$, $m < 0$, or $m > n$. In Fig. 8.1, our only response when we found an error in the arguments was to raise one of two exceptions and cause computation to halt.

A better approach is to declare an exception `OutOfRange`, which takes a pair of integers as parameters. When we raise this exception, we let the function arguments n and m be the arguments of the exception as well. We can then handle the error as follows. For $n = m = 0$, we shall treat the value of $\binom{0}{0}$ as 1. Otherwise, we print an error message telling the user what values n and m had when the error occurred. However, we let `comb` return the value 0 in the hope that it will be possible for computation to proceed.[1]

Figure 20.1 shows the program. Line (1) declares the exception constructor `OutOfRange` and says that its argument type is `int*int`, that is, a pair of integers. Lines (2)–(6) define the function `comb1`, which is like `comb` in Fig. 8.1. However, lines (3) and (4) detect possible errors and raise the exception

---

[1] We should be very sure that no unexpected errors will be introduced by the chosen value 0, or hard-to-diagnose bugs may result.

```
(1)    exception OutOfRange of int*int;
```
exception OutOfRange

```
(2)   fun comb1(n,m) =
(3)        if n <= 0 then raise OutOfRange(n,m)
(4)        else if m < 0 orelse m > n then raise OutOfRange(n,m)
(5)        else if m=0 orelse m=n then 1
(6)        else comb1(n-1,m) + comb1(n-1,m-1);
```
*val comb1 = fn : int * int → int*

```
(7)   fun comb(n,m) = comb1(n,m) handle
(8)        OutOfRange(0,0) => 1 |
(9)        OutOfRange(n,m) => (print("out of range: n=");
(10)          print(n); print(" m="); print(m); print("\n"); 0);
```
*val comb = fn : int * int → int*

```
(11)   comb(4,2);
```
val it = 6 : int

```
(12)   comb(3,4);
```
out of range: n=3 m=4
val it = 0 : int

```
(13)   comb(0,0);
```
val it = 1 : int

Fig. 20.1. Combinatorial function handled by an exception.

OutOfRange(n,m) so the arguments that caused the error will be transmitted with the exception when it is raised.

In line (7) we define the function comb, which calls comb1 and then handles the exceptions that are raised by comb1. Line (8) shows the first pattern of the match, where both arguments are 0, and the result is 1. Lines (9) and (10) handle all other cases of the exception. We print the message "out of range" and the values of n and m as a side-effect.

The last expression on line (10) is 0. Recall it is the value of the final expression in a list of expressions that is returned. Thus the value returned by comb is 0 in all exceptional cases besides $m = n = 0$.

Line (11) shows a correct use of comb. Here, comb1 computes the value 6 and raises no exception. There is no exception to handle, so 6 is produced by comb, and ML tells us that 6 is the value of it.

Line (12) shows an erroneous use of comb, where comb1 raises the exception OutOfRange(3,4) at line (4). This exception fails to match the pattern on line (8), but matches the pattern of (9), which gives n the value 3 and m the value 4. We see two lines of response. The first is the side-effect resulting from the sequence of print-expressions in lines (9) and (10). The second is the value of it, which is 0. This integer is the value returned by comb because 0 is the last expression on lines (9) and (10).

Finally, line (13) shows an erroneous situation where the pattern of line (8) is matched. The exception OutOfRange(0,0) is raised on line (3). It matches the pattern on line (8), and the value 1 is produced. Thus, 1 becomes the value of it in the ML response. There is no side-effect as there was when the pattern of line (9) was the correct match. □

Scoping Rules for Exceptions

Every time we bind a value to an identifier, there is an associated *scope* for that binding, which defines when that binding is available in the environment. The principal rules for the scopes of bindings are:[2]

1.   When a binding is made in the top-level environment, it remains there forever, although a new binding for the same identifier will obscure it and make it effectively unavailable.

2.   When a function is called, its arguments are bound to the parameters of the function. These bindings exist for the duration of the function call, but not after the function returns. The parameters may be referred to within the function, unless obscured by a local definition. Binding of parameters to arguments was introduced in Chapter 5.

3.   When a local definition is made, such as let...in...end discussed in Chapter 7 or local...in..end from Chapter 15, the bindings made between the let or local and the in are available until the matching end is reached.

Exception identifiers are not exempt from these rules, and there are some consequences for the way exceptions are handled. As a case in point, let us reconsider the version of function comb in Fig. 8.3, which used local exceptions. Although the exceptions BadN and BadM can be printed if raised, there is no way to handle them. If we try to write comb1 of Fig. 20.1 in an analogous way, with a local exception OutOfRange, we find that we cannot handle this exception in function comb when it is raised.

That is, suppose we replace comb1 of Fig. 20.1 with the function comb2 in Fig. 20.2. Then the scope of OutOfRange in Fig. 20.2 does not extend beyond the function comb2. In particular, when comb tries to handle exception OutOfRange in Fig. 20.2, its identifier OutOfRange will not match the identifier of the exception raised by comb2. As a result, if we call the function comb of Fig. 20.2 with an improper argument, the exception raised by comb2 will *not* be handled and execution will halt with an uncaught exception.

---

[2] Strictly speaking, these rules mix issues of *dynamic* scope (when things exist) with *static* or *lexical* scope (where in the program a thing can be referred to). However, both issues are important, and we need to follow the rules of each.

```
fun comb2(n,m) =
    let
        exception OutOfRange of int*int
    in
        if n <= 0 then raise OutOfRange(n,m)
        else if m<0 orelse m>n then raise OutOfRange(n,m)
        else if m=0 orelse m=n then 1
        else comb2(n-1,m) + comb2(n-1,m-1)
    end;
```
*val comb2 = fn : int * int → int*

```
fun comb(n,m) = comb2(n,m) handle
    OutOfRange(0,0) => 1 |
    OutOfRange(n,m) => (print("out of range: n=");
        print(n); print(" m="); print(m); print("\n"); 0);
```
*val comb = fn : int * int → int*

Fig. 20.2. This function raises an exception that cannot be handled.

Summary of Built-In Exceptions

The SML/NJ system provides a collection of built-in exceptions, most of which are common to many other ML implementations as well. We shall list them here, grouped by the type of data to which they apply.

1. *System-level exceptions*

   a) **Io.** An error has occurred during an input or output operation. A string argument will provide information about the error.

   b) **Bind.** A pattern has failed to match the expression to which it must be bound. For example, **val x::xs = nil** raises this exception.

   c) **Match.** A match has no pattern that matches the expression to which it is applied.

2. *Arithmetic errors*

   a) **Div.** A division by zero has occurred. This exception can be caused by either of the division operators, **div** or **/**, or by the **mod** operator.

   b) **Overflow.** The result of an arithmetic operation on integers or reals does not fit in the number of bytes allocated for that type of number in the computer executing the ML system.[3]

---

[3] Some ML systems make a distinction among operations that cause the overflow, defining exceptions such as **Sum**, **Prod**, **Diff**, **Neg**, and **Floor** for the operations addition, multiplication, subtraction, negation, and floor. Incidentally, in most machines negation can cause an overflow because in the common "two's complement" integer representation there is one negative value whose positive counterpart is not representable.

c)   **Sqrt, Exp, Ln.** Certain real operations can cause errors because particular arguments are invalid. Functions **sqrt** (square root), **exp** (e^x), and **ln** (natural logarithm) are given exceptions of their own. For example, **Sqrt** will be raised if the argument to **sqrt** is negative.

3.   *Character and string errors*

a)   **Chr.** The function **chr** was given an integer that is out of the range 0–255, for example **chr(270)**.

b)   **Ord.** The function **ord** was given the empty string to convert to an integer.

c)   **Substring.** The function **substring** (not discussed until item II(d) in Chapter 25) was given a range of positions, at least some of which are not found in the string. For example,

```
substring("abc",2,4)
```

raises this exception.

d)   **Range.** In a "bytearray" (not previously discussed, but similar to an array of characters; see part VIII of Chapter 25), we attempted to store an integer that is not in the range that represents a character. The appropriate range is the same as for **chr**.

4.   *List and array errors*

a)   **Hd, Tl.** These exceptions are raised when we use the functions **hd** or **tl** respectively, to find the head or tail of an empty list.

b)   **Nth, NthTail.** There are two functions on lists, **nth** and **nthtail** (discussed in items IV(c) and IV(d) of Chapter 25), that find the nth element from the front or the tail starting at the nth element of a list. However, we begin counting elements from 0, so the first element is 0, the second 1, and so on. The exceptions are raised when the desired position is not on the list. For example, **nth([10,20,30],1) = 20**, and **nth([10,20,30],5)** raises the **Nth** exception.

c)   **Subscript.** An array reference uses a subscript that is out of the subscript range for the array.

Exercises

20.1*: Write a factorial function that produces 1 when its argument is 0, produces 0 for a negative argument while printing an error message, and produces $n!$ for a positive argument n. Organize your code so a function **fact1** does the work of computing $n!$ and raises an exception **Negative(n)** if n is a negative integer.

! 20.2: Modify Fig. 18.2 to raise the exception `NotFound` with an argument that is the name of the person not found on the list. Handle this exception in another function that calls `getID`. If the exception is raised, create an ID for the person by converting the first five characters of the name to integers. Treat characters as digits in base 128 to form an integer. Then create a new record with the given person's name, the new ID, and an empty set of courses. Add this record to the given list and return the new ID. *Note*: in order to modify the given list, your new function must take as argument a reference to the list to be searched.

! 20.3*: In Fig. 9.8 we wrote a program to read nonnegative integers and signal the end of file with the integer -1. It is better to handle this signal with an exception. Modify Fig. 9.8 by declaring an exception `Eof` and raising it in function `startInt` when the end of file is found. Modify function `getInt` to handle `startInt` before passing the result of `startInt` to `finishInt`. If `startInt` has raised `Eof`, then `getInt` also raises `Eof` and otherwise `getInt` calls `finishInt`. Finally, `sumInts1` must handle the result of `getInt` to tell whether the end of file has been reached.

20.4: Write a function `inverse` that computes $1/x$ for real number x, but handles the `Div` exception that is raised when division by 0 occurs, producing the "large" value 10^{10}.

21 Computing With Functions as Values

We have seen that types in ML include functions with any given domain type and any given range type. That is, if D and R are any types, then $D \to R$ is the type of a function that takes an argument of type D and returns a value of type R. Since functions are ordinary values in ML, it is possible to "compute" with them. That is, we can create new functions not only by the conventional means of function definition but also by special operations found in ML. In this chapter we shall study two of these mechanisms: function composition and Currying.

Function Composition

The composition of functions was introduced in Chapter 11, where we showed how is it possible to define a function `comp` that composes functions. Recall that if $F(x)$ is a function that takes an argument of type T_1 and produces a value of type T_2, while $G(y)$ is a function that takes an argument of type T_2 and produces a value of type T_3, then $G(F(x))$ is the *composition* of G and F. We compute $G(F(x))$ by applying F to an argument x of type T_1, producing a value y of type T_2. Then we apply G to y, and $G(y)$ is the value of type T_3 produced from x by the composition of G and F.

ML provides the lowercase "Oh" as a function composition operator, so it was not necessary for us to define function `comp` explicitly. The composition of G and F is expressed in ML by `G o F`. If F and G are respectively of types $T_1 \to T_2$ and $T_2 \to T_3$, then `G o F` is of type $T_1 \to T_3$. The expression `G o F` can be used anywhere an expression of this type is appropriate. For example, it could be bound as the value of a variable by a val-declaration, or passed as an argument to another function that has a parameter of type $T_1 \to T_3$.

◇ **Example 21.1.** In Fig. 21.1 we see the definition of three functions: f, g, and h. Function f adds 1 to its argument, but it expects a character string consisting of one digit as its argument and produces an integer. Function g doubles its argument, but in so doing it converts from integer to real. Finally, function h is the composition of g and f. In the setting above, the types T_1, T_2, and T_3 are `string`, `int`, and `real` respectively.

At the end of Fig. 21.1 we see a use of h. To compute the value, ML first computes `f("5")`, which is 6, since the difference between `ord("5")` and `ord("0")` is 5. Then, ML computes $g(6)$, which is 12.0; that number is printed as the result. □

```
fun f(x) = (ord(x)-ord("0")) + 1;
val f = fn : string → int

fun g(y) = 2.0 * real(y);
val g = fn : int → real

val h = g o f;
val h = fn : string → real

h("5");
val it = 12.0
```

Fig. 21.1. Composing functions.

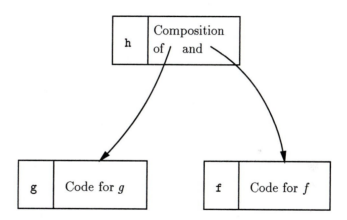

Fig. 21.2. Representing function values in an environment.

It is useful to consider the way the values of f, g, and h are represented by ML. Since functions are defined by code, the identifiers f and g are bound to a value that is code. However h, being defined by a composition, is bound to a value that is a notation saying it is the composition of f and g. The situation is suggested in Fig. 21.2.

- Note that the value for h refers to the values bound to f and g in the current environment, not to the names **f** and **g**. The distinction becomes important if we bind identifier f or g to a new value. Since h is bound to the particular environment entries suggested in Fig. 21.2, and entries in an environment (other than references) never change their values, the value of h does not change.

Curried Functions

Until now, we have considered only functions that have a single parameter, although that parameter often is a tuple written with parentheses and commas. Thus, we have written many ML functions that looked like multiparameter functions of languages like C or Pascal. Technically, these ML functions really have a single parameter, of a product type. However, in practice there is little harm in pretending they are ordinary multiparameter functions.

However, ML provides a more general way to connect a function name to its parameters or arguments. It is sometimes useful to express multiparameter functions in *Curried form*,[1] where the function name is followed by the list of its parameters with no parentheses or commas. The following example illustrates the difference between the Curried and uncurried form of functions. We shall be introduced to the important advantage of the Curried form when we discuss partially instantiated functions next.

◇ **Example 21.2.** Let us write a two-parameter function that computes x^y. In lines (1) and (2) of Fig. 21.3 we see such a function **exponent1** in the style we have been using. This function takes a parameter that is a pair consisting of a real x and an integer y, and returns x^y. It is not carefully designed because it loops forever on a negative integer y.

Exponentiation

(1)
```
fun exponent1(x,0) = 1.0
```
(2)
```
|    exponent1(x,y) = x * exponent1(x,y-1);
```
    val exponent1 = fn : real * int → real

(3)
```
fun exponent2 x 0 = 1.0
```
(4)
```
|    exponent2 x y = x * exponent2 x (y-1);
```
    val exponent2 = fn : real → int → real

(5)
```
exponent1(3.0,4);
```
    val it = 81.0

(6)
```
exponent2 3.0 4;
```
    val it = 81.0

Fig. 21.3. Two styles for exponentiation functions.

The Curried function **exponent2** in lines (3) and (4) of Fig. 21.3 does exactly the same computation as the uncurried function **exponent1**. The parameters of **exponent2** are not surrounded by parentheses or separated by commas, either in the definition on lines (3) and (4) or in the recursive use on line (4).

---

[1] Named after the mathematician H. Curry, who investigated this form of function definition.

- The parentheses around **y-1** on line (4) are necessary for ML to group arguments properly. Without parentheses around **y-1**, the second argument in the recursive call to **exponent2** will be regarded as **y**. Constant 1 will be subtracted from the result of the call, leading to a type error. The reason for this interpretation is that juxtaposition of expressions, which is function application in ML, is an operator of higher precedence than the arithmetic operators.

Lines (5) and (6) show appropriate calls to the two functions. Each computes $3^4 = 81$. □

Partially Instantiated Functions

Curried functions are useful because they allow us to construct new functions by applying the function to arguments for a proper subset of its parameters. To begin our exploration of this matter, notice the subtle difference between the responses to the two functions in Fig. 21.3. ML finds the type of **exponent1** to be a function that takes a pair of type **real * int** as parameter and returns a real. However, the type of **exponent2** is given as **real -> int -> real**. Remembering that the **->** operator associates from the right, we interpret this type as **real -> (int -> real)**, that is, a function taking a real as argument and returning a function from integers to reals.

This type suggests how the function **exponent2** is interpreted. In the call of line (6) in Fig. 21.3, the first argument, 3.0, is given to the function **exponent2**, resulting in a new function g. This function, of type **int -> real**, takes an exponent y as its argument and produces the result $g(y) = 3^y$. The function g is a value in its own right and can, under the right circumstances, be isolated and bound to a variable as its value.

The process of forming new functions by binding one or more of the parameters of an existing function is called *partial instantiation*. In the general mathematical setting, we can take a function f of n arguments, say $f(x_1, x_2, \ldots, x_n)$. We bind the first k of those arguments to constants $a_1, \ldots, a_k$ to form a new function, which we may call $f_{a_1,\ldots,a_k}(x_{k+1}, \ldots, x_n)$. The definition of function $f_{a_1,\ldots,a_k}$ is as expected:

$$f_{a_1,\ldots,a_k}(x_{k+1}, \ldots, x_n) = f(a_1, \ldots, a_k, x_{k+1}, \ldots, x_n)$$

In ML, Curried functions can be partially instantiated by applying them to values, one for each of the first n parameters. It is only possible to instantiate the parameters from the left, not in any order.[2]

◇ **Example 21.3.** Having made the definition of **exponent2** in Example 21.2, we can proceed to create a new function by instantiating its first argument. An example is

---

[2] However, any function — Curried or not — can be partially instantiated by defining a new function using **fun**.

```
val g = exponent2 3.0;
val g = fn : int → real
```

Now g is a function that takes an integer y as argument and returns 3^y. Figure 21.4 suggests what has happened. Identifier g has been bound to a value that is a notation representing the function **exponent2** applied to 3.0.

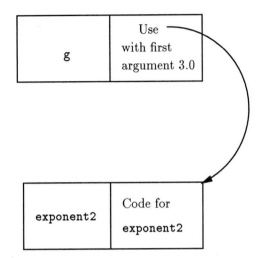

Fig. 21.4. Partially instantiating a function.

We can use g like any other function if we provide its proper argument. For example,

```
g 4;
val it = 81.0
```

applies g to the integer 4, producing 3^4, or 81. □

- Note that we are not restricted to the no-parentheses form. We could have written **g(4)** instead of **g 4**, and we could have defined new functions from **exponent2** with parentheses. For instance,

  ```
  val h = exponent2(10.0)
  ```

  makes h a function that computes powers of 10.

- The value of the function g does not change if we define a new function called **exponent2**, because the definition of g refers to the specific value shown in Fig. 21.4.

Folding Lists

Let us now take up an example of how functions can be built from other functions by examining the function **fold** that is provided by SML/NJ. This function is related to the function **reduce** that we mentioned in Chapter 11, but they are different in important ways.

The purpose of **fold** is to take a list $L = [a_1, \ldots, a_n]$ and treat each element a_i as if it were a function, call it F_{a_i}. Then **fold** with L as an argument constructs the function that is the composition of all the functions $F_{a_1}, \ldots, F_{a_n}$, that is, by $F_{a_1} \circ F_{a_2} \circ \cdots \circ F_{a_n}$.

◇ **Example 21.4.** Suppose $L = [a_1, \ldots, a_n]$ is a list of integers, and the function F_{a_i} is the function that multiplies its argument by a_i. Then the function $F_{a_1} \circ F_{a_2} \circ \cdots \circ F_{a_n}$ multiplies its argument by the product of the elements of the list L, that is, $a_1 \times a_2 \times \cdots \times a_n$. If we apply this function to 1, we can compute the product of the elements of a list. To make this use of **fold** work, we must specify properly how F_{a_i} is determined by a_i.

As another example, suppose instead that F_{a_i} is the function that adds 1 to its argument, regardless of what a_i is. Then the function $F_{a_1} \circ F_{a_2} \circ \cdots \circ F_{a_n}$ adds n to its argument. In particular, applied to 0 it computes the length of the list L. Thus, **fold** also lets us define the length function if we correctly specify the functions F_{a_i}. □

The missing element in Example 21.4 is the method of going from a_i to the proper F_{a_i}. In effect, we need to reverse the effect of partial instantiation of these functions, by writing one function $F(a, x)$ such that $F(a, x)$ equals $F_a(x)$ for all a and x.

◇ **Example 21.5.** Let us consider the two problems in Example 21.4. If F_{a_i} is to multiply its argument x by a_i, then we want $F(a, x) = ax$, or in ML:

```
fun F(a:int,x) = a*x;
val F = fn : int * int → int
```

In the second problem, where we want each F_{a_i} to add one to its argument, we define $F(a, x) = x + 1$, or:

```
fun F(a,x) = x+1;
val F = fn : 'a * int → int
```

in ML. □

Now we are ready to understand how the function **fold** of SML/NJ works. First, we want to be able to create from a function F a function that applies to a list and an initial value and performs the sequence of function applications described above. Before we learned the Curried form of functions, we used a "trick" involving a let-expression in Figs. 11.6 and 11.7 to define some higher-order functions. Now, with the Curried form available, we have an easier way to describe higher-order functions.

```
(1)        fun fold F nil y = y
(2)         |    fold F (x::xs) y = F(x, (fold F xs y));
```
$$\textit{val fold} = \textit{fn} : ((\textit{'a} * \textit{'b}) \rightarrow \textit{'b}) \rightarrow \textit{'a list} \rightarrow \textit{'b} \rightarrow \textit{'b}$$

Fig. 21.5. Definition of `fold`.

Figure 21.5 defines the function `fold`. It takes three parameters.

1. Function F is of type `'a * 'b -> 'b`. Type `'a` is the type of list elements, and the functions F_a that we create from F as discussed in Examples 21.4 and 21.5 have domain and range types `'b`.

2. List L is the list of elements of type `'a` that represent the functions to be composed.

3. Value `y` is of type `'b`. It is the initial value to which the composed functions are applied.

Line (1) of Fig. 21.5 covers the case of an empty list. Then, the list of functions to be composed is empty. The composition of an empty list of functions is the identity function. When the identity is applied to initial value y, the result is y.

Line (2) covers the inductive case, where the list L has a head element **x** and a tail **xs**. To compute the result we do the following:

a) Apply `fold` to function F, the tail of the list, and the initial value y. The result is computed recursively by applying the function associated with each element of the tail in turn to the initial value y.

b) Apply the function F to the list head x and the result of (a). As a result, all the functions associated with the entire list L are applied to the initial value y. They are applied in the reverse of the order in which they appear on the list, with the last element applied first.

Because `fold` is defined in Curried form, we can partially instantiate `fold` with a function F and get another function that takes a list L and an initial value y as arguments. Moreover, we can partially instantiate that function with a list L and get a function that takes only the initial value y as argument.

◇ **Example 21.6.** We can use `fold` to define a product-of-list-elements function:

```
val prod = fold (fn(a:int,x) => a*x);
```
$$\textit{val prod} = \textit{fn} : \textit{int list} \rightarrow \textit{int} \rightarrow \textit{int}$$

Here, `fold` has been applied to an anonymous function that takes a pair of arguments (a, x) and returns their product. This application of `fold` defines a function `prod`.

The type of `prod` is `int list -> int -> int`. Thus, `prod` takes as argument a list of integers, and returns a function from integers to integers; this function happens to multiply its argument by the product of the elements of the list.

Now, we can apply **prod** to a specific list:

```
val prod0 = prod [2,3,4,5];
val prod0 = fn : int → int
```

Here, the function **prod0** is defined to be **prod** applied to the list [2,3,4,5]. As a result, **prod0** is the function that multiplies its integer argument by 120. We can see this fact by applying **prod0** to an integer, such as the expected argument 1:

```
prod0 1;
val it = 120
```

The result produced is 120 times the argument. Similarly, **prod0(2)** produces 240. □

◇ **Example 21.7.** Similarly, we can define a function that computes the length of lists by:

```
val len = fold (fn(a,x) => x+1);
val len = fn : 'a list → int → int
```

If we apply **len** to a specific list, the result will be a function that adds the length of this list to whatever integer it is given.

Should we want the usual **length** function, we must arrange to apply **len** to a list and 0. We can do so by defining

```
fun length(L) = (len L)(0);
val length = fn : 'a list → int
```

Note that it is not possible simply to apply **len** to 0, since ML's **fold** is defined so the function G it produces has the list as its first argument. Had the list been the second argument, then we could have defined **length** to be **len** 0 □

Exercises

! **21.1***: Suppose we define

```
fun comp F G = G o F;
fun add1 x = x+1;
```

Give the type and value for each of the following functions or constants.

a) `val compA1 = comp add1;`

!! b) `val compCompA1 = comp compA1;`

c) `val f = compA1 add1;`

d) `f(2);`

!! e) `val g = compCompA1 compA1;`

f) `val h = g add1;`

g) `h(2);`

! **21.2**: Repeat Exercise 21.1 for the following expressions. The functions `compA1` and `compCompA1` are as defined in Exercises 21.1(a) and (b).

a) `val f = compA1 real;` where `real` is the built-in function that converts integers to equivalent reals.

b) `val compT = comp truncate;` where `truncate` is the built-in function that converts a real to an integer, rounding towards 0 if necessary.

!! c) `val g = compCompA1 compT;`

d) `val h = g real;`

e) `f(2);`

f) `h(3.5);`

g) `h(~3.5);`

! **21.3***: Write a function `makeFnList` that takes a function F whose domain type is D and whose range type R is a function type $T_1 \rightarrow T_2$. The result of `makeFnList` is a function G that takes a list of elements $[d_1, \ldots, d_n]$ of type D and produces a list of functions $[f_1, \ldots, f_n]$ of type R, such that $f_i = F(d_i)$.

21.4*: Write a function `applyList` that takes a list of functions and a value and applies each function to the value, producing a list of the results.

Substring

21.5*: Write a function `substring` that takes two parameters, in the uncurried style, and tests whether the first is a substring of the other. String x is a *substring* of string y if we can write y as the concatenation of strings w, x, and z. It is permissible for any of the strings to be empty. For example, `"abc"` has substrings including `""`, `"b"`, and `"ab"`. Using `makeFnList` of Exercise 21.3, construct a function f that takes a list of strings $[s_1, \ldots, s_n]$ and produces a list of functions $[F_1, \ldots, F_n]$, such that $F_i(x)$ tells whether s_i is a substring of x.

! **21.6***: From f of Exercise 21.5 create a list of functions that, respectively, check whether one of the words `"he"`, `"she"`, `"her"`, `"his"` is a substring of a given string.

21.7*: Apply your list from Exercise 21.6 to the string `"hershey"`, using function `applyList` from Exercise 21.4. What is the result?

Subsequence   **! 21.8**: Repeat Exercise 21.5 for *subsequences* in place of substrings. String x is a subsequence of string y if x is formed by striking out zero or more positions of y. For example, `"ac"` is a subsequence of `"abc"` but is not a substring. Then, as in Exercise 21.6, create a list of functions that test whether the following strings are subsequences of a given string: `["ear","part","trap","seat"]`. Finally, apply your list of functions to the string `"separate"`.

21.9: Show how the `fold` function of Fig. 21.5 can be used to define the function `implode`.

! 21.10: Write a function like `fold` that composes its functions from the front of the list rather than the rear as the function in Fig. 21.5 does.

! 21.11: Write a function that takes a list of reals $[a_0, a_1, \ldots, a_{n-1}]$ and produces a function that takes an argument b and evaluates the polynomial

$$a_0 + a_1 x + a_2 x^2 + \cdots + a_{n-1} x^{n-1}$$

at b; that is, it computes $\sum_{i=0}^{n-1} a_i b^i$.

! 21.12: It is actually quite easy to convert a function from Curried to uncurried form. Write the following higher-order functions that perform the translations.

a)* Given a function F that takes one parameter whose type is a product type with n components, the function `curry` applied to F produces a function G that takes n arguments in Curried form. $G\ x_1\ x_2\ \cdots\ x_n$ produces the same value as $F(x_1, x_2, \ldots, x_n)$.

b) Given a Curried function F that takes n parameters, the function `uncurry` applied to F produces a function G that takes one parameter that is a tuple with n components. $G(x_1, x_2, \ldots, x_n)$ produces the same value as $F\ x_1\ x_2\ \cdots\ x_n$.

22   More About Input and Output

We were introduced to input and output operations in Chapter 9. In the present chapter, we shall expand our knowledge of the input/output operations of ML, including some useful operations that are provided by SML/NJ but may not be available in all implementations of ML.

Instreams and Outstreams

We met the type **instream** in Chapter 9. Normally, an instream represents a file of characters that has been opened for input. We may imagine an instream to be represented by the token (normally an integer) used by the operating system to refer to that file. However, we are not allowed by ML to see this token or even to compare it to another instream value.

Similarly, there is a type **outstream** that normally represents a file of characters that has been opened for output. We may also think of an outstream as represented by an internal token representing this file. The types **instream** and **outstream** are two of the ML primitive types, on a par with **int**.

open_in,
open_out

We open files for reading or writing by the operators **open_in** and **open_out**. Each takes as argument a string that is the path name of a file. The operator **open_in** returns an instream, while **open_out** returns an outstream.

◇ **Example 22.1.** We gave several examples of **open_in** in Chapter 9. The following is a similar example of **open_out**.

```
val OUT = open_out("/u/ullman/foo");
val OUT = - : outstream
```

Notice that the value of **OUT** is not shown; it is represented by a dash, because it is an internal token whose value we are not allowed to know. Its type is identified as **outstream**.

The effect of the **open_out** statement is to empty the file that is its argument, **/u/ullman/foo** in this case. An outstream is returned and bound to the identifier **OUT**. In the future, we can write characters onto the end of file **/u/ullman/foo** by referring to **OUT**. □

open_append

- SML/NJ also provides an operation **open_append** that is like **open_out**, but does not empty the file beforehand. This operation may not be available in other implementations of ML.

close_in,
close_out

After reading or writing from a file, we can close the file by `close_in(F)` or `close_out(F)`, respectively. Here `F` is the instream or outstream token that we received from `open_in` or `open_out` when we opened the file.

◇ **Example 22.2.** We close the file `/u/ullman/foo` mentioned in Example 22.1 with `close_out(OUT)`. We use `close_out` because the file was opened for writing by `open_out`, and we refer to the file by `OUT` because that identifier was bound to the outstream for the file `/u/ullman/foo` in the call to `open_out` that declared outstream `OUT`. □

flush_out

- SML/NJ also has an operation `flush_out` that can be applied to an outstream. We would normally use `flush_out` if the outstream were a terminal or other device whose output is buffered. This command assures that any characters waiting in the buffer are written at the time `flush_out` is executed, even if we do not immediately close the outstream.

Input and Output Commands

Function `output(F,s)` appends the string s to the end of the outstream F. The reading of input from an opened input file is accomplished by the operation `input(F,i)`. The result of this operation is the next i characters on the instream F. If there are fewer than i characters remaining, and the input file is a character source such as a terminal, the input operation will wait, perhaps forever, until that many characters appear in the instream or an explicit end-of-file is encountered. If the instream is a conventional file with fewer than i remaining characters, then whatever remains is returned.

exception Io

- It is an error that raises the exception `Io` if we try to read from or write to a file that has been closed.

- It is not really possible to read or write a file that has never been opened because there is no instream or outstream token with which to refer to that file.

Standard Input and Output

std_in, std_out

UNIX has a notion of a "standard" input and output for a process, normally the terminal or window in which the process originates. In ML, the identifiers `std_in` and `std_out` are an instream and an outstream, respectively, that allow us to refer to the standard input and output without opening them.

◇ **Example 22.3.** We did several examples of the use of the `input` operation in Chapter 9. Let us consider an example using function `output` and the standard output `std_out`. In Fig. 22.1 we see a quick version of the `comb` function (no error checking) that with each call prints a line of `X`'s of length equal to the value of n with that call. The output helps us picture the sequence of calls made by an initial call to `comb(n,m)`.

```
(1)        fun put(0) = output(std_out,"\n")
(2)         |    put(n) = (output(std_out,"X"); put(n-1));
           val put = fn : int → unit

(3)        fun comb(n,m) = (
(4)            put(n);
(5)            if m=0 orelse m=n then 1
(6)            else comb(n-1,m) + comb(n-1,m-1)
           );
           val comb = fn : int * int → int

(7)        comb(5,2);
           XXXXX
           XXXX
           XXX
           XX
           XX
           X
           X
           XXX
           XX
           X
           X
           XX
           XXXX
           XXX
           XX
           X
           X
           XX
           XXX
           val it = 10 : int
```

Fig. 22.1. Printing a profile of calls to comb.

Lines (1) and (2) are the function put(n), which prints n X's and then a newline on the standard output. We see in line (1) the basis case, where $n = 0$ and we print just the newline. In line (2) is the case where $n > 0$. We print one X then recursively print $n - 1$ more X's and the newline.

Lines (3)–(6) is the modified function comb. On line (4) it prints n X's, and then on lines (5) and (6) does the normal recursion for comb. Finally, line (7) is an example call to comb(5,2). The original call of line (7) and each recursive call it makes is reflected by a line of X's, and at the end is ML's response to the original call. Note that because put prints to the standard output, the X's appear on the terminal mixed with ML's own responses, which also go to the standard output. □

• Note that Example 22.3 uses only single characters as output strings in lines (1) and (2) of Fig. 22.1. In general, strings of any length may be used.

• When using standard input, we must be careful how we call ML. If we use the UNIX command `sml <foo`, then file `foo` becomes the standard input, and `input(std_in,i)` will read i characters from file `foo`, not from the terminal. If we want to read from the terminal, we need to invoke `sml` without an input file, and then get the file `foo` by `use("foo")`. Now, the terminal will be referred to by `std_in`.

Looking Ahead on the Input

Sometimes it is essential to be able to check what is waiting in some instream without actually trying to read from that instream. For example, the instream might be a terminal or other source that will never produce another character, and the program will block if it tries to execute `input` on this character source.

The following simple tool for checking input without reading was introduced in Chapter 9. If `I` is an instream, we can execute `end_of_stream(I)`, and the Boolean-valued result will be true if and only if the end of the file has been reached. However, when reading from a terminal, there currently might be no characters waiting to be read, even though we have not reached the end of file. SML/NJ (but possibly not other ML implementations) provides the operator `can_input(I)`, which returns an integer, the number of characters that can be read from the instream `I` at the moment `can_input` is executed.

can_input

In other situations we may be sure there is another character to be read, yet the logic of our program may be simpler if we look at the next character without consuming it from the instream as a call to `input` would. The function `lookahead(I)` returns the next character on instream `I`, but leaves this character on the instream. If there is no waiting character, then `lookahead` returns `""`, the empty string. The following is an extended example that shows the use of `lookahead`. It also introduces a grammatical notation that we shall use in Chapter 26 to summarize the syntax of the entire ML language.

lookahead

◇ **Example 22.4.** The problem we shall address is how to read arithmetic expressions from the input and compute their value. For simplicity, we assume all operands are integers, and there are no blanks or other white space between characters (it is easy to remove white space in a preprocessing operation, should we wish). The operators are *, +, -, and /.[1]

We shall describe the structure of expressions using a graphical notation equivalent to context-free grammars; it is illustrated in Fig. 22.2. Each *syntac-*

---

[1] Of course, ML would use `div` for integer division, but that is unimportant because we are not reading ML programs in this example.

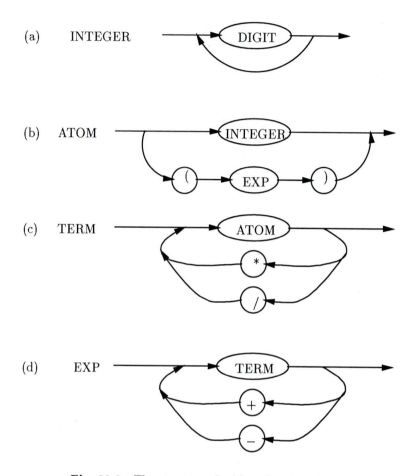

(a)   INTEGER

(b)   ATOM

(c)   TERM

(d)   EXP

Fig. 22.2. The structure of arithmetic expressions.

Syntactic category

tic category is named on the left; we have in Fig. 22.2 four syntactic categories: INTEGER, ATOM, TERM, and EXP (expression). A syntactic category represents a set of sequences of elements. Each element can be a string of characters or it can be another syntactic category. The possible instances of a syntactic category are indicated by the possible paths from the left end of the graph to the right end; each path represents a sequence of elements that is an instance of the syntactic category named at the left.

For instance, in Fig. 22.2(a) the graph for INTEGER requires us to go through DIGIT once. Then we can continue to the right end or we can cycle back to pass through DIGIT any number of additional times. That is, an INTEGER is a string consisting of one or more DIGIT's. The syntactic category DIGIT is not defined by a graph, but we define it to consist of any of the digits 0 through 9.

In Fig. 22.2(b) we see that an ATOM is defined to be either an INTEGER or a sequence consisting of a left parenthesis, an EXP, and a right parenthesis. That is, an ATOM is an integer or a parenthesized expression.

Next we see that a TERM is an ATOM followed by zero or more additional elements, each consisting of a multiplication or division sign and another ATOM. That is, a TERM is a sequence of one or more ATOM's separated by multiplication and/or division signs. Similarly, an EXP is a sequence of one or more TERM's separated by plus and/or minus signs.

Figure 22.3 shows a program that computes the value of an expression.[2] Its functions carefully choose between the **lookahead** operator and the **input** operator to make sure that input characters are consumed only at the appropriate time. We have omitted comments and the ML responses, to allow the program to fit on the page.

Line (1) is the definition of an exception that will be raised when an ill-formed input is found. Line (2) is a function that tests whether a character is a digit. Then come six functions — the last five are mutually recursive — that collectively implement the diagrams of Fig. 22.2. Each takes a parameter **IN** that is the instream on which the expression appears. Some functions take an additional parameter that helps the function return the integer value of some portion of the input. This additional parameter, if present, will be referred to as "the parameter" or "the argument" of the function, even though **IN** is also a parameter.

Let us introduce the functions, and then later return to the details of their implementation. The six functions, each of which returns the value of whatever input it consumes, are:

1. **integer** consumes whatever prefix of the current input is a sequence of digits. The parameter i is the integer value of any digits that have been seen and consumed on the input immediately before the current call to **integer**. The result returned is the value of the digits seen so far (as represented by i) and any further digits found consecutively on the input. An initial call to **integer** with $i = 0$ implements the diagram of Fig. 22.2(a) and returns the value of the digits read.

2. **atom** looks on the input for either

    a) An integer or
    b) A left parenthesis, followed by any expression, followed by a right parenthesis.

    It thus implements the diagram of Fig. 22.2(b).

3. **term** looks for an atom on the input and, after consuming one, calls **termTail**. The argument i for **termTail** is the value of the atom found. Together, **term** and **termTail** implement the diagram of Fig. 22.2(c).

---

[2] This program implements a parsing method called "recursive descent." The reader may consult *Compilers: Principles, Techniques, and Tools*, A. V. Aho, R. Sethi, and J. D. Ullman, Addison-Wesley, Reading, Mass., 1986 for an explanation of this technique.

```
(1)    exception Syntax;

(2)    fun digit(c) = ("0" <= c andalso c <= "9");

(3)    fun integer(IN,i) =
(4)        if digit(lookahead(IN)) then
(5)            integer(IN, 10*i+ord(input(IN,1))-ord("0"))
(6)        else i;

(7)    fun atom(IN) =
(8)            if digit(lookahead(IN)) then
(9)                integer(IN,0)
(10)           else if lookahead(IN) = "(" then (
(11)               input(IN,1);
                   let
(12)                   val e = expression(IN)
                   in
(13)                   if lookahead(IN) = ")" then (input(IN,1); e)
(14)                   else raise Syntax
                   end
               )
(15)           else raise Syntax
       and
(16)       term(IN) = termTail(IN,atom(IN))
       and
(17)       termTail(IN,i) =
(18)           case lookahead(IN) of
(19)               "*" => (input(IN,1); termTail(IN,i*atom(IN))) |
(20)               "/" => (input(IN,1);
                               termTail(IN,i div atom(IN))) |
(21)               _ => i
       and
(22)       expression(IN) = expTail(IN,term(IN))
       and
(23)       expTail(IN,i) =
(24)           case lookahead(IN) of
(25)               "+" => (input(IN,1); expTail(IN,i+term(IN))) |
(26)               "-" => (input(IN,1); expTail(IN,i-term(IN))) |
(27)               _ => i;

(28)   val I = open_in("test");

(29)   expression(I);
```

Fig. 22.3. Parser for arithmetic expressions.

4. **termTail** looks for and consumes from the input zero or more groups consisting of a * or / sign and an atom. It takes a parameter i, which is the value of all atoms found so far, multiplied or divided as dictated by the signs that connect them. If **termTail** finds a * or / as the next input character, it consumes it and calls **atom**. The value i is multiplied or divided, as appropriate, by the value of the atom found. The result becomes the argument of a recursive call to **termTail**. If **termTail** does not find a * or / as the next input character, it does nothing but return its argument i.

5. **expression** looks for a term on the input and, after consuming one, calls **expTail** with argument i equal to the value of the term found. Together, **expression** and **expTail** implement the diagram of Fig. 22.2(d).

6. **expTail** looks for and consumes from the input zero or more groups consisting of a + or − sign and a term. It takes a parameter i, which is the value of all terms found so far, added or subtracted as dictated by the signs that connect them. Its operation is analogous to that of **termTail**.

Let us now examine the code of Fig. 22.2 in more detail. Function **integer** is in lines (3)–(6). Line (4) uses **lookahead** to see if there are any more digits on the input. If so, then on line (5) we read the next digit by **input(IN,1)**, convert it to an integer with **ord**, and add the result to $10i$, where i is the argument representing the value of digits read so far. That is, if digits $c_1 c_2 \cdots c_k$ have been read so far, and these have value i treated as a decimal integer, then after reading the new digit c on line (5) the representation of the integer read so far is $c_1 c_2 \cdots c_k c$. This value is $10i + \text{ord}(c) - \text{ord}("0")$. Finally, if there is no digit waiting on the input, then all digits have been seen and the value i itself is returned on line (6).

•   Note that **integer** is only called on line (9), where on line (8) we have already determined that at least one digit waits on the input. Thus **integer** properly implements the diagram of Fig. 22.2(a), which requires that at least one digit be consumed.

The function **atom** appears in lines (7)–(15). In lines (8) and (9) we test if there is a digit waiting on the input and call **integer** if so. Using argument 0 in this call is correct, since there are no previous digits when the initial call to **integer** is made. Recursive calls to **integer** from itself will increase the value of the argument.

The other kind of atom begins with a left parenthesis, and this character is checked for at line (10). If found, then we execute a sequence of two steps. The first, at line (11), consumes the character, which we know is a left parenthesis. The second step, a let-expression in lines (12)–(14), calls **expression** and binds its value to identifier **e** at line (12). Then in line (13) we check if the character following the expression is a right parenthesis. If so, we do two things:

1.   Consume the right parenthesis with `input(IN,1)`.
2.   Return the value `e` produced by the expression on line (12).

If a right parenthesis is not found, there is a syntax error and we raise an exception on line (14).

The final case of `atom` is seen on line (15). Here we have seen on the input neither the beginning of an integer nor the beginning of a parenthesized expression. We therefore raise the **Syntax** exception.

Line (16) is the entire function **term**. It first calls `atom` to consume an atom from the input and return the value of that atom. This value becomes the argument of `termTail`, which multiplies or divides the value of the first atom by the sequence of zero or more atoms it finds on the input.

- We have used a succinct but subtle style in designing the function **term**. The call to `atom` occurs within a call to `termTail`, so the call to `atom` is executed first. We could have separated the two steps more transparently, but less succinctly by code such as

    ```
    let val i = atom(IN) in termTail(IN,i) end
    ```

Function `termTail` begins on line (17). On line (18) it looks at the next input, which becomes the basis of a 3-way case-statement. Line (19) covers the case where the next character is `*`. This character is consumed by `input(IN,1)`. Then `atom` is called to read and evaluate the next atom on the input. The value of this atom is multiplied by i, which is the value of the argument to `termTail`, and this product becomes the argument in a recursive call to `termTail`.

Line (20) handles the case where the next character is / analogously to line (19). Line (21) handles all other possible values of the next character. If the next character is other than `*` or /, the term is complete. In this case, `termTail` returns its own argument as the value of the entire term that has just been seen on the input.

Finally, lines (22)–(27) are functions **expression** and **expTail**. Their workings are analogous to those of **term** and **termTail**, and we omit the details.

On line (28) we begin to use the functions we have written. Identifier **I** is bound to an instream representing the opened file **test**; this file contains an expression that we wish to evaluate. A call to **expression(I)** on line (29) results in the value of the expression in file **test** being returned by ML. □

Exercises

22.1: Write expressions that will do the following.

a)* Open file **zap** for reading.
b)   Open file **baz** for writing.
c)* Open file `/usr/spool/mail/fred` for appending.
d)   Close the file whose outstream is `out1`.
e)* Close the file whose instream is `in2`.

f)   Read 5 characters from the instream `in3`.

g)* Write the string `"super"` to the outstream `out4`.

h)   Find the first character waiting on the standard input.

i)* Find how many characters are presenting waiting on the standard input.

! 22.2: Give the grammatical diagram(s) for the form of real constants of ML as described in Chapter 1.

! 22.3*: Write a function to read integers i and b separated by a single nondigit and print the representation of i in base b. If $b > 10$, then represent digits ten and above by their decimal representation surrounded by parentheses. For example, 570 in base 12 is 3(11)6; that is, $570 = 144 \times 3 + 12 \times 11 + 6$. You should read from an instream `IN` and write to outstream `OUT`.

! 22.4: ML allows us to construct values from integers using list-formation (with square brackets) and tuple-formation (with parentheses). An example is `[(1,2),(3,4)]`.

a)   Give grammatical diagrams for the set of values that can be formed by these two construction rules. You do not need to enforce the ML requirement that list elements have the same type.

b)   Implement a parser for this class of character strings. You should read the input from an instream `IN`. The response of your parser is a Boolean indicating whether the input is or is not of the proper form. Your program should allow white space among the integers, parentheses, commas, and brackets, but not in the middle of an integer. The entire value will be terminated by the character `$`.

◇◇◇
23   Creating Executable Files

When we develop a program in any language, we need to compile the program and store the compiled program in an executable file. By so doing, we avoid having to waste time recompiling the program every time we run it. SML/NJ provides two operators that allow us to create such executable files: `exportFn` and `exportML`.

Exporting Functions

exportFn

The function `exportFn` takes two arguments:

1. The name f of a file in which to write the compiled program.
2. A function F.

When executed, the file f does exactly what the function F would have done if executed in the environment that existed when `exportFn` was called. The type of function `exportFn` is

$$\text{fn : string * (string list * string list -> unit) -> unit}$$

That is, the first argument, the file name, is a string. The second argument, the function F, has to be of the type that takes a pair of lists of strings as an argument and returns a unit. Function `exportFn` also returns a unit.

Command line

To understand what the string-list arguments of the function F are, we have to consider how UNIX handles commands. When you type a command in response to the UNIX prompt, the system treats the first string on the command line as the name of the file to be executed. Any other strings on the command line are arguments to be passed to the executing program. The main program of each file executed by UNIX has a parameter that is the list of elements on the command line. Thus, if there are n arguments on the command line, then the 2nd through $(n+1)$st elements of this list are these arguments in order, and the first element of the list is the command itself. This list of $n + 1$ elements is the first argument of the function F.

Unix environment

The second list of strings that is an argument to the function F has elements that tell about the UNIX environment in which the function is executing. For example, when the author executes such a function, the first element of the second argument to F is `"HOME=/u/ullman"`, saying that `/u/ullman` is the author's home directory.

234

◇ **Example 23.1.** Let us take a simple example of the use of **exportFn**. In Fig. 23.1 we see an ML program that, when executed, will create a file called **combfile**. When executed, **combfile** computes $\binom{n}{m}$ for the integers n and m that appear on the command line. For instance if in response to the UNIX prompt we type,

        combfile 10 5

combfile will be executed. It will print the value of $\binom{10}{5}$ and halt.

```
(1)    fun comb1(n,m) =
           let
(2)            exception BadN;
(3)            exception BadM;
           in
(4)            if n <= 0 then raise BadN
(5)            else if m < 0 orelse m > n then raise BadM
(6)            else if m=0 orelse m=n then 1
(7)            else comb1(n-1,m) + comb1(n-1,m-1)
           end;
```
*val comb1 = fn : int * int → int*

```
       (* scanInt(L) converts a list of decimal digits to the
               integer that is the value of the string in reverse *)
(8)    fun scanInt(nil) = 0
(9)    |   scanInt(x::xs) = ord(x)-ord("0")+10*scanInt(xs);
```
val scanInt = fn : string list → int

```
       (* stringToInt(s) converts string s of decimal digits to
               its equivalent integer *)
(10)   fun stringToInt(s) = scanInt(rev(explode(s)));
```

```
(11)   fun comb([_,n,m],_) = (
(12)           print(comb1(stringToInt(n), stringToInt(m)));
(13)           print("\n")
           );
```
*val comb = fn : string list * string list → unit*

```
(14)   exportFn("combfile",comb);
```

Fig. 23.1. Exporting the comb function.

Lines (1)–(7) contain the definition of the combinatorial function we have seen several times before. The only difference is that we have renamed the function **comb1**.

Lines (8) and (9) are a function `scanInt` that takes as argument a list of characters that are the digits of an integer, in reverse; the result it produces is the value of that integer. The basis is line (8), where the value of an empty list is 0. For the induction, on line (9), we convert the first element x of a list to its integer value by `ord(x)-ord("0")`. We then add to this value 10 times the value of the tail of the list. Note that this formula is correct, because the digits are presented in reverse order — least significant digit first.

- Compare `scanInt` with function `integer` of Fig. 22.3. Since here the digits are available in reverse order, we do not need to carry along the extra parameter that was needed for `integer`.

Line (10) is the function `stringToInt` that converts a string s consisting of digits into the equivalent integer. It is the cascade of three simple steps:

1. Explode string s so it becomes a list of digits rather than a string of digits.

2. Reverse the list. We use the built-in function `rev` that is equivalent to the function `reverse` that we wrote in Example 6.2.

3. Apply `scanInt` to convert the reversed list of digits to an integer with the appropriate value.

Lines (11)–(13) define the function `comb`, which is the function we actually export. Function `comb` must take its arguments from the UNIX shell, so its arguments will be two lists described above. The first list is the arguments on the command line, and the second is a list of descriptors from the current UNIX environment. We ignore the latter, so the second parameter in the definition of `comb` is the anonymous variable `_`.

We assume that the function `comb` will be called with the values of n and m written on the command line in that order. Thus, `comb` will be passed a list of three strings:

1. The name of the file in which the exported function `comb` exists (this file is called `combfile` in the export call on line (14) of Fig. 23.1, but of course the code could be moved to another file later).

2. The value of n as a string of digits.

3. The value of m as a string of digits.

The first of these strings is not used by `comb`, so the pattern for the first argument `[_,n,m]` identifies variables `n` and `m` with the second and third elements of the list.

- Note that `comb` is written in such a way that if the exported file is called from UNIX with anything but two arguments, there will be no matching pattern and the exception `Match` will be raised. We also get a warning that the patterns are not exhaustive when we compile the program of Fig. 23.1.

- A more careful design would have a second pattern for `comb`, say `comb(_,_)`, with an associated action to print an error message. Alternatively, we could handle the `Match` exception by printing the error message.

On line (12) `comb` converts each of the character strings n and m to the equivalent integer using `stringToInt`. Having made these conversions, `comb` then applies `comb1` to the integers n and m and prints the resulting value. Finally, at line (13) `comb` ends by printing a newline character.

Line (14) is the export statement. It takes two arguments:

1. The file name `combfile` into which the executable code is to be placed, and

2. `comb`, the ML function that constitutes the program in the file `combfile`.

After SML/NJ executes the program of Fig. 23.1, it returns to the UNIX prompt, as usual. However, we shall find, in the same directory from which ML was called, a file named `combfile`. As mentioned previously, if in response to the UNIX prompt we type

```
combfile 10 5
```

then the result 252, which is $\binom{10}{5}$, will be printed. What actually happens is that a compiled version of the function `comb` is called with first argument equal to the list `["combfile","10","5"]`. The second argument is a long list of environment information that is ignored. □

Exporting the ML Environment

exportML

SML/NJ also allows us to create executable files with the function `exportML`. This function takes one argument, a string that names the file into which the compiled program is written. The difference between `exportFn` and `exportML` is that the former produces code to execute a particular function. The latter reproduces the ML system with its environment equal to whatever it was when the `exportML` function was executed.

If we export the ML system into a file `foo` and execute `foo` at the UNIX level, it will do whatever was in the program that caused ML to be exported into `foo`. We then get the ML prompt, -, and may proceed to execute ML code in the existing environment.

◇ **Example 23.2.** Figure 23.2 shows a simple use of `exportML`. We begin with our usual definition of the combinatorial function; we have returned to calling it `comb`. The definition of `comb` is now part of the environment.

At the last line, we export the ML environment into the file `newsml`. Note the response of the system. The function `exportML` is of type

```
fn : string -> bool
```

```
fun comb(n,m) =
    let
        exception BadN;
        exception BadM;
    in
        if n <= 0 then raise BadN
        else if m < 0 orelse m > n then raise BadM
        else if m=0 orelse m=n then 1
        else comb(n-1,m) + comb(n-1,m-1)
    end;
```
val comb = fn : int * int → int

```
exportML("newsml");
```
val it = false

Fig. 23.2. Exporting the ML system with a loaded `comb` function.

It returns **false** when it is called with a file it did not previously create, in which case it actually creates the file **newsml** that will serve as an ML environment.

When we execute **newsml** in response to the UNIX prompt, we get the response

val it = true

The value **true** tells us that we are running a file created by **exportML** rather than creating such a file. We get the ML prompt and are now able to write top-level expressions in an environment where **comb** is defined. For example, we may type

```
comb(10,5);
```
val it = 252

We may also type any definitions or expressions we wish into the top-level ML system, just as we can when we invoke **sml** from UNIX. □

Exercises

23.1*: Write a function to print the environment list. Export this function into a file **printenv** so invoking **printenv** in response to the UNIX prompt will cause the current UNIX environment to be printed.

23.2: Modify the program of Fig. 23.1 so the exceptions **BadN**, **BadM**, and **Match** are handled by printing appropriate error messages. Recall that **Match** is raised when function **comb** is applied to a list whose length isn't three, that is, when file **combfile** is called with other than two arguments. Also, remember that local exceptions cannot be handled.

23.3*: Write and export a function that takes a list of any number of integers on the command line and computes their sum.

23.4: Write and export a function that takes on the command line

1.   A real number x represented by digits with a decimal point somewhere in the middle, followed by

2.   An integer y,

and prints x^y.

◇◇◇ 24   Controlling Operator Grouping

Functions like + that are used as binary (two-argument) infix (between-the-operands) operators in arithmetic expressions are a staple of almost every programming language, and ML is not an exception. The binary-infix style of expressions is useful because there are familiar conventions, embodied in associativity and precedence rules, that allow us to group operands to their operators with relatively few parentheses needed to force grouping.

ML allows us to extend this power to operators that we define as functions. We are also able to change the grouping strategy for existing operators, and we can turn infix operators back into ordinary functions. This chapter discusses the mechanisms for doing so.

Precedence

Grouping operands

It is conventional to give infix operators a *precedence*, which is an integer associated with that operator. When we group operands to operators, we group the higher-precedence operators first. To *group* an occurrence of an operator to its operands, we look to the immediate right of the operator. We then find the shortest sequence of operators, operands, and parentheses that form an expression with balanced parentheses; this sequence is the *right operand*. Looking to the immediate left of the operator we find the *left operand*, which is the shortest sequence of symbols on the left that constitutes a well-formed expression. These left and right operands are grouped with the operator occurrence by placing a left parenthesis just before the left operand begins and placing a right parenthesis just after the right operand ends.

◇ **Example 24.1.** Consider the expression $a + b - c$. If we choose to group the + first, we look to the right and find the symbol b, which is an expression by itself. Thus we need go no further; b is the right operand. Similarly, looking to the left of the + we find that a is the shortest well-formed expression and thus constitutes the left operand. We group the operands of the + by rewriting the expression as $(a + b) - c$.

Now, let us group the operands of the − operator. The right operand is c. Looking left, we first find a right parenthesis. We must go as far left as the matching left parenthesis, and we therefore identify $(a + b)$ as the left operand. The grouping for − thus gives us the fully parenthesized expression $((a + b) - c)$. □

The order in which we choose to group an operator occurrence to its operands usually affects how we evaluate the expression, so we must know the proper order to do the grouping. One important convention is that of operator precedence. We assign to each binary infix operator a precedence, and we group the operator occurrences in order of their precedence, highest first. Each language has its own policy regarding precedence of operators, but they tend to be fairly similar. Multiplicative operators such as * and / have higher precedence than the additive operators + and -. These arithmetic operators have higher precedence than the comparison operators like <=, and the comparison operators have higher precedence than the logical operators like **andalso**.

PRECEDENCE	OPERATOR	COMMENTS
0	`before`	Second argument executed only for side-effects
3	`o` `:=`	Function composition Assignment, for **ref** values
4	`=, <>, <,` `>, <=, >=`	Comparison operators
5	`::, @`	Concatenation and Cons for lists
6	`+, -` `^`	Additive operators String concatenation
7	`*, /, mod, rem` `div, quot`	Multiplicative operators

Fig. 24.1. Precedence of binary infix operators.

Precedence Levels in SML/NJ

Figure 24.1 gives the precedence levels of the SML/NJ infix operators. Precedence levels are represented by nonnegative integers.[1] The operators are positioned as shown, with nothing at levels 1 and 2. Since it is possible for the user to define new operators, levels 1 and 2 can be populated as can levels above 7. We may also add new operators at the levels 0 or 3 through 7.

Three of the operators listed in Fig. 24.1 are not formally part of standard ML:

---

[1] Later implementations of SML/NJ and some other implementations use only the single digits 0 through 9 as precedence levels.

before

1. **before** executes its left argument then its right argument but produces the value of the left argument as its own value. Therefore, the right argument is executed only for side-effects.

quot

2. **quot** is a variant of **div** that behaves differently when the result is negative. That is, while **div** always produces the next lower integer when the result is nonintegral, **quot** produces the integer that is closer to 0.

rem

3. **rem** is a variant of **mod** that behaves differently when the result is negative. To be precise, a **mod** b is the integer we must add to $b \times (a$ **div** $b)$ to get a, for any positive or negative integers a and b, while a **rem** b is the integer we must add to $b \times (a$ **quot** $b)$ to get a.

◇ **Example 24.2.** To illustrate the point,

        8 div ~3;
        val it = ~3

But

        8 quot ~3;
        val it = ~2

Note that for a negative result **quot** rounds toward positive infinity, while **div** rounds toward negative infinity. For positive results, these two operators both round down.

Here are the values of the **mod** and **rem** operators applied to all combinations of plus or minus 8 and plus or minus 3:

        8 mod 3 = 2   ~8 mod 3 = 1   8 mod ~3 = ~1   ~8 mod ~3 = ~2
        8 rem 3 = 2   ~8 rem 3 = ~2   8 rem ~3 = 2   ~8 rem ~3 = ~2

For example, we know that ~8 **div** 3 = ~3, and 3*~3 = ~9. Since ~9+1 = ~8, we see why ~8 **mod** 3 = 1. On the other hand, ~8 **quot** 3 = ~2 and

        ~2*3 = ~6

Since ~8 = ~6+~2, we see why ~8 **rem** 3 = ~2. □

Complicating matters is the fact that not all the symbols we think of as binary infix operators are represented by the "main sequence" of precedences represented by Fig. 24.1. The complete story appears in Fig. 26.1. If we look ahead to Chapter 26, we find that the operators **andalso** and **orelse** are deemed to have precedence below any on the main sequence, with **andalso** having higher precedence than **orelse**. In effect, we can think of **andalso** as having precedence −1 and **orelse** as having precedence −2.

In addition, we see in Fig. 26.1 that the operator defined by juxtaposition of expressions, which is the way we apply a function to its argument, has higher precedence than any on the main sequence. It is as if function application had infinite precedence.

Associativity of Operators

Left, right associativity

Precedence is only one of the two ways that order of evaluation is controlled. We normally group operators of equal precedence from the left; such operators are said to be *left-associative*. It is also possible to have operators group from the right; these operators are *right-associative*.

◇ **Example 24.3.** In Fig. 24.1 all the operators are left-associative except for :: and **@**, which are right-associative.[2] Thus $3 - 4 - 5$ is grouped from the left as $(3 - 4) - 5$. Its value is -6 rather than 4, as would be the case if we incorrectly grouped from the right as $3 - (4 - 5)$.

On the other hand, `a::b::cs` groups from the right as `a::(b::cs)`. Thus this expression makes sense if `a` and `b` are elements of some type T and `cs` is a list of elements of type T, as we have conventionally assumed. If we were to group from the left as `(a::b)::cs`, we would have to interpret `a` as an element of some type T, `b` as a list of elements of type T, and `cs` as a list of lists of elements of type T.

There is another example of a right-associative operator from the type expressions of ML. The operator `->`, which constructs function types, is right-associative. Thus $T \rightarrow S \rightarrow R$ is interpreted as a function with domain type T and range type equal to functions from type S to type R. □

Creating New Infix Operators

infix

We can define any function, data constructor, or exception constructor to be an infix operator with the statement

> `infix` <level> <identifier list>

Here <level> is the precedence level, an integer. The operator or operators being defined to have this precedence form the <identifier list>. These operators will be left-associative. Of course, each function or constructor so declared must be binary; that is, it must have two arguments.

infixr

- If we wish an operator or operators to be right-associative, we use the keyword `infixr` in place of `infix`.

- We may omit the <level> from the declaration, in which case the precedence level is taken to be 0.

- A negative level is illegal.[3]

---

[2] In some implementations of ML, **@** may be left-associative. In fact, the formal definition of standard ML calls for left-associativity of this operator, although it has been implemented in SML/NJ as right-associative to mesh better with the :: operator.

[3] Some ML implementations treat negative levels as 0.

nonfix

- To remove the infix property from an identifier or identifiers, use the keyword **nonfix** followed by the list of identifiers we wish to turn back into ordinary identifiers.

- It is also possible to turn an identifier *temporarily* into a nonfix function name by preceding it by the keyword **op** as discussed in Chapter 11.

◇ **Example 24.4.** Suppose we define the function **comb** in our conventional way as in Fig. 23.2. We can then declare it to be a left-associative infix operator by

> ```
> infix 2 comb;
> ```
> *infix 2 comb*

We have given **comb** precedence level 2 so its arguments are grouped after any of the usual arithmetic operators. For instance:

> ```
> 5 comb 2 comb 4;
> ```
> *val it = 210 : int*

This expression is grouped as (`5 comb 2`) `comb 4`, or

$$\binom{\binom{5}{2}}{4}$$

Since $\binom{5}{2} = 10$ and $\binom{10}{4} = 210$, we see that the correct result is computed.

The identifier **comb** no longer has its normal syntax as a function. If we try to use it that way, as

> ```
> comb(5,2);
> ```
> *Error: nonfix identifier required*

we are told this function application requires a "nonfix" identifier, one that is used as a normal function preceding its arguments. If we wish to turn **comb** back into such an identifier, we may declare

> ```
> nonfix comb;
> ```
> *nonfix comb*

Alternatively, we could leave **comb** as an infix operator, but use it once as a function by writing **op comb(5,2)**.

The operator **comb** can also be used with other infix operators. For instance

> ```
> 5 comb 2 comb 2 + 2;
> ```
> *val it = 210 : int*

Notice that +, with precedence 6, takes precedence over **comb**, with precedence 2, so the subexpression $2 + 2$ is grouped first.

However, functions that are not defined to be infix apply to their operators before binary infix operators are applied. For example, suppose we define the function **square** in the usual way:

```
fun square(x:int) = x*x;
```
val square = fn : int → int

Then we could write an expression like

```
square 2 comb 2 comb 4;
```
val it = 15 : int

The use of **square** is grouped with its operand first, so this expression is interpreted as

$$\binom{\binom{2^2}{2}}{4} = \binom{\binom{4}{2}}{4} = \binom{6}{4}$$

or 15. □

◇ **Example 24.5.** We can also make built-in functions become infix operators if they take two arguments. For example,

```
infix 3 sub;
```
infix 3 sub

declares the **sub(A,i)** function to be a left-associative, infix operator.[4] Then we can write the more natural **A sub i** in place of **sub(A,i)**. As another example, line (20) of Fig. 17.4, which is the program to upper-triangulate a matrix, can be written

```
val ratio = (M sub !j sub !i)/(M sub !i sub !i);
```

instead of the original

```
val ratio = sub(sub(M,!j),!i)/sub(sub(M,!i),!i);
```

The left-associativity of **sub** gives this expression the correct interpretation.

Because we have defined the precedence level of **sub** to be 3, which is lower than that of the arithmetic operators, we get a specific behavior of expressions that involve **sub**. For example, **A sub i+1** is grouped as **A sub (i+1)**. If we would prefer to have such an expression grouped as **(A sub i)+1**, then we need to give **sub** a high precedence, such as 8 or 9. □

Infix Data Constructors

If in the definition of a datatype we use a data constructor that takes two arguments, we may declare this constructor to be an infix operator and write instances of the datatype in a form similar to arithmetic expressions.

---

[4] In fact, early versions of SML/NJ and some other ML implementations define **sub** in exactly this way.

```
(1)    datatype 'a btree = T of 'a btree * 'a btree |
(2)                Leaf of 'a;
```
datatype 'a btree
con Leaf : 'a → 'a btree
*con T : 'a btree * 'a btree → 'a btree*

```
(3)    infix 2 T;
```
infix 2 T

```
(4)    fun printTree(Leaf(x:int)) = print(x)
(5)    |   printTree(t1 T t2) = (
(6)            print("(");
(7)            printTree(t1);
(8)            print(",");
(9)            printTree(t2);
(10)           print(")")
            );
```
val printTree = fn : int btree → unit

```
(11)   val t = Leaf(1) T Leaf(2) T Leaf(3);
```
val t = Leaf 1 T Leaf 2 T Leaf 3 : int btree

```
(12)   printTree(T);
```
((1,2),3)val it = () : unit

```
(13)   val t =
           Leaf(1) T (Leaf(2) T Leaf(3) T (Leaf(4) T Leaf(5)));
```
val t = Leaf 1 T (Leaf 2 T Leaf 3 T (Leaf 4 T Leaf 5)) : int btree

```
(14)   printTree(t);
```
(1,((2,3),(4,5)))val it = () : unit

Fig. 24.2. An infix tree-construction operator.

◇ **Example 24.6.** In Fig. 24.2 we see a definition of a simple kind of binary tree, where only leaves have labels. The definition of datatype **btree** is in lines (1) and (2). In line (1) the data constructor **T** is defined; it has two arguments, both of which are binary trees. This data constructor is used for interior nodes. Line (2) has the data constructor **Leaf**, which takes a label of the arbitrary type **'a**.

In line (3), we define constructor **T** to be a binary infix operator of low precedence. Thus, although **Leaf** will still precede its argument, the constructor **T** will be placed between the left and right subtrees that form the tree it constructs.

Lines (4)–(10) describe a function **printTree** that prints the leaves of a binary tree, from left to right. This function requires that the labels be of type integer. Line (4) handles the basis case where the tree is a leaf; we simply print the label. Line (5) covers the case of a tree constructed by T. Note that the pattern on line (5) shows T between its operands, as it must be. In lines (6) through (10) we call `printTree` recursively on the left and right subtrees. A comma is placed between the results at line (8) and the entire output is surrounded by parentheses on lines (6) and (10).

Line (11) creates a value of type `int btree`. Since constructor T associates from the left, the value of identifier t represents the tree shown in Fig. 24.3. On line (12) we print the leaves of this tree from the left. They appear with the proper parentheses to suggest the structure of the tree. Since for simplicity we have not printed a newline after the complete tree, the response of ML giving the value of `it` appears on the same line.

Fig. 24.3. The binary tree defined on line (11) of Fig. 24.2.

A more complicated example of a tree is shown in lines (13) and (14). Here parentheses are used to guide the order of grouping for the various occurrences of constructor T. This grouping is reflected in the output on line (14). The grouping of leaves 2 and 3 is implicit in the left-associativity of T. □

Exercises

24.1: If we instead define `infixr 3 T` at line (3) of Fig. 24.2, would the interpretation change for

a)* Line (11)?
b) Line (13)?

! **24.2:** Suggest a way to redefine the precedence and/or associativity of + and * so that

a)* $a + b * c$ is interpreted as $(a + b) * c$, and $a * b + c$ is interpreted as $(a * b) + c$.
b) $a + b * c + d$ is interpreted as $a + ((b * c) + d)$.

24.3*: Figure 6.2 gave three functions that operated on polynomials: `padd` (polynomial addition), `smult` (multiplication of a scalar by a polynomial), and `pmult` (multiplications of polynomials). Each is a function of two parameters, so we can make them be infix operators.

a) Suggest a way to define these operators so that

    1.   `pmult` takes precedence over `padd`.

    2.   `smult` takes precedence over `pmult`.

    3.   All three are left-associative.

    4.   The arithmetic operators on reals take precedence over the polynomial operators. For example, `2.0 + 3.0 smult P` is interpreted as $(2+3)P$ rather than an erroneous attempt to add 2 to the polynomial $3P$.

b) Show how to write the expression $(P+2Q) \times R$, where P is the polynomial $3x^4 + 5x^2 - 6$, $Q = x^3 + 2x^2 - 3x + 4$, and $R = x + 1$, using the infix operators and using parentheses only when necessary.

24.4: Repeat Exercise 24.3 but require that all operators be right-associative and that polynomial operators take precedence over arithmetic operators.

24.5: For the binary tree datatype of Fig. 24.2, write a function that

a)* Sums the labels of the leaves of a tree, assuming labels are reals.

Sibling   ! b) Sums the labels of those leaves that have a leaf for a *sibling*. Siblings are nodes that have the same parent.

25   Built-In Functions of SML/NJ

In this chapter, we shall enumerate the predefined functions of SML/NJ. Some of these functions may not be available in other ML implementations, or they may differ in type or meaning in other implementations. The set of available functions includes the binary infix operators listed in Fig. 24.1, but we do not reenumerate those functions here.

Some of the functions appearing in this chapter have not been mentioned previously. We call attention to those by listing them in the margin. Functions we have seen before are enumerated but not flagged in the margin.

I. Functions for Integers and Reals

The binary arithmetic and comparison operators were mentioned in Fig. 24.1, and their meanings were described in Chapter 1. In addition there are:

a)   ~, of type `int -> int` or type `real -> real`, negates its argument.

b)   **min** and **max**, of type `int * int -> int`, produce the minimum or maximum, respectively, of their two arguments. Note that these functions are not defined for reals.

c)   **abs**, of type `int -> int` or type `real -> real`, turns a number into its absolute value.

d)   **real**, of type `int -> real`, turns an integer into a real of the same value as discussed in Chapter 2.

e)   **floor**, **ceiling**, and **truncate**, each of type `real -> int`, turn reals into neighboring integers. See Chapter 2 for the distinctions among these three functions and their exact definitions.

f)   **sin**, **cos**, and **arctan**, each of type `real -> real`, apply the trigonometric functions of the same name. Angles are measured in radians.

g)   **sqrt**, **exp**, and **ln**, of type `real -> real`, compute $\sqrt{x}$, e^x, and $\log_e x$ for argument x.

h)   **chr**, of type `int -> string`, produces a character with the ASCII code equal to the given integer as discussed in Chapter 2. Its inverse, **ord**, is listed under string functions.

i)   **makestring**, of type `int -> string` or type `real -> string`, produces a string representing an integer or real. For example,

Margin notes: min, max · abs · sin, cos, arctan · sqrt, exp, ln · makestring

```
makestring(24+35);
```
val it = "59" : string

```
makestring(1000000000000000.0);
```
val it = "1.0E15" : string

Note that values of 10^{15} or more are expressed as strings in exponential notation.

j)   `print`, of type `int -> unit` or type `real -> unit`, prints the value of its argument as a side-effect and returns the unit as its value.

II. Functions on Strings

In addition to the concatenation operator and the comparison operators mentioned in Fig. 24.1, there are the following functions.

a)   `explode`, of type `string -> string list`, creates a list of characters from a string as discussed in Chapter 4.

b)   `implode`, of type `string list -> string`, concatenates the elements of a string list to produce a single string as discussed in Chapter 4.

size

c)   `size`, of type `string -> int`, returns the length of (number of positions in) the string that is its argument. For example,

```
size("abcabc");
```
val it = 6 : int

substring

d)   `substring`, of type `string * int * int -> string`, takes a string and two integers as arguments. It returns characters starting at the position indicated by the first integer; the number of characters returned is indicated by the second integer. However, in this and other functions involving positions in strings, we count starting at position 0. For example,

```
substring("abcdefg",2,3);
```
val it = "cde" : string

That is, the character `"c"` appears in the position numbered 2. The string of length 3 beginning at that position is `"cde"`.

e)   `ord`, of type `string -> int`, converts the first character of a given string to the integer that is its ASCII code as discussed in Chapter 2. Its inverse, `chr`, was listed as a function on integers.

ordof

f)   `ordof`, of type `string * int -> int`, gives the ASCII code for the character in the given string that is at the position indicated by the integer argument. As discussed in (d) above, positions are counted starting at 0. For example,

```
ordof("abcde",3);
```
val it = 100 : int

Note that 100 is the ASCII code for "d".

g) **print** is an overloaded function that can be of type **string -> unit**. Applied to a string, it prints that string.

III. Functions on Booleans

The basic operations on Boolean values **true** and **false**, which were discussed in Chapter 1, are summarized below.

a) **andalso** and **orelse** are of type **bool * bool -> bool** and are essentially logical AND and OR, respectively. However, they evaluate their second argument only if the truth value of the result has not been determined by the first argument. This distinction is important if the expression that is the second argument has side-effects or raises an exception.

b) **not**, of type **bool -> bool**, performs logical negation.

makestring   c) **makestring**, of type **bool -> string**, turns a Boolean value into the string that spells its name. For example,

```
makestring(true);
val it = "true" : string
```

d) **print** can also be of type **bool -> unit**; it prints the given truth value.

IV. Functions on Lists

We saw many of the important functions that operate on lists in Chapter 4. Two of these, the binary infix operators : : (cons) and **@** (concatenation), were listed in the table of Fig. 24.1. The **explode** and **implode** operations to convert between strings and lists were mentioned in the section for strings. The other operations are:

a) **hd**, of type **'a list -> 'a**, produces the head of a given list.

b) **tl**, of type **'a list -> 'a list**, produces the tail of a given list.

nth   c) **nth**, of type **'a list * int -> 'a** produces the element of the given list whose position is given by the integer argument. As usual, positions are counted starting at 0. For example,

```
nth([1,2,3],2);
val it = 3 : int
```

nthtail   d) **nthtail**, of type **'a list * int -> 'a list**, produces the tail of the list starting at the position given by the integer. For example,

```
nthtail([1,2,3,4],2);
val it = [3,4] : int list
```

e) **null**, of type **'a list -> bool**, tells whether a list is the empty list.

length

f)   **length**, of type `'a list -> int`, gives the length of a list.

rev

g)   **rev**, of type `'a list -> 'a list`, produces the reverse of the given list.

h)   **map**, of type `('a -> 'b) -> 'a list -> 'b list`, is similar to the function of the same name described in Chapter 11. However, the built-in **map** function takes its arguments in Curried form (see Chapter 21). For example, if **square** is the function that squares integers, then:

> map square [1,2,3];
> *val it = [1,4,9] : int list*

app, revapp

i)   **app** and **revapp**, of type `('a -> 'b) -> 'a list -> unit`, are functions like **map**, but they return a unit rather than the list with the given function applied. For example,

> app square [1,2,3];
> *val it = () : unit*

Thus, these functions only make sense if we wish to apply a function to each element of a list for its side-effects, such as printing of the element. Function **revapp** is like **app**, but the list is first reversed.

j)   **fold** and **revfold** are functions of type

$$((`a * `b) -> `b) -> `a list -> `b -> `b$$

revfold

The function **fold** was discussed in Chapter 21. Function **revfold** is similar but it first reverses the list to which it is applied. Each of these functions effectively treats the elements of a list as function names and composes these functions.

exists

k)   **exists**, of type `('a -> bool) -> 'a list -> bool`, takes a predicate P (i.e., a function from some type T to the type **bool**) and a list of elements of type T. It returns true if at least one of the elements satisfies the predicate P. For example, suppose P is the function that returns true if and only if its argument is larger than 3, defined by:

> fun P(x) = x>3;
> *val P = fn : int → bool*

Then we can apply **exists** as:

> exists P [1,2,3];
> *val it = false : bool*

> exists P [1,4,2];
> *val it = true : bool*

V. Functions on Arrays

Recall from Chapter 16 that arrays are an abstraction provided with SML/NJ.

Array types and functions are not available unless we execute

```
open Array;
```

Below are the functions provided in this abstraction; we discussed the first three in Chapter 16.

a) **array**, of type `int * 'a -> 'a array`, returns an array whose number of elements is given by the integer argument, and whose initial value for each element is given by the second argument. Recall that elements are indexed starting at 0. There are some limitations on function types for elements of arrays, but the commonly used types for array elements are supported.

b) **sub**, of type `'a array * int -> 'a`, takes as argument an array and an integer. It returns the element at the array position indexed by that integer.

c) **update**, of type `'a array * int * 'a -> unit`, takes an array, an integer indexing a position within the array, and a new value for that position. As a side-effect, **update** changes the value of the selected array element to be that given by its third argument.

length

d) **length**, of type `'a array -> int`, produces the length (i.e., the number of elements) of the given array.

arrayoflist

e) **arrayoflist**, of type `'a list -> 'a array`, takes a list of elements and produces an array whose elements are the same as those of the list, in order. For example,

```
val A = arrayoflist([1,2,3]);
val A = prim? : int array
```

Now, A is an array of three elements indexed 0, 1, and 2. Their values are 1, 2, and 3 respectively. For instance, **sub(A,1)** has value 2.

VI. Functions for References

The reference and its functions were described in Chapter 17. For review, they are the following.

a) The dereferencing function **!**, of type `'a ref -> 'a`, takes a reference and produces the thing referred to.

b) The assignment function **:=**, of type `'a ref * 'a -> unit`, takes a reference and a suitable value and makes the reference refer to this value. The operation is performed as a side-effect, and the unit is returned.

c) **inc** and **dec**, each of type `int ref -> unit`, respectively increment and decrement a reference to an integer. The operation is performed as a side-effect.

VII. Functions on Bit Strings

It is possible to treat integers as bits strings if we use the abstraction **Bits**. This abstraction of SML/NJ must be opened by

    open Bits;

to make its functions available without using a full name starting with **Bits** and a dot. To understand these functions, we must imagine that integers, which we write in decimal, are converted to their binary equivalents. We may then operate on these binary numbers as if they were bit strings. The following functions may be used.

andb, orb, xorb a) **andb**, **orb**, and **xorb** are each of type **int * int -> int**. Each takes two integer arguments and converts them to binary notation, that is, to bit strings. The shorter of the two bit strings is padded out at the left end with 0's, if necessary, so they are the same length. Then we operate on the two bit strings, bitwise. The result is a new bit string that is interpreted as an integer and becomes the result of the function. For the **andb** function, the bitwise operation is to make the resulting bit 1 if and only if both given bits strings have 1 in that position. For example,

    andb(14,7);
    val it = 6 : int

What has happened is that decimal integers 14 and 7 have been converted to binary: 1110 and 111, respectively. The latter is padded at the front to make 0111. When we compare 1110 and 0111, we find that the middle two positions have 1 in both bit strings, but the first and fourth positions do not. Thus, the result as a bit string is 0110. This bit string, interpreted as a binary integer, is 6 in decimal. Similarly, **orb** produces a 1 in a particular position if either or both of the given bit strings has 1 there. For example,

    orb(12,5);
    val it = 13: int

We take the bitwise OR of 1100 and 0101, which is 1101, or 13 in decimal. Finally, the **xorb** (exclusive-or) function puts a 1 in a position if and only if exactly one of the given strings has 1 in that position. Thus,

    xorb(5,14);
    val it = 11 : int

The integers 5 and 14 represent bit strings 0101 and 1110, whose exclusive-or is 1011, or 11 in decimal.

lshift, rshift b) **lshift** and **rshift**, each of type **int * int -> int**, treat their first argument as a bit string and their second argument as a number of positions to shift left or right respectively. For example,

```
lshift(23,2);
```
val it = 92 : int

```
rshift(23,2);
```
val it = 5 : int

Here, `lshift` has shifted the binary representation of 23 two positions left, in effect multiplying by 4. Also, `rshift` has shifted the binary representation of 23 two positions right, throwing away the two low-order bits, in effect computing `23 div 4`.

VIII. Functions for Byte Arrays

A final abstraction provided by SML/NJ is the *byte array*. This type is an array of integers, restricted so each element of the array is in the range 0 to 255. That is, an element may be interpreted as a character and stored in a single byte of memory to save space and time. Thus, byte arrays can be an efficient implementation of character strings with operations more powerful than those provided for strings by standard ML. The types and functions for byte arrays become available without using dotted names if we execute

```
open ByteArray;
```

Having done so, we have the following functions available.

a) `array` of type `int * int -> bytearray`. This function is essentially the same as the function of the same name for ordinary arrays. The first integer argument is the number of elements of the array, indexed starting at 0. The second argument is the initial value of these elements, and it must be in the range 0 to 255. Note that an integer, not a character, is expected as the second argument, even though it is natural to think of elements of a byte array as characters. For example,

```
val B = array(10,ord("a"));
```
val B = - : bytearray

We should notice that because the abstraction `ByteArray` has just been opened, its definition of function `array` takes priority over the definition from the abstraction `Array`, and ML correctly interprets B as a byte array. We can use the dot notation described in Chapter 14 to refer to the functions in abstraction `Array`.

b) `sub`, `update`, and `length` are the same as for ordinary arrays, but the element values must be integers in the range 0 to 255.[1] For example,

```
sub(B,2);
```
val it = 97 : int

---

[1] In some implementations sub will appear as an infix operator of precedence 3, even if for ordinary arrays, sub is nonfix.

Note that the ASCII code for "a", not the character "a", is produced.

extract

c)   **extract**, of type **bytearray * int * int -> string**, takes a bytearray, an integer denoting the first desired position of the array (counting from 0, as usual), and another integer denoting the number of positions desired, starting from the position indicated by the first integer. For example, suppose we were to store in the byte array **B** the characters "a", "b", ..., "j". A sample extraction is:

> **extract(B,2,3);**
> *val it = "cde" : string*

We start at the position indexed by 2, which is the third position since we start at 0. The third position holds "c". We extract the three characters starting at this position, that is, the string "cde". Note that unlike the other operations described in (a) and (b) above, **extract** automatically converts the stored integers into characters.

d)   Functions **fold** and **revfold**, of type

> **((int * 'a) -> 'a) -> bytearray -> 'a -> 'a**

act on byte arrays like the functions of the same name defined for general lists.

e)   Functions **app** and **revapp**, of type **(int -> 'a) -> bytearray -> unit**, likewise behave on byte arrays as the functions of the same name for lists.

Exercises

In this chapter we give exercises only for the functions that have not been covered in earlier chapters.

25.1: Write the following functions as simply as possible, using built-in functions on integers or reals where possible.

a)* The function that is the maximum of the absolute values of integers x and y.

b)   The function that is the absolute value of the minimum of integers x and y.

! c)* The arc sine of x, that is, the angle whose sine in radians is x.

! d)   The arc cosecant of x, that is, the angle whose inverse cosine is x.

e)* e^{e^x} for real x.

f) $\log_e \log_e x$ for real x.

25.2: Show how to use the function **makestring** to produce the following strings:

a) `"123"`
b) `"123.45"`
c) `false`

25.3*: Use the functions `ordof` and `size` to write a function that computes the sum of the ASCII codes for the characters of a string without using `explode`.

25.4: Use function `substring` and your answer to Exercise 25.3 to produce a function that sums the ASCII codes of a string s between positions i and j.

25.5*: What is the value of `null(nthtail(L,length(L)))` for any list L?

! **25.6**: Write a function that takes an integer list and determines whether for any i the ith element has value i.

25.7*: Use `app` and `print` to print each element of an integer list without writing a recursive function.

25.8: Write a function using `exists` to tell whether there is an element whose absolute value is less than $\sqrt{2}$ on a given list of reals.

! **25.9***: use `arrayoflist` to write a function that takes a real x and an integer n and produces the array with elements 1.0, x, x^2, x^3, ..., x^{n-1}.

25.10: Give the values of the following expressions on bit strings.

a)* `andb(43,19)`
b) `orb(43,19)`
c)* `xorb(43,19)`
d) `andb(orb(43,19),xorb(43,19))`

25.11: Suppose we have a byte array `caps` of length 10 whose elements are, in order, the ASCII codes for the characters `"A"` through `"J"`. What are the values of the following expressions?

a)* `extract(caps, 3, 4)`
b) `extract(caps, 1,6)`

◇◇◇ 26 Summary of ML Syntax

We shall now summarize the structure of the ML language. We begin with the lexical features — the way identifiers, constants, and other simple classes are formed. Then, we give the syntax of the language, using the grammatical notation that was introduced in Example 22.4. In this notation, we use capital letters to indicate syntactic categories; these are either lexical concepts like ID (identifier), or concepts defined by a graph like that of Fig. 22.2.

Lexical Categories

In our description of ML, we shall refer to the following classes of character strings without giving a grammatical description.

1. *Identifiers* (ID). The alphanumeric and symbolic identifiers were described in Chapter 3. However, we exclude from the class ID those identifiers that begin with an apostrophe and therefore are type variables, covered in item (5) below.

2. *Constants* (CONST). These are integers, reals, character strings, Booleans, and the unit (). Their legal forms were described in Chapter 1.

3. *Labels* (LABEL). These are either identifiers or positive integer constants as described in Chapter 18.

4. *Infix operators* (INFIX). These are the usual arithmetic and other operators that we mentioned in Chapter 24, plus any other identifiers defined to be infix by the `infix` or `infixr` declarations that we also described in Chapter 24.

5. *Type variables* (TYVAR). These are identifiers that begin with an apostrophe and stand for types.

6. *Integers* (INT). There is a context where only an integer constant is permitted, and we indicate that constraint by the class INT.

Some Simplifications to the Grammatical Structure

To eliminate some of the complexity in describing the syntactic structure of ML, we begin by listing some understandings about identifiers. These modifications to the possible forms of identifiers will then be omitted from the grammatical description throughout this chapter.

Long identifier

1. An identifier that comes from a structure may have that structure name placed in front of it, separated by a dot, as described in Chapter 14. For example, the function `insert` from structure `Tree` could be referred to as `Tree.insert`. We shall continue to refer to such identifiers, called *long* identifiers in the formal description of ML simply as "identifiers."

2. An infix identifier can be made to have the syntax of a normal function application by preceding it by the keyword `op` as mentioned in Chapters 11 and 24. The use of `op` binds tighter than any other symbol, so it applies only to the identifier that follows. We shall speak only of identifiers in what follows; the reader should understand that if it makes sense to do so, the identifier may be preceded by `op`.

3. An identifier, expression, or pattern can be followed by a colon and a type. This colon acts like an infix operator, but its precedence is lower than that of any of the operators listed in Fig. 24.1. It is, however, higher than the precedence of `andalso` or `orelse` or of other keywords that appear in expressions. Thus, for example, `x+y:int` is grouped `(x+y):int`, but `x andalso y:bool` is grouped `x andalso (y:bool)`.[1]

Expressions

Figure 26.1 presents the grammatical diagram for expressions (EXP) in ML. As a general convention, we list the alternative forms for a syntactic category in order of highest precedence first, from the top of the diagram. Since many of the forms are more complex than infix operators applied to two expressions, the notion of precedence is not precise. However, as a rule, to parse an expression, we form the subexpressions of the higher paths in the diagram before the lower paths.

◇ **Example 26.1.** Because the expression form EXP `orelse` EXP is above the form `while` EXP `do` EXP in Fig. 26.1, we group an expression like

$$\text{while } E_1 \text{ do } E_2 \text{ orelse } E_3$$

as

$$\text{while } E_1 \text{ do } (E_2 \text{ orelse } E_3)$$

not

$$(\text{while } E_1 \text{ do } E_2) \text{ orelse } E_3. \quad \square$$

The paths through the diagram of Fig. 26.1 represent the following forms of expressions, from top to bottom of the diagram. The numbers in the following enumeration are keyed to path numbers along the left edge of Fig. 26.1.

---

[1] Note, however, that in these examples ML can infer the types of x and y regardless of how the grouping is done.

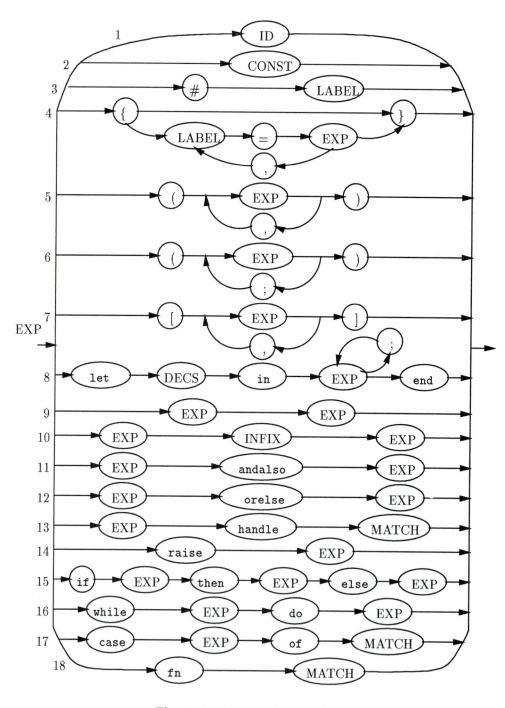

Fig. 26.1. Structure of expressions.

1. An identifier.

2. A constant.

3. A label preceded by a pound sign. This type of expression produces a record selector, which is a function for extracting the value of the field with this label from records as discussed in Chapter 18.

4. A record, consisting of curly brackets surrounding zero or more fields, each consisting of a label, an equal sign, and an expression. The fields are separated by commas. Record expressions were discussed in Chapter 18.

5. A parenthesized, comma-separated list of expressions, representing a tuple. As a special case, if there is only one expression in the list, then we have an ordinary parenthesized expression, rather than a tuple. Tuples were discussed in Chapter 4.

6. A parenthesized semicolon-separated list of expressions, which is a sequence of "statements" as discussed in Chapter 9.

7. A comma-separated list of expressions, surrounded by square brackets. These are list-expressions as discussed in Chapter 4.

8. A let-expression, consisting of the keyword **let**, a DECS — that is, a list of declarations of a form to be described later — the keyword **in**, a semicolon-separated list of expressions, and the keyword **end**. The form of this expression was introduced in Chapter 7, but the most general form is as given in Fig. 26.1.

9. A pair of expressions, juxtaposed with no intervening symbol. This form represents function application. The first expression must denote a function, and the second is its argument. Recall all ML functions have only one argument, although this argument may be a tuple (i.e., of form 5 described above).

10. Two expressions separated by an infix operator. This form represents the "main sequence" of operators that appeared in Fig. 24.1, along with any other identifiers declared to be infix operators.

11. Two expressions separated by the operator **andalso**.

12. Two expressions separated by the operator **orelse**.

13. An expression, followed by the keyword **handle** followed by a MATCH. The meaning of this expression form, whereby we "handle" an exception, was described in Chapter 20. We shall give the grammar for the syntactic category MATCH next, but the intuitive structure was described in Chapter 19.

14. An expression preceded by the keyword **raise**, which is an expression that raises an exception. The value of the expression following **raise** must evaluate to an exception as discussed in Chapter 8.

15. An if-then-else expression as described in Chapter 1.

16. A while-do expression as described in Chapter 17.

17. A case-expression as described in Chapter 19.

18. The keyword **fn** followed by a MATCH. The result is a value that is a function as discussed in Chapters 11 and 19.

Matches and Patterns

We discussed the notion of a match in Chapter 19. Its formal structure is described by the lower diagram of Fig. 26.2. A match consists of one or more groups of the form PAT => EXP, where PAT is a pattern and EXP is an expression. Each group is separated from the next by a vertical bar.

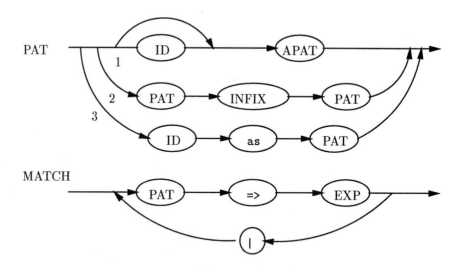

Fig. 26.2. Structure of matches and patterns.

Atomic pattern   The syntactic category PAT is defined recursively with the related syntactic category APAT, or *atomic pattern*. We see from the upper diagram in Fig. 26.2 that a PAT has one of the following three forms, keyed to the numbers of the paths in that diagram.

1.   An atomic pattern optionally preceded by an identifier. This form represents any atomic pattern as defined in Fig. 26.3. It also represents a data or exception constructor preceding an atomic pattern. For example, if `Node` is a data constructor that takes two arguments, then `Node(t1,t2)` is a pattern. Here, `(t1,t2)` is an atomic pattern and `node` is a single identifier preceding this atomic pattern.

2.   Two patterns connected by an infix operator. Most of the common infix operators, such as arithmetic or comparison operators, cannot appear in patterns because they make no sense. However, the infix operator could be `::`, and as we have seen, patterns like `x::xs` are very common. It could also be a data or exception constructor that has been defined to be an infix operator.

3.   An identifier `x` followed by keyword `as` and a pattern P says that identifier `x` must be bound to any value matched by the pattern P. The pattern P is interpreted according to the rules for PAT.

Atomic patterns include most of the pattern forms we have seen. Note that a PAT can be an APAT, and an APAT can be a parenthesized PAT, so the only real difference between the two is in the use of parentheses that they require. Here are the forms of atomic pattern, in order of highest precedence. The numbers of the forms are keyed to the numbers on the diagram of Fig. 26.3.

1.   An identifier, which matches anything.

2.   A constant, which matches only itself.

3.   The wildcard symbol _ that matches anything. The difference between an identifier and the wildcard is that the latter cannot be referred to elsewhere, and every use of the wildcard represents a different, anonymous identifier.

4.   A list of one or more patterns separated by commas and surrounded by parentheses. This form represents a tuple pattern. In the special case that there is one pattern only, it is simply a parenthesized pattern.

5.   A list of zero or more patterns separated by commas and surrounded by square brackets. This form represents a list pattern.

6.   A comma-separated list of one or more elements, surrounded by curly braces. This form of pattern is a record pattern. Each element represents a field in one of two forms. The usual form is LABEL = PAT, that is, a label representing a field, followed by the pattern that the value of this field must match. Another possible form is a single identifier. Recall from Chapter 18 that identifier `x` in this context stands for `x=x`; that is, `x` is both the label and the variable that is the pattern. Finally, an identifier `x` followed by keyword `as` and a pattern says that `x` is both the field name and the pattern. However, the pattern following `as` is another pattern that the field value must match. We also see from the complicated sixth group

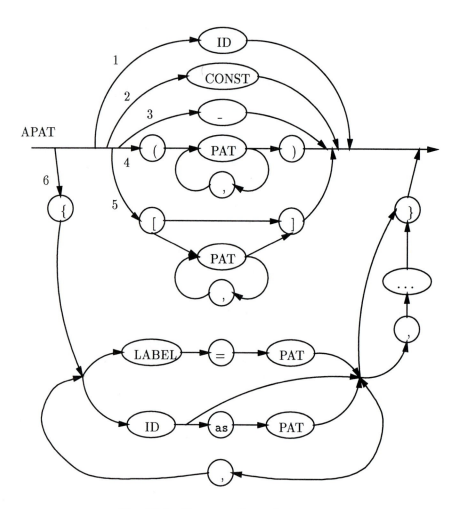

Fig. 26.3. Structure of atomic patterns.

of paths in Fig. 26.3 that this list of elements may optionally be followed by a comma and the wildcard for fields .... .

Types

Another essential element of ML programs is an expression that denotes a type. Types can be concrete like **int**, or polymorphic like **'a list**. ML has ten predefined types:

1. **bool**, a Boolean. This type is actually a datatype with the data constructors **true** and **false**.

2. **int**, an integer.

3.   **real**, a real number.

4.   **string**, a character string.

5.   **list**, the datatype defining lists. Note that this datatype has two data constructors, **nil** and **::**. It could be defined as

      ```
      datatype 'a list = nil | :: of 'a * 'a list;
      ```

      although we must then define **::** to be an infix operator.

6.   **ref**, a reference, as described in Chapter 17.

7.   **exn**, an exception.

8.   **instream**, a file or other data source opened for input, as discussed in Chapters 9 and 22.

9.   **outstream**, a file or other data source opened for output, as discussed in Chapter 22.

10.   **unit**, the value **()**, as discussed in Chapter 1.

Note that SML/NJ defines certain other types through the structure mechanism. Examples are the array discussed in Chapter 16 and several other structures described in Chapter 25.

From these types we can build arbitrarily complex types, using the recursive grammatical structure of Fig. 26.4. The forms of a type expression are as follows, from highest to lowest precedence. Again, the numbers below are keyed to the numbers on paths in Fig. 26.4.

1.   A type variable, that is, an identifier beginning with an apostrophe.

2.   A record type consisting of a comma-separated list of elements, surrounded by curly brackets. Each element defines the type of a field. The field name, a LABEL, is followed by a colon and the type expression describing the field.

3.   An identifier, which is a type constructor, optionally preceded by one or more type expressions. If there are two or more preceding type expressions, they must be surrounded by parentheses. If there is only one type expression, the parentheses are optional. This form includes concrete types like **int**, where the identifier (**int**) is not preceded by any type expressions. It also includes forms like **'a list**, **('a) list**, and **(int, real) mapping**.

4.   Two types separated by *****'s. This form represents product types. Recall that grouping of components of tuples is significant. For instance, a type like **int * int * int** should not be confused with **(int * int) * int**. We can create either form by using rules (4) and (6) in the proper order. Rule (6) introduces the needed parentheses.

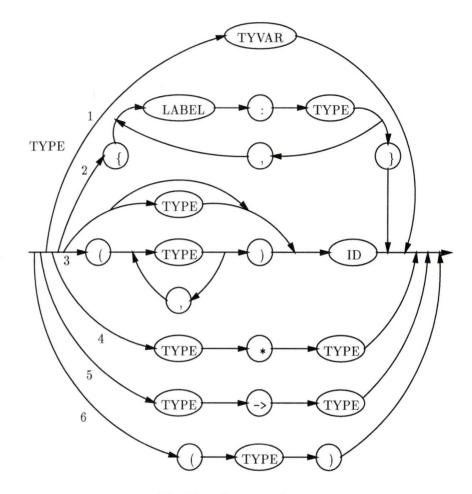

Fig. 26.4. Structure of types.

5. Two types separated by the operator ->. This form represents function construction; it defines a type that is a function from the first type to the second. Recall that -> is right-associative. Also, * takes precedence over ->, as we can infer from the fact that the path for * is above the path for -> in Fig. 26.4.

6. A parenthesized type.

Declarations

Value binding   Let us now take up the structure of declarations in ML. Because this structure is complex, we shall first look at three important kinds of *value bindings* defined in ML. In general, a value binding is an expression that describes a particular value. A value binding is preceded by a keyword such as **val** to form a declaration.

In Fig. 26.5 we see the diagrams for the three most complex forms of value bindings; simpler forms are included in Fig. 26.6, where we define the syntactic category DEC of declarations.

Type binding

Type bindings (TBIND) must be preceded by the keyword `type` to define a new type. The simplest form of binding consists of an identifier (the name of the new type), an equal sign, and a type expression. An example is `ilist = int list`. Here, `ilist` is the ID, and `int list` is the type expression.

Optionally, a type binding can have one or more type variables as parameters preceding the identifier that names the type. Two or more type variables must be surrounded by parentheses, although parentheses are optional for a single type variable. Additionally, a type binding may be a sequence of type bindings of the above forms, separated by the keyword `and`. This structure is shown in the first diagram of Fig. 26.5.

datatype binding

Datatype bindings (DTBIND) are preceded by the keyword `datatype` or `abstype` to describe a datatype. The informal description of this ML feature is in Chapter 12. The simplest form consists of an identifier, the name of the datatype, and an equal-sign, followed by one or more elements separated by vertical bars. Each element defines a data constructor for this datatype and is an ID optionally followed by the keyword `of` and a type expression. Here, the ID is the data constructor, and the TYPE describes the type of the values to which the constructor is applied.

◇ **Example 26.2.** The binding `tree = Leaf | Node of tree * tree` is of this form. Here, `tree` is the datatype name, and `Leaf` and `Node` are two data constructors. The latter has an optional `of` followed by the type of nodes, which is a pair of trees. □

However, datatype bindings may be preceded by one or more type variables as parameters. The form of these parameters is the same as for type bindings; parentheses around one type variable are optional, but they are required for two or more type variables. Finally, it is also possible for a datatype binding to be several datatype bindings of the type described above, separated by keyword `and`. The structure of datatype bindings is shown in the second diagram of Fig. 26.5.

Function binding

The third kind of binding in Fig. 26.5 is the *function binding*. This form follows the keyword `fun`. The binding for a single function consists of one or more groups separated by `|`. In each group is an ID (the function name), followed by one or more atomic patterns, an equal-sign, and an expression.

The atomic patterns are the arguments of the function. It is common for there to be only one atomic pattern and for this atomic pattern to be a parenthesized pattern representing all the arguments of the function. However, as discussed in Chapter 21, it is possible to write a function definition in Curried form, where the function name is followed by each of its arguments with no

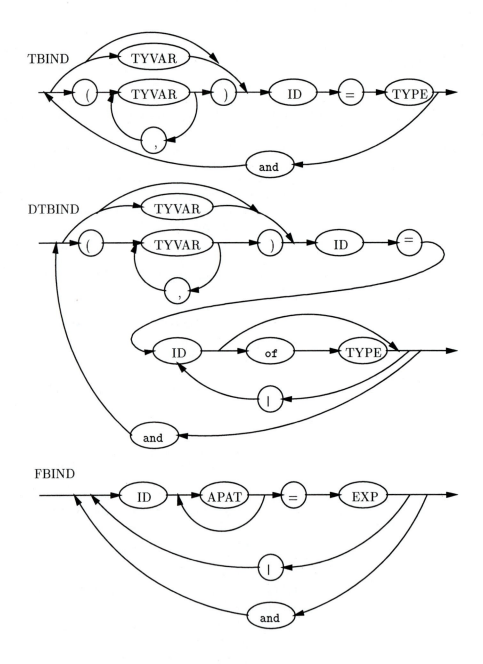

Fig. 26.5. Three kinds of value bindings.

parentheses or commas. In this case, each argument is an atomic pattern by itself.

Following the atomic patterns is the equal sign and an expression. The expression is the definition of the function for arguments that match the given pattern.

The groups separated by | form the definition of one function, and the name of this function must be the ID in each group. However, several functions may be defined in one function binding, and if so, these definitions are separated by **and**.

In Fig. 26.6 is the structure diagram for declarations (DEC). This syntactic category is mutually recursive with the category DECS, or list of declarations, which has the simple definition shown in Fig. 26.7. That is, a list of declarations is zero or more declarations separated by optional semicolons. (Nothing separates declarations if the semicolon is not there.)

The forms of declarations given in Fig. 26.6 are as follows. Again, the numbers below are keyed to the numbers on the paths of Fig. 26.6.

1. *Value declarations.* The keyword **val** is followed by a pattern, an equal-sign, and an expression. This declaration binds the variables appearing in the pattern to whatever values they acquire by matching the pattern with the expression in the manner described in Chapter 6. Several value bindings can be made with one val-declaration if they are separated by **and**. Also, the word **rec** (recursive) optionally may appear after **val**; it is essential if one or more of the values are recursive functions.

2. *Function declarations.* The keyword **fun** is followed by a function binding. The latter is the structure just described in connection with the third diagram of Fig. 26.5.

3. *Type declarations.* The keyword **type** is followed by a type binding. The latter was described in connection with the first diagram of Fig. 26.5.

4. *Datatype declarations.* The keyword **datatype** is followed by a datatype binding as described in connection with the second diagram of Fig. 26.5. This binding optionally may be followed by the keyword **withtype** and a type binding. The latter clause, which we have not previously discussed, allows us to define some types as abbreviations and use them in the definition of the datatype itself. For example, the following datatype has values consisting of one or two string-integer pairs, and we use the type **pair** as an abbreviation for **string * int**.

    withtype

```
datatype oneOrTwoPairs = One of pair |
        Two of pair * pair
withtype pair = string * int;
```

5. *Abstract type declarations.* The keyword **abstype** is followed by a datatype binding and an optional withtype-clause, just as for datatype declarations

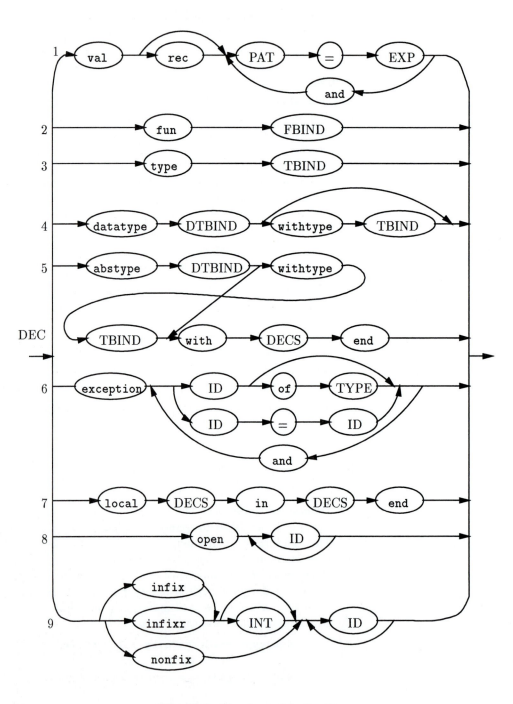

Fig. 26.6. Structure of declarations.

described in (4) above. Recall that the abstract type, described in Chapter 14, is like a datatype but with the possibility that functions on this type are used to encapsulate the type. These functions are defined following the datatype definition. They are preceded by the keyword **with** and followed by **end**.

6. *Exception declarations.* The keyword **exception** is followed by the declaration of one or more exceptions. The simplest form of an exception binding is an identifier, which becomes the name of the exception. We can also add the keyword **of** and a type expression to give the exception a parameter of a particular type. Another form of exception binding is ID = ID, where the first identifier is defined to be a synonym for the second identifier, which must be an exception. There is occasional purpose to this definition because the scopes of the two identifiers may be different as discussed in Chapter 20. Finally, several exception bindings may be connected by **and**.

7. *Local declarations.* The keyword **local** is followed by some declarations, the keyword **in**, more declarations, and the keyword **end**. As discussed in Chapter 15, this construct allows information hiding.

8. *Structure opening.* The keyword **open** is followed by one or more names of structures that are opened. Opened structures allow their identifiers to be used without the dot notation as discussed in Chapter 14.

9. *Fixity declarations.* An identifier can be declared to be an infix operator, associating from the left or right, by the keywords **infix** and **infixr**, respectively. An integer precedence level is optionally specified after either of these keywords. We can also remove the infix property by the keyword **nonfix**.

Figure 26.7 gives the definition of the syntactic category DECS in terms of DEC. As we see, DECS are one or more declarations, with optional semicolons separating them.

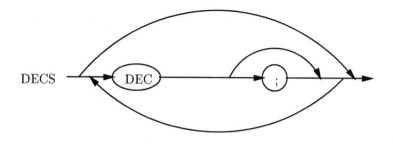

Fig. 26.7. Structure of a declaration list.

Signatures

The signature is a description of the form of a structure; both structures and signatures were introduced in Chapter 14. A signature is essentially a list of *specifications* (SPEC's). Each specification (SPEC) has one of the forms shown in Fig. 26.8. Many specifications describe an identifier, perhaps a function or a datatype, that are part of a structure with this signature.

The possible forms of a specification are the following. They appear from top to bottom in the diagram of Fig. 26.8, keyed as usual to the numbers of the paths in the diagram.

1. *Variable descriptions.* The keyword **val** followed by one or more groups, separated by **and**. Each group describes the type of one identifier, and the form of a group is ID : TYPE.

2. *Type descriptions.* One of the keywords **type** or **eqtype** is followed by an identifier that is the name of some type. If **eqtype** is used, then in the structure described, this type must be an equality type (one that allows tests for equality between values; see Chapter 10). The type may be polymorphic, in which case it will be preceded by one or more type variables. If there is more than one type variable, the list of type variables must be surrounded by parentheses. Several types may be specified at once if they are separated by **and**.

3. *Datatype descriptions.* The keyword **datatype** is followed by a datatype binding, an expression whose form is given by the DTBIND diagram in Fig. 26.5.

4. *Exception descriptions.* The keyword **exception** is followed by one or more identifiers that are the names of exceptions. The identifiers are separated by **and**, and each has an optional **of** TYPE clause describing the type of its argument.

5. *Substructure descriptions.* A signature can specify that one of the elements of a described structure is another structure. This specification consists of the keyword **structure**, the name of the nested structure, a colon, and the signature of the nested structure. Several structures may be specified at once if their descriptions are separated by **and**.

6. *Sharings.* A signature may specify that certain of its identifiers must refer to the same thing in any structure described by this signature. This specification consists of the keyword **sharing**, the optional keyword **type** (used if the identifiers being equated are the names of types), and a list of two or more identifiers separated by equal-signs. The identifiers in this list are asserted to stand for the same substructure or type.

7. *local specifications.* For information hiding, some specifications may be local, indicated by a **local-in-end** construct.

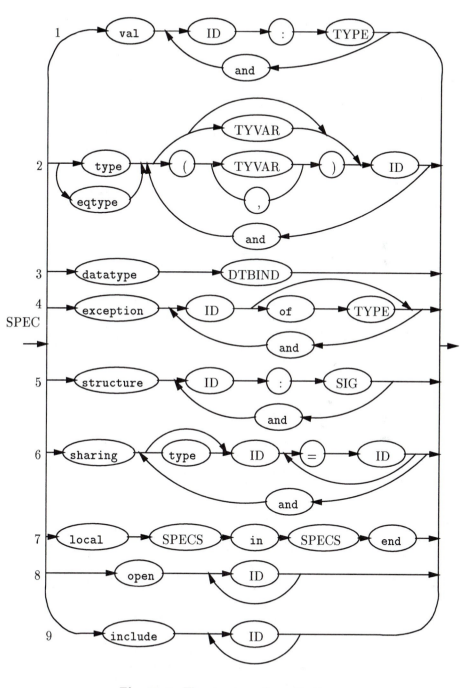

Fig. 26.8. The structure of specifications.

8. *Opening of structures.* In a list of specifications we can open one or more structures to make their identifiers available. The syntax is the keyword **open**, followed by the structure names.

include

9. *Inclusion of other signatures.* With the keyword **include**, followed by a list of identifiers that are the names of signatures, we can include within one signature the specifications of others.

Figure 26.9 completes the grammatical structure of signatures. The diagram for SPECS indicates that a list of specifications is zero or more specifications (SPEC), optionally terminated by semicolons.

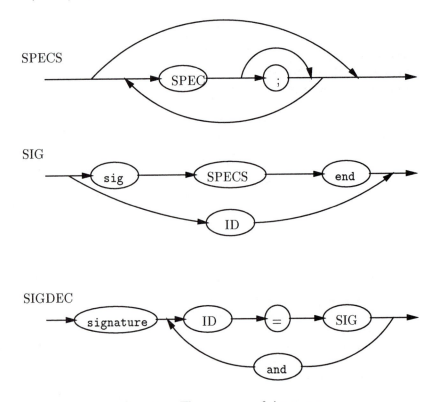

Fig. 26.9. The structure of signatures.

The syntactic category SIG (signature) is shown in the second diagram of Fig. 26.9 to be of one of two forms. Either it is a list of specifications surrounded by the keywords **sig** and **end**, or it is an identifier that has previously been declared to be a signature using a "signature declaration," which will be described next.

Signature declaration   In the last diagram of Fig. 26.9 we see the structure of a *signature declaration* (SIGDEC). It consists of one or more groups separated by **and**. Each group equates an identifier to a signature; that signature can either be described explicitly by **sig**-SPECS-**end** or by a name, as we saw when we examined the middle diagram, for SIG, in Fig. 26.9.

Structures

We also studied in Chapter 14 the notion of a structure, which is the actual description of the collection of types, functions, and other elements whose general form is specified by a signature. The syntax for structures is found in Fig. 26.10. There are three mutually recursive syntactic categories:

a)   STRUCT, a structure analogous to SIG for signatures,

b)   STRDEC, a structure declaration analogous to a combination of SPEC and SIGDEC for signatures, and

c)   STRDECS, a list of structure declarations analogous to SIGDECS for signatures.

In the first diagram of Fig. 26.10 we see the four possible forms of a structure.

1.   Zero or more structure declarations surrounded by keywords **struct** and **end**. This form is the common, explicit way to describe a structure.

2.   An identifier that has previously been defined to be the name of a structure.

3.   A functor application as was described in Chapter 14. This form consists of an identifier — the functor name — and a parenthesized argument for the functor. The argument of a functor may be a single structure, following the simple form as in Example 14.11. Alternatively, the argument may be zero or more structure declarations, using the more general form illustrated by Example 14.13.

4.   A structure defined with the help of some local definitions, using the **let-in-end** construct.

Now let us consider the form of a structure declaration (STRDEC), as in the second diagram of Fig. 26.10. One common form of a declaration within a structure is a DEC, that is, one of the ordinary kinds of declaration that were described in the diagram of Fig. 26.6. This form is the middle path of the middle diagram.

The upper path describes the declaration of a structure, which is not among the "ordinary" declarations of Fig. 26.6. This type of declaration consists of the keyword **structure**, an identifier (the name of the structure), an optional colon and signature describing the structure, an equal-sign, and the structure itself. The lower path in the second diagram describes the possibility of using some local declarations to help make a structure declaration using the **local-in-end** construct.

The third diagram in Fig. 26.10 defines the syntactic category STRDECS. These are zero or more structure declarations separated by optional semicolons.

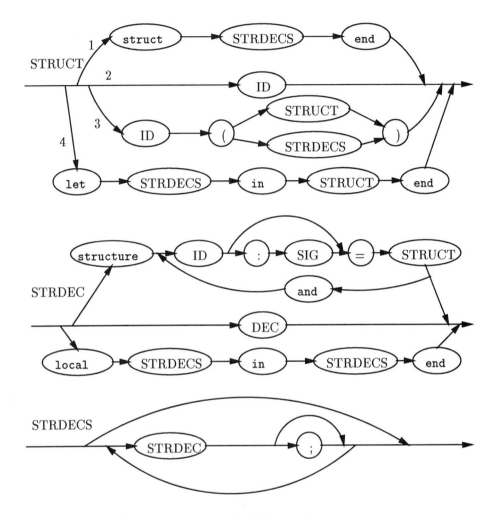

Fig. 26.10. Grammatical diagrams for structures.

Functors

Figure 26.11 gives the form of a functor declaration (FUNDEC). It consists of the keyword `functor` followed by one or more groups, separated by **and**. Each group defines a functor by the elements:

a)   An identifier, the functor name.

b)   A parameter for the functor, surrounded by parentheses. A functor parameter may have the simple form of a structure name, a colon, and a signature. For example, this form was illustrated in line (1) of Fig. 14.6. The more general form of functor parameter is a list of zero or more specifications; these are the elements used in signatures. We saw some examples

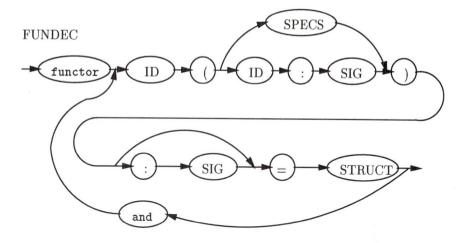

Fig. 26.11. The structure of functors.

of this type of functor parameter in Example 14.12.

c) An optional colon and a signature describing the structure that is the result of applying the functor.

d) An equal sign and a structure. This structure is the expression that describes the result of the functor in terms of the argument of the functor.

Modules

A *module* is a separately compilable piece of ML code. Its form is shown in the lower diagram of Fig. 26.12. Normally, it is a semicolon-separated sequence of declarations of functors, structures, and signatures. Note that STRDEC includes DEC as a special case, so ordinary declarations are included among the options.

Functor specification

However, there is a fourth type of element, called a *functor specification* (FUNSPEC). Its syntax is shown in the second diagram of Fig. 26.12; it is similar to the simple form of a FUNDEC. However, at the end we do not have the "= STRUCT" that actually defines the result of applying the functor. FUNSPEC's are used to describe externally defined functors, giving just enough information to allow compilation to occur. They can be viewed as a more complex version of **extern** declarations in C.

Programs

Finally, the structure of a program is given by Fig. 26.13. A program is a list of declarations of functors, structures, and signatures. The elements of this list are separated by optional semicolons. Note again that common declarations — of functions, datatypes, and so on — are included in the syntactic category

FUNSPEC

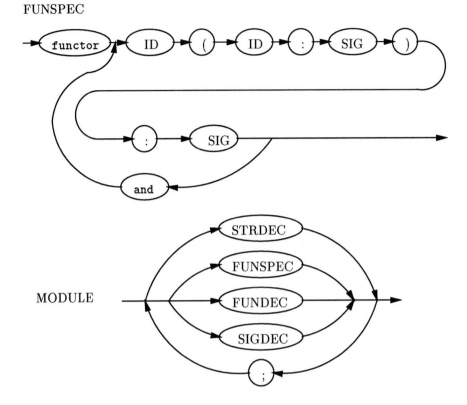

MODULE

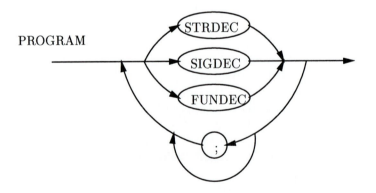

Fig. 26.12. The structure of modules.

PROGRAM

Fig. 26.13. The structure of programs.

STRDEC, so all the usual kinds of ML program elements are included in the diagram of Fig. 26.13.

The reader may note that expressions, which are a common example of a program element when we write code at the top level, appears to be missing. In practice, the ML compiler turns an expression E at the top level into the declaration

```
val it = E;
```

Thus, expressions are included as a special kind of STRDEC. This convention also explains why the value of identifier `it` is given in the ML response to an expression.

Solutions to Selected Exercises

Solutions for Chapter 1

1.1a: *val it = 7 : int*

1.1c: *val it = 2 : int.* We group operators from the left, so we first compute `11 div 2`, or 5, and then compute `5 mod 3`, which is 2.

1.1e: *val it = false : bool.* The `andalso` groups its operands before `orelse`. Thus, the whole expression is grouped

```
3>4 orelse (5<6 andalso (not 7<>8))
```

We begin by evaluating the left operand of the outermost operator, `orelse`. That operand `3>4` is false, so we must evaluate the right operand,

```
5<6 andalso (not 7<>8)
```

The left operand `5<6` is true, so we consider the right operand: `not 7<>8`. Since `7<>8` is true, `not 7<>8` is false, and the result of the `andalso` is false. Thus, both operands of the `orelse` are false and the entire expression is false.

1.2a: The `/` operator applies only to reals, not integers. Use `div` instead.

1.2c: The `and` operator has a meaning not discussed in Chapter 1; it cannot be applied to Boolean values. Use `andalso`.

1.2e: A real number needs to have digits both before and after the decimal point. Instead of `4.`, use `4.0`.

1.3: There are many ways to break the string. Here is one:

```
"\t\"\\\\\\\" stands for the double-quote \
\character, \\\n\t\\which otherwise \
\would be interpreted \\\n\t\\as the \
\string ender.\""
```

If you didn't "get this," now that you see the tricks, try creating a string that will print the four displayed lines above.

Solutions for Chapter 2

2.1a: `floor(123.45)` or `truncate(123.45)`.

280

2.1d: `ceiling(~123.45)` or `truncate(~123.45)`.

2.1e: `ord("Y")`.

2.1g: `real(ord("N"))`.

2.2a: The function `ceiling` requires a real argument, e.g. `ceiling(4.0)`.

2.2c: The argument of `chr` must be in the range 0 to 255. Thus, 256 is not an acceptable argument. It is not clear how to "fix" the expression, since there is no obvious intent.

2.2e: Function `ord` must take a character string as an argument. It converts the first character while ignoring others. Perhaps `ord("3")` was meant. The result would be 51, the ASCII code for the character `"3"`.

Solutions for Chapter 3

3.1a: An alphanumeric identifier suitable for "ordinary" values.

3.1c: Comma is not permitted in an identifier of any sort.

3.1e: The characters of alphanumeric and symbolic identifiers may not be combined in a single identifier. `a<=b` is interpreted as the sequence of three identifiers: `a`, `<=`, and `b`. The first and third are alphanumeric identifiers. The second is the identifier of the comparison operator "less than or equal to" that is part of the top-level environment.

3.1g: `#1` is not an identifier since it combines characters of symbolic and alphanumeric classes.

Solutions for Chapter 4

4.1a: 4

4.1c: `[4,5]`

4.1e: `"foobar"`

4.1g: `["c","o","b","o","l"]`

4.2a: There is no fourth component. The number following the `#` must be 1, 2, or 3.

4.2c: `(1)` is not a tuple; it is an integer. The component-extraction operator `#` does not apply to integers, so an error results.

4.2e: `implode` applies only to lists; here the argument is a tuple. Perhaps `implode(["a","b"])` was meant.

4.2g: The operator `@` applies to lists, not integers. Perhaps `[1]@[2]` was intended.

4.3a: `real * (string * (int list))`. This expression is the type for a pair whose first component is an integer and whose second component is a pair consisting of a string and a list of integers.

4.3c: `(int * real) list`. This expression is the type of a list of pairs. The first component of the pair is an integer and the second component is a real.

4.4: `(1,2)` and `(1,2,3)` are not the same type. The first is of type `int * int` and the second is of type `int * int * int`. However, `[1,2]` and `[1,2,3]` are of the same type, `int list`.

4.5a: `[[[1,2],[3,4]], [[5,6],[7,8]]]`

4.5c: `(["a","b"], (1,(2.5,"c")), 3)`

Solutions for Chapter 5

5.1a:

```
fun cube(x:real) = x*x*x;
```

5.1c:

```
fun third(L) = hd(tl(tl(L)));
```

5.1e:

```
fun thirdChar(s) = third(explode(s));
```

5.2a:

```
fun fact(n) =
        if n<=1 then 1 else n*fact(n-1);
```

5.2c:

```
fun duplicate(L) =
    if L=nil then nil else hd(L)::hd(L)::duplicate(tl(L));
```

5.2e: The function defined in Fig. S1 will serve. There are considerably simpler ways to solve this problem if we use the let-construct described in Chapter 7.

5.3: In the second line we have expression $c + 1$. Since 1 is an integer, c must also be an integer. In the third line, the expressions following the **then** and **else** must be of the same type. One of these is c, so the type of both is integer. Thus, expression $b+d$ is of integer type. Therefore b and d must also be integers. Finally, since a and b are compared on lines 2 and 3, they must be of the same type. Hence a is also an integer.

5.5a:

```
fun round(x) = real(floor(x+0.5));
```

```
fun maxList(L: real list) =
    if tl(L)=nil (* L is a single element *)
        then hd(L) (* the single element is the maximum *)
        else (* assume there are at least 2 elements *)
            if hd(L)>hd(tl(L)) (* the first element
                    exceeds the second *)
                then maxList(hd(L)::tl(tl(L))) (* eliminate
                        second element *)
                else maxList(tl(L)) (* eliminate first
                        element *);
```

Fig. S1. Solution to Exercise 5.2(e).

Solutions for Chapter 6

6.1a: The solution is almost like padd in Fig. 6.2. However, when the first polynomial is empty and the second is not, we need to negate each of the coefficients of the second polynomial to produce the answer. Thus, in place of the simple line (2) of Fig. 6.2 we have a recursion that negates the first component and recursively negates the elements of the tail of the second polynomial. The code is as follows:

```
fun diff(P,nil) = P
  | diff(nil,q::qs) = ~q::diff(nil,qs)
  | diff((p:real)::ps, q::qs) = (p-q)::diff(ps,qs);
```

6.1c: If the list of roots is empty, the polynomial 1, represented by the list [1.0], is appropriate. If the list is not empty, then let p be the first root. We may recursively construct the polynomial for the rest of the roots and multiply it by $x - p$, or in list representation [~p,1.0]. The following lines implement this idea.

```
fun polyFromRoots(nil) = [1.0]
  | polyFromRoots(p::ps) =
        pmult([~p,1.0],polyFromRoots(ps));
```

6.2a: Yes; x="a", y="b", zs=["c"], and w=["d","e"].

6.2c: No; the expression y::zs in the pattern is forced to match nil in the expression. We fail, since constant symbols :: and nil cannot be matched. Put another way, the first component of the pair has to be a list of length at least 2 in order to match the pattern x::y::zs.

6.5:

```
fun square(0) = 0
  | square(n) = square(n-1)+2*n-1;
```

6.7:

```
fun flip(nil) = nil
  | flip((x as (a:int,b))::xs) =
        if a<b then x::flip(xs) else (b,a)::flip(xs);
```

6.10a: We first check to see whether the set S is empty, that is, whether the list is `nil`. If so, x is not in S. If not, then we compare x with the head of the list. If the head equals x, then x is in S. Otherwise, we recursively test whether x is in the tail of the list.

```
fun member(_,nil) = false
  | member(x,y::ys) = (x=y orelse member(x,ys));
```

We might be tempted to replace the second line by

```
  | member(x,x::xs) = true
  | member(x,_::xs) = member(x,xs);
```

However, it is not permitted to use an identifier like **x** twice in one pattern.

6.10c:

```
fun insert(x,nil) = [x]
  | insert(x,S as y::ys) =
        if x=y then S else y::insert(x,ys);
```

6.11, 6.12: The solutions are in Fig. S2. Function `insertAll`, the solution to Exercise 6.11, uses as an inductive step the idea that we can insert a onto the front of the first list L. Then we recursively insert a onto each of the remaining lists, which is the list of lists Ls.

```
fun insertAll(a,nil) = nil
  | insertAll(a,L::Ls) = (a::L)::insertAll(a,Ls);

fun powerSet(nil) = [nil]
  | powerSet(x::xs) =
        powerSet(xs)@insertAll(x,powerSet(xs));
```

Fig. S2. Solution to Exercises 6.11 and 6.12.

Then we compute the power set as follows. For a basis, the power set of the empty set is the set containing the empty set. The latter is represented by the list `[nil]`, as in the first line of function `powerSet` in Fig. S2. If the given list is not empty, we take the first element x, compute the power set of the remaining elements, and concatenate this list with the list of all sets with x added. Thus, all the sets that have x and those that do not are included in the overall list. Incidentally, there is a better way to write this function that does not require us to compute powerSet(xs) twice. However, we do not discuss the needed construct, the "let"-expression, until the next chapter.

6.13:

```
fun prodDiff1(_,nil) = 1.0
  | prodDiff1(a,b::bs) = (a-b)*prodDiff1(a,bs);

fun prodDiff(nil) = 1.0
  | prodDiff(b::bs) = prodDiff1(b,bs)*prodDiff(bs);
```

6.14:

```
fun emptyList(nil) = true
  | emptyList(_) = false;
```

Solutions for Chapter 7

7.1: The function in Fig. S3 is about as succinct as can be managed.

```
fun thousandthPower(x) =
        let
            val x = x*x*x*x*x;
            val x = x*x*x*x*x;
            val x = x*x*x*x*x
        in
            x*x*x*x*x*x*x*x*x*x
        end;
```

Fig. S3. Solution to Exercise 7.1.

7.3: A solution is in Fig. S4. Function insertAll is from Fig. S2.

```
fun powerSet(nil) = [nil]
  | powerSet(x::xs) =
        let
            val L = powerSet(xs)
        in
            L @ insertAll(x,L)
        end;
```

Fig. S4. Solution to Exercise 7.3.

7.5: A solution is in Fig. S5. Note that we could have written the recursive case simply as

```
|   doubleExp(x,i) = doubleExp(x,i-1) * doubleExp(x,i-1);
```

However, it would take considerably more time to compute the function this way, as computations would then be repeated an exponential number of times.

```
fun doubleExp(x:real,0) = x
|   doubleExp(x,i) =
        let
            val y = doubleExp(x,i-1)
        in
            y*y
        end;
```

Fig. S5. Solution to Exercise 7.5.

Solutions for Chapter 8

8.1: A solution appears in Fig. S6.

```
exception Negative;

fun fact(0) = 1
|   fact(n) =
        if n>0 then n*fact(n-1)
        else raise Negative;
```

Fig. S6. Solution to Exercise 8.1.

8.3: A solution is in Fig. S7.

Solutions for Chapter 9

9.1: There is no type error. The value returned by the expression on line (3) of Fig. 9.2 is whatever `printList` returns on the tail of the given list. Thus, an easy induction on the length of the list shows that `printList` always returns 0. Another way to look at it is that the 0 in line (1) is the only concrete value ever produced by `printList`.

9.3: A solution is found in Fig. S8.

```
exception Unnormalizable;


exception Misshaped;


(* normalize(a,L) divides each element of list L by a *)
fun normalize(a,nil) = nil
|   normalize(a,r::rs) = r/a::normalize(a,rs);


(* condense1(b,L1,L2) subtracts from the jth element of L2
    b times the jth element of L1 for all j and produces
    the resulting L2 *)
fun condense1(b:real,nil,nil) = nil
|   condense1(b,x::xs,y::ys) = (y-b*x)::condense1(b,xs,ys)
|   condense1(_) = raise Misshaped (* one list is longer
            than the other *)


(* condense2(L,M) takes a list L and a list of lists M, and
    considers each list L' on M. For L', we subtract from
    each element in the tail of L' the product of the head
    of L' and the corresponding element of list L *)
fun condense2(L,nil) = nil
|   condense2(L,(x::xs)::Rs) =
            condense1(x,L,xs)::condense2(L,Rs);


(* condense(M) applies pivotal condensation to matrix M *)
fun condense([[a]]) = a
|   condense((0.0::_)::_) = raise Unnormalizable
            (* normalization impossible *)
|   condense((b::bs)::Rs) =
        let
            val L = normalize(b,bs);
            val M' = condense2(L,Rs)
        in
            b*condense(M')
        end
|   condense(_) = raise Misshaped; (* the number of rows
            does not equal the length of each row *)
```

Fig. S7. Solution to Exercise 8.3.

```
(* test if a character is white space *)
fun white(" ") = true
|   white("\t") = true
|   white("\n") = true
|   white(_) = false

fun getWord(file) = (* read one word *)
        if end_of_stream(file) then ""
        else
            let
                val c = input(file,1)
            in
                if white(c) then ""
                else c^getWord(file)
            end;

fun getList1(file) = (* read all words from an instream *)
        if end_of_stream(file) then nil
        else getWord(file) :: getList1(file);

(* read all words from a file given the file name *)
fun getList(filename) = getList1(open_in(filename));
```

Fig. S8. Solution to Exercise 9.3.

9.5: This version of function `white` appears at the top of Fig. S8.

Solutions for Chapter 10

10.1a: We have an error. Function `rev1` requires an equality type, and lists of functions are not of an equality type.

10.1c: This is a legal expression in ML and it produces the list `[rev2, rev1]` as an answer. The ML response to expression `rev2([rev1,rev2])` is actually

$$val\ it = [fn,\ fn]\ :\ (''a\ list \rightarrow ''a\ list)\ list$$

Notice what has happened. Function `rev1`, with the more restrictive type (`''a list → ''a list` versus `'a list → 'a list`), forces the type of the list elements to be the former.

10.2a: For (*i*), the expression `'a * 'a * int` is the only example. For (*ii*) there are many examples, such as `'a * real list * int`. For (*iii*) there are again numerous examples, of which (`'c * 'd list) * 'b * int` is one.

10.3a: `fun f(x,y,z) = (z(x)=y);`

10.3c:

```
fun f(nil,_,z) = z
|    f(x::xs,_,_) = x;
```

10.4a: Yes; it is constructed from basic types using the list and product-type mechanisms for constructing new equality types.

10.4c: No; the values of this type are functions. Incidently, note the domain type for these functions is integer and the range type is functions that take a real argument and produce the unit as value.

10.5a: True. Both sides have the value `[(1,2), (3,4)]`.

10.5c: True. Both sides have the same value as in Exercise 10.5(a).

Solutions for Chapter 11

11.1: A solution is in Fig. S9.

```
(* print a table with rows
           x+i*delta, F(x+i*delta)
 for i = 0, 1,...,n-1 *)
fun tabulate(x,delta,0,F) = ()
|   tabulate(x,delta,n,F) = (
        print(x:real);
        print("\t");
        print(F(x):real);
        print("\n");
        tabulate(x+delta,delta,n-1,F)
    );
```

Fig. S9. Solution to Exercise 11.1.

11.3a: A solution is found in Fig. S10. Note that the local function `trap1(x,i)` computes the area of the i trapezoids of width δ, starting at x.

11.5a: `map(fn(x)=>if x<0.0 then 0.0 else x, L);`

11.5c:

```
map(fn(c)=>if c>="a" andalso c<="z" then chr(ord(c)-32)
           else c,
    L);
```

11.6a: `reduce(fn(x,y)=> if x<y then y else x, L);`

```
fun trap(a,b,n,F) =
        if n<=0 orelse b-a<=0.0 then 0.0
        else
            let
                val delta = (b-a)/real(n);
                fun trap1(x,0) = 0.0
                |   trap1(x,i) = delta*(F(x)+F(x+delta))/2.0
                        + trap1(x+delta,i-1)
            in
                trap1(a,n)
            end;
```

Fig. S10. Solution to Exercise 11.3a.

11.6c: `reduce(op ^, L);`

11.7a: `filter(fn(x)=>x>0.0, L);`

11.7c: Here is a way to write a suitable anonymous function to do the job. Note the importance that the test for s="" is forced, by the **orelse**, to occur before the test that s does not begin with "a". If we could not rely on the order of the tests, we might accidently try to find the head of an empty list.

```
filter(fn(s)=>not(s="" orelse hd(explode(s))<>"a"), L);
```

Of course, one could define the desired test by a function with two patterns, such as:

```
fun init_a("") = false
|   init_a(s) = (hd(explode(s))="a");
```

11.9: The following code works by looking for the first two elements of the list (if they exist), applying F to them to form one element, and recursively reducing the list with the first two elements replaced by one.

```
exception EmptyList;

fun lreduce(F,nil) = raise EmptyList
|   lreduce(F,[x]) = x
|   lreduce(F,x::y::zs) = lreduce(F, F(x,y)::zs);
```

11.11:

```
fun reduceB(g,F,nil) = g
|   reduceB(g,F,x::xs) = F(x, reduceB(g,F,xs));
```

11.12a: `reduceB(0,fn(x,y)=>y+1, L);`

11.12b: `reduceB([nil],fn(x,y)=>(x::hd(y))::y, L);`. That is, we compute the suffixes of the tail of a list L. We then take the first of the resulting suffixes and make a copy of it to which the head of L is prepended. This new suffix is the longest possible suffix and is prepended to the list of suffixes of the tail.

11.16a:

```
fun eval(plus,times,[c],x) = c
|   eval(plus,times,c::cs,x) =
        plus(c,times(x,eval(plus,times,cs,x)));
```

11.16b:

```
eval(fn(x:int,y)=>x+y, fn(x:int,y)=>x*y, [1,2,3,4], 5);
```

Solutions for Chapter 12

12.1a: `type 'a setOfSets = 'a list list;`

12.2a: `Node(1, Node(2,Empty,Empty), Node(3,Empty,Empty))` is one possible answer.

12.3: Define the type by

```
type ('d, 'r) mapTree = ('d * 'r) btree;
```

Then, we can define the desired tree by

```
val t1 =
    Node(("a",1), Empty, Empty): (string, int) mapTree;
```

Note the subtle difference in the two steps. In the definition of **mapTree**, we use type `('d * 'r) btree`. That is, we use the * to construct a product type to refer to a btree with type variable **'label** replaced by the expression `'d * 'r`. In the construction of tree **t1**, the type is `(string, int) mapTree`, using the comma to separate the domain and range types. That is, the type `(string * int) btree` has become `(string, int) mapTree`. The reason for the difference is that **btree** takes a single type parameter, while **mapTree** was defined to take two type parameters.

12.5: A solution is found in Fig. S11. The strategy is similar to Fig. 9.8, and we have omitted the comments to save space. The only significant difference is the way **sumInts1** has become mutually recursive with a function **testEof** that tests whether the next "integer" is really **Eof** and returns 0 as a sum if so. If the end of file has not yet been reached, then we have a real integer, so it is added to the result of calling **sumInt1** on the remainder of the file. The effect of these two functions is the same as that of **sumInt1** alone in Fig. 9.8.

```
exception BadChar;

datatype intOrEof = Eof | Int of int;

fun white(c) = (c=" " orelse c="\n" orelse c="\t");

fun digit(c) = (c>="0" andalso c<="9");

fun startInt(file) =
        if end_of_stream(file) then Eof
        else let
                val c = input(file,1)
            in
                if digit(c) then Int(ord(c)-ord("0"))
                else if white(c) then startInt(file)
                else raise BadChar
            end;

fun finishInt(Eof,file) = Eof
|   finishInt(Int(i),file) =
    if end_of_stream(file) then Int(i)
    else let
            val c = input(file,1)
        in
            if digit(c) then
                finishInt(Int(10*i+ord(c)-ord("0")), file)
            else if white(c) then Int(i)
            else raise BadChar
        end;

fun getInt(file) =
        finishInt(startInt(file), file)

fun sumInts1(file) =
        testEof(getInt(file),file)
and
    testEof(Eof,file) = 0
    | testEof(Int(i),file) = i + sumInts1(file);

fun sumInts(filename) =
        sumInts1(open_in(filename));
```

Fig. S11. Solution to Exercise 12.5.

12.6a: We need a datatype that takes no type parameters, similar to the **fruit** datatype of Example 12.3. The appropriate declaration is

```
datatype suit = Club | Heart | Diamond | Spade;
```

12.6c: We need a recursive datatype with a basis data constructor, say **Int**, to wrap integers, and an inductive data constructor, say **Thing**, to wrap a list of things. An appropriate declaration is

```
datatype thing =
        Int of int |
        Thing of thing list
```

Here is a typical value of the datatype **thing**.

```
Thing([Int(1), Thing([Int(2)]), Int(3)]);
```

Solutions for Chapter 13

13.1a:

```
fun lookup(a:int,Empty) = raise Missing
  |   lookup(a,Node((b,c),left,right)) =
          if a=b then c
          else if a<b then lookup(a,left)
          else (* b<a *) lookup(a,right);
```

13.3: A solution is shown in Fig. S12. The strategy behind **search1** is a little tricky. First, if L is empty, then there is no more searching to be done. We return the list R of nodes already reached. If L is nonempty, look at the head element x. If x is already on R, we need not search from x. We delete x from L and recursively call **search1**. However, if x is not on R then we add x to R, replace x on L by the successors of x in G, and recursively call **search1**.

Incidentally, if the auxiliary functions **succ**, **member**, and **search1** are not needed for any other purpose, we can make them local to **search** by writing the latter function as in Fig. S13.

13.5:

```
fun nodeSum(node(a:int,L)) = a + listSum(L)
and
    listSum(nil) = nil
  | listSum(t::ts) = nodeSum(t) + listSum(ts);
```

13.6a: We can define the auxiliary function **preOrder1** as follows.

```
fun preOrder1(Empty,L) = L
  |   preOrder1(Node(a,left,right),L) =
          a::preOrder1(left,preOrder1(right,L));
```

```
type 'node graph = ('node * 'node list) list;

exception NotANode;

(* succ(a,G) looks up the list of successors of
   node a in graph G *)
fun succ(a,nil) = raise NotANode
|   succ(a,(b,L)::tail) =
       if a=b then L else succ(a,tail);

(* member(a,L) determines whether a is on list L *)
fun member(a,nil) = false
|   member(a,b::bs) =
       if a=b then true else member(a,bs);

(* search1(L,R,G) finds all the nodes reachable from any
   of the list of nodes L in graph G, but does not search
   from the set R of nodes that have already been reached.
   R is included in the set of reached nodes that is
   eventually returned. *)
fun search1(nil,R,G) = R
|   search1(x::xs,R,G) =
       if member(x,R) then search1(xs,R,G)
       else (* x is a new node, never before seen *)
           search1(succ(x,G)@xs, x::R, G);

(* search(a,G) finds the set of nodes reachable from
   a in graph G *)
fun search(a,G) = search1([a],nil,G);
```

Fig. S12. Solution to Exercise 13.3.

```
fun search(a,G) =
       let
           fun succ (* definition of succ *) ;
           fun member (* definition of member *) ;
           fun search1 (* definition of search1 *)
       in
           search1([a],nil,G)
       end;
```

Fig. S13. Making functions local.

If the tree is empty, list produce the list L. If the tree is not empty, call **pre-Order1** recursively on the right subtree and the given list L. This call produces the preorder listing of the right subtree ahead of L. Then call **preOrder1** a second time, with the left subtree and the list that resulted from the first call as arguments. Finally, attach the label of the root to the front of the resulting list. Notice that this step is the only one where lists actually grow, and it uses cons, not concatenation.

Then the function **preOrder** itself is defined in terms of **preOrder1** quite simply:

```
fun preOrder(T) = preOrder1(T,nil);
```

13.7a, 13.8a: The following function satisfies both conditions.

```
fun lookup(_,Empty,_) = false
|   lookup(x,Node(y,left,right),lt) =
        if lt(x,y) then lookup(x,left,lt)
        else if lt(y,x) then lookup(x,right,lt)
        else (* x must equal y *) true;
```

Its type is `'a * 'a btree * ('a * 'a -> bool) -> bool`.

Solutions for Chapter 14

14.1: A solution is in Fig. S14.

```
structure Tree = struct
    exception Missing;

    datatype 'label tree =
        Node of 'label * 'label tree list;

    (* create a one-node tree *)
    fun create(a) = Node(a,nil);

    (* build a tree from a label and a list of trees *)
    fun build(a,L) = Node(a,L);

    (* find the ith subtree of a tree *)
    fun subtree(i,Node(a,nil)) = raise Missing
    |   subtree(1,Node(a,t::ts)) = t
    |   subtree(i,Node(a,t::ts)) = subtree(i-1,Node(a,ts));
end;
```

Fig. S14. Solution to Exercise 14.1.

14.2: An appropriate signature is:

```
signature SIMPLE = sig
    exception Missing;
    datatype intTree =
        Node of int * intTree list;
    val build : int * intTree list -> intTree;
    val subtree : int * intTree -> intTree
end;
```

We can then use this signature to create the desired structure by

```
structure SimpleTree: SIMPLE = Tree;
```

14.3: Here is one possible sequence of steps.

```
open SimpleTree;
val t2 = build(2,nil);
val t3 = build(3,nil);
val t1 = build(4,nil);
val t4 = build(1,[t1,t2,t3]);
subtree(2,t4);
```

14.6: A solution appears in Fig. S15. Note that we have written `isEmpty` as we did, rather than the more succinct `fun isEmpty(Q) = (Q=nil)`, because by matching patterns we avoid the equality test and therefore allow the type of `Q` to be anything, even a non-equality type.

```
structure Queue = struct
    exception EmptyQueue;

    type 'a queue = 'a list;

    val create = nil;

    fun enqueue(x,Q) = Q@[x];

    fun dequeue(nil) = raise EmptyQueue
    |   dequeue(q::qs) = (q,qs);

    fun isEmpty(nil) = true
    |   isEmpty(_) = false;
end;
```

Fig. S15. Solution to Exercise 14.6.

14.9a:

```
signature SIM = sig
    type element;
    val sim : element * element -> bool
end;
```

14.9b: A solution appears in Fig. S16. Note that the code for **sim** will produce a warning because ML thinks that when we explode x and y, one or both could result in the empty list, which would not match the patterns like **xhead::xtail**. However, we have caught such cases in the preceding patterns that check for one or both strings being empty.

14.9c:

```
structure MisspellSet =
    MakeSimSet(Sim = Misspell);
```

Solutions for Chapter 15

15.1: A solution appears in Fig. S17(a) and (b). To understand what is going on, note that in the datatype **tttree** the integer components are the separators, and the **tttree** components are the subtrees. Then, the datatype **oneOrTwo** either wraps one tree in **S** or two trees and a separator in **P**.

Function **lookup** is straightforward. We use the separators to guide us to the proper leaf. Function **insert** requires a lot of work. The heart is in a function **insert1** that finds the proper subtree into which the insertion occurs and returns a **oneOrTwo**, that is, either a single tree or a pair, wrapped appropriately. The five auxiliary functions **group** test whether there is a single or a pair and produce a wrapped tree or pair, as appropriate. The only time a pair is produced is in the case where three subtrees become four, as was illustrated in Fig. 15.5. Note that the five **group** functions are named with a code where **U** stands for "unknown" (we get either a single or a pair) and **T** (we get a single tree).

15.6: Here is a possible structure called **Pair** with signature **ELEMENT**. We have chosen pairs of integers as the type **element**, and the function **similar** checks equality of the first components only.

```
structure Pair: ELEMENT = struct
    type element = int * int;
    fun similar((x1,x2), (y1,y2)) = (x1=y1)
end;
```

Then, the following is a sketch of a structure that uses **Pair** as its substructure called **Element** and defines the local type **elt** to be the same type as appears in structure **Pair**.

```
functor MakeSimSet(Sim: SIM):
    sig
        open Sim;
        type set;
        val create : set;
        val insert : element * set -> set;
        val findSim : element * set -> set
    end

=

struct
    open Sim;
    type set = element list;
    val create = nil;
    fun insert(x,S) = x::S;
    fun findSim(x,nil) = nil
    |   findSim(x,s::ss) =
            if sim(x,s) then s::findSim(x,ss)
            else findSim(x,ss)
end;


structure Misspell: SIM =
    struct
        type element = string;
        fun sim("","") = true
        |   sim("",_) = false
        |   sim(_,"") = false
        |   sim(x,y) =
            let
                val xhead::xtail = explode(x);
                val yhead::ytail = explode(y);
                val xs = implode(xtail);
                val ys = implode(ytail)
            in
                if xhead=yhead then sim(xs,ys)
                else xs=ys
            end
    end;
```

Fig. S16. Solution to Exercise 14.9(b).

```
structure TTTree = struct
    datatype tttree = Two of int * tttree * tttree |
        Three of int * int * tttree * tttree * tttree |
        Leaf of int;

    datatype oneOrTwo = S of tttree |
        P of int * tttree * tttree;

    (* create(i) creates a 2-3 tree with one leaf,
    labeled i *)
    fun create(i) = Leaf(i);

    (* lookup(x,T) tells whether integer x is at a leaf of
    2-3 tree T *)
    fun lookup(x,Leaf(i)) = (x=i)
    |   lookup(x,Two(i,T1,T2)) =
            if x<i then lookup(x,T1)
            else lookup(x,T2)
    |   lookup(x,Three(i,j,T1,T2,T3)) =
            if x<i then lookup(x,T1)
            else if x<j then lookup(x,T2)
            else (* x>=j *) lookup(x,T3);

    (* the following 5 "group" functions are auxiliaries
    used in the function insert1 below.
    See explanation in the text. *)
    fun groupUT(i,S(T1),T2) = S(Two(i,T1,T2))
    |   groupUT(i,P(j,T1,T2),T3) = S(Three(i,j,T1,T2,T3));

    fun groupTU(i,T1,S(T2)) = S(Two(i,T1,T2))
    |   groupTU(i,T1,P(j,T2,T3)) = S(Three(i,j,T1,T2,T3));

    fun groupUTT(i,j,S(T1),T2,T3) = S(Three(i,j,T1,T2,T3))
    |   groupUTT(i,j,P(k,T1,T2),T3,T4) =
            P(i,Two(k,T1,T2),Two(j,T3,T4));

    fun groupTUT(i,j,T1,S(T2),T3) = S(Three(i,j,T1,T2,T3))
    |   groupTUT(i,j,T1,P(k,T2,T3),T4) =
            P(k,Two(i,T1,T2),Two(j,T3,T4));

    fun groupTTU(i,j,T1,T2,S(T3)) = S(Three(i,j,T1,T2,T3))
    |   groupTTU(i,j,T1,T2,P(k,T3,T4)) =
            P(j,Two(i,T1,T2),Two(k,T3,T4));
```

Fig. S17a. Solution to Exercise 15.1 (beginning).

```
(* insert1(x,T) inserts integer x into 2-3 tree T and
returns a oneOrTwo, that is, a 2-3 tree wrapped in S
or two 2-3 trees wrapped in P *)
fun insert1(x,Leaf(i)) =
        if x<i then P(i,Leaf(x),Leaf(i))
        else if x>i then P(x,Leaf(i),Leaf(x))
        else S(Leaf(i))
|   insert1(x,Two(i,T1,T2)) =
        if x<i then
            groupUT(i,insert1(x,T1),T2)
        else (* x>=i *)
            groupTU(i,T1,insert1(x,T2))
|   insert1(x,Three(i,j,T1,T2,T3)) =
        if x<i then
            groupUTT(i,j,insert1(x,T1),T2,T3)
        else if x<j then
            groupTUT(i,j,T1,insert1(x,T2),T3)
        else (* x>=j *)
            groupTTU(i,j,T1,T2,insert1(x,T3));

(* unwrap(X) either removes the one tree from an S or
creates a new node with the two subtrees found
inside a P. *)
fun unwrap(S(T)) = T
|   unwrap(P(i,T1,T2)) = Two(i,T1,T2);

(* insert(x,T) inserts x into 2-3 tree T. *)
fun insert(x,T) = unwrap(insert1(x,T))
end;
```

Fig. S17b. Solution to Exercise 15.1 (end).

```
structure BinaryTree: BTREE = struct
    structure Element = Pair;
    type elt = int * int;
    (* suitable definitions for btree and the functions *)
end;
```

However, should we replace **type elt = int * int** in structure **BinaryTree** by any other type, for example **type elt = real * int**, then we would get an error indicating a violation of a sharing constraint.

Solutions for Chapter 16

16.1a: val A = array(20, nil: real list)

```
open Array;

signature HASHFUNCTION = sig
    eqtype element;
    val b : int;
    val h : element -> int
end;

functor MakeHash(HashFunction: HASHFUNCTION):
    sig
        open HashFunction;
        val A : element list array;
        val lookup : element -> bool;
        val insert : element -> unit;
        val delete : element -> unit
    end
=
    struct
        open HashFunction;
        val A = array(b, nil: element list);
        local
            (* functions insertList, deleteList, and lookup-
                List as in lines (7)-(15) of Fig. 16.4 *)
        in
            fun insert(x) = (* body as in Fig. 16.4 *)
            fun delete(x) = (* body as in Fig. 16.4 *)
            fun lookup(x) = lookupList(x,sub(A,h(x)))
        end
    end;

structure StringHT: HASHFUNCTION = struct
    type element = string;
    val b = 10;
    fun h(x) =
        let
            fun h1(nil) = 0
            |   h1(x::xs) = (ord(x)+h1(xs)) mod b
        in
            h1(explode(x))
        end
end;

structure HashTable =
    MakeHash(HashFunction = StringHT);
```

Fig. S18. Solution to Exercise 16.2.

16.1c: `sub(A,29)`. Remember that the entries of every ML array start with 0, so the 30th entry has index 29.

16.1e: `update(A,10,43)`.

16.2: A solution to the complete exercise is in Fig. S18. At the beginning we have the signature `HASHFUNCTION`, which is the answer to Exercise 16.2(a). Then comes the functor itself, which is the response to 16.2(b). Note that the code for the critical operations `insert`, `delete`, and `lookup` are the same as in Fig. 16.4, but the array `A` is not an argument of these functions. Rather, the array `A` that serves as the hash table is a value of the structure that is output of the functor. Then comes the answer to 16.2(c), the structure `StringHT` that defines an appropriate hash function and sets the number of buckets to 10.

The last step defines the desired hash table `A` with attendant functions `insert`, `delete`, and `lookup` by applying the functor to structure `StringHT`. This hash table is now in the resulting structure `HashTable`, which can be opened to access the array `A` and the functions mentioned above, which will work only on `A`.

16.5: All we have to do is replace the hash function h defined in lines (4)–(6) of Fig. 16.4 by a hash function that is suitable for integers. A simple hash function for integers is to take the remainder when the integer is divided by the number of buckets. That is, we could use

```
fun h(x) = x mod b;
```

in place of lines (4)–(6).

```
exception EmptyList;

fun install(A,_,nil) = A
  | install(A,i,y::ys) = (
            Array.update(A,i,y);
            install(A,i+1,ys)
        );

fun arrayoflist(nil) = raise EmptyList
  | arrayoflist(L as x::xs) =
        let
            val A = Array.array(length(L),x)
        in
            install(A,1,xs)
        end;
```

Fig. S19. Solution to Exercise 16.6.

16.6: A solution appears in Fig. S19. The strategy we have used for function **arrayoflist** is to initialize the array **A** to have all its entries equal to the first element on the list. Then we call the function **install** to take the tail of the list and update the entries of the array, starting at the second entry (with index 1), and finally to return the resulting array.

Function **install** works by returning the array if the list is exhausted. If there are remaining elements, it puts the first element in the entry indexed by the second argument i and calls **install** recursively on the tail of the list, after incrementing the index by 1.

Notice that we have not opened the structure **Array**, but have addressed its identifiers such as **update** by **Array.update**. The reason we have done so is rather subtle. Structure **Array** has a function **length** that is different from the usual SML/NJ function **length**, which computes the length of a list. Since we wanted to use the latter function, we could not open the structure **Array**; it would have obliterated from view the **length** that works on lists in favor of one that works on arrays.

Solutions for Chapter 17

17.1a: val i = ref 10

17.1c: inc(i)

17.1e: i := 20

17.2a: (!x + !y)*(!x + !y). Note that it is unnecessary to indicate the type of **x** or **y**. Since these variables already refer to values, ML can figure out the type of values to which they refer and thus disambiguate overloaded symbols like + and *.

17.3: The heart of the solution is shown in Fig. S20. Function **pivot(M,m,n)** takes an array of arrays **M** that we assume represents a matrix of side n. Thus, each of the rows is represented by an array of n reals, indexed 0 through $n-1$. There are n rows, which we also take to be indexed 0 through $n-1$. The middle parameter, m, indicates where we are in the pivotal condensation process. That is, we have eliminated the first m rows and columns and can now concentrate on the matrix consisting of the $(n-m) \times (n-m)$ square in the lower right corner, as if it were the entire matrix. We use the function **pivot** by calling **pivot(M,0,n)**, if M is the $n \times n$ matrix whose determinant we wish to take.

Function **pivot** works in three phases. The first normalizes the row indexed m by letting a be M_{mm} and dividing all the entries $M_{m,m+1}$ through $M_{m,n-1}$ by a. The second phase subtracts $M_{im} \times M_{mj}$ from M_{ij} for all i and j between $m+1$ and $n-1$. The final phase recursively calls **pivot** on the last $n-m-1$ rows and columns (i.e., on the previous matrix with row and column m deleted), and multiplies the result by M_{mm}.

```
open Array;

fun pivot(M,m,n) =
    if m>=n then 0.0
    else if m=n-1 then sub(sub(M,m),m)
    else (* 0<m<n-1 *) (
        let (* normalize row m to right of diagonal *)
            val i = ref (m+1);
            val a = sub(sub(M,m),m)
        in
            while !i<n do (
                update(sub(M,m), !i, sub(sub(M,m),!i)/a);
                inc(i)
            )
        end;
        let (* subtract M[i,m]*M[m,j] from M[i,j]
                for all i and j such that m<i,j<n *)
            val i = ref (m+1);
            val j = ref (m+1)
        in
            while !i<n do (
                while !j<n do (
                    update(sub(M,!i),!j,sub(sub(M,!i),!j)-
                        sub(sub(M,!i),m)*sub(sub(M,m),!j));
                    inc(j)
                );
                j := m+1;
                inc(i)
            )
        end;
        (* result is M[m,m] times recursive call on matrix
            starting at row and column m+1 *)
        sub(sub(M,m),m)*pivot(M,m+1,n)
    )
```

Fig. S20. Solution to Exercise 17.3.

17.4: The functions **condense** of Fig. S7 and **pivot** of Fig. S20 each take time proportional to n^3 on a matrix of side n. Observe that in Fig. S7, functions **normalize** and **condense1** each take time proportional to n. Function **condense2** calls **condense1** no more than n times and thus takes time proportional to n^2. Finally, **condense** calls **normalize** and **condense2** no more than n times each, and thus takes time proportional to n^3.

Function **pivot** of Fig. S20 uses two nested loops, each of which repeats no more than n times. Function **pivot** thus takes time proportional to n^2 before calling itself recursively with the next higher value of m. Since m ranges from 0 to $n-1$, there are n recursive calls. Each takes time proportional to n^2, so the total time is proportional to n^3. Not only is the growth rate of the running time of the list-based algorithm as good as that of the array-based algorithm, but the way Ml is implemented makes it likely that list-based solutions will run slightly faster than the corresponding array-and-reference-based solutions if the growth rates are the same.

17.5: An expression must follow the **do**, and a val-declaration is not an expression. ML will not accept this code.

```
structure Matrix = struct
    type mat = real Array.array Array.array;
    fun matrix(n,m,v) =
        let
            val M = Array.array(n,Array.array(m,v));
            val i = ref 1
        in
            (while !i<n do (
                Array.update(M,!i,Array.array(m,v));
                inc(i)
            );
            M: mat)
        end
    fun sub(M:mat,i,j) = Array.sub(Array.sub(M,i),j);
    fun update(M:mat,i,j,v) =
            Array.update(Array.sub(M,i),j,v)
end;
```

Fig. S21. Solution to Exercise 17.7.

17.7: A solution is in Fig. S21. Note that since we are defining functions named **sub** and **update** that appear in the structure **Array**, we do not open that structure; to do so would introduce errors. Rather, we refer to the functions of **Array** by their full name, including the structure name **Array** and a dot.

17.10a: for(1, 10, fn(i)=>(print(i); print("\n")));

Solutions for Chapter 18

18.1a: type dino = {name:string, height:real, weight:real}

18.1c:
```
val brachio:dino =
    {name="Brachiosaurus", height=40.0, weight=50.0}
```

18.1e: `#weight(brachio)`

```
type student = {name:string, ID:int, courses: string list};

(* findName(n,L) produces those student records with
    name field n *)
fun findName(n,nil) = nil
|    findName(n,(r:student)::rs) =
        if n = #name(r) then r::findName(n,rs)
        else findName(n,rs);

(* enrollment(c,L) produces the names in those of the
    records on list L that have a course list including
    course c *)
fun enrollment(c,nil) = nil
|    enrollment(c,(r:student)::rs) =
        if #courses(r) = nil then enrollment(c,rs)
        else if c = hd(#courses(r)) then
            #name(r)::enrollment(c,rs)
        else enrollment(c, {name = #name(r), ID = #ID(r),
            courses=tl(#courses(r))}::rs);
```

Fig. S22. Solution to Exercises 18.2(a) and (c).

18.2a: Figure S22 shows the function **findName**. It uses the definition of type **student** that appears at the top of Fig. S22. It is essential that the record structure be defined for each function that applies to this type of record. Otherwise ML cannot be sure that the type does not include any fields that the function doesn't mention, and therefore cannot establish the exact type of the function parameters.

Also, if we have the higher-order function **filter** of Fig. 11.5 available, then we can write **findName** more simply as

```
fun findName(n,L) =
        filter(fn(r:student) => (n = #name(r)), L)
```

18.2c: A solution is in Fig. S22; it is the function **enrollment**. This function uses a trick that first appeared in Fig. 13.9, where we operated upon a tree by modifying the tree to remove one node at a time. Here, we could have written a function that tests whether a given course is present in a list of courses, and used that in the function **enrollment**. Instead, we have chosen to write only one function, which, when it does not find the desired course c at the head of the list of courses, calls itself recursively with the head of the course list removed. The first two cases of this function handle the situations where the list of courses is empty (when c is surely not among them), and where the head of the list equals c (when c surely is among the courses).

18.3a:

```
datatype 'a linkedList = Nil |
    Cell of {element: 'a, next: 'a linkedList ref};
```

18.3c:

```
fun skip(Nil) = raise BadCell
  | skip(Cell({next=(ref Nil),...})) = raise BadCell
  | skip(Cell({next=x as (ref(Cell({next=y,...}))),...})) =
        x := !y;
```

Solutions for Chapter 19

19.1a:

```
val rec padd = fn
        (P,nil) => P |
        (nil,Q) => Q |
        ((p:real)::ps, q::qs) => (p+q)::padd(ps, qs);
```

19.1c:

```
val rec printList = fn
        nil => () |
        x::xs => (print(x:int); print("\n"); printList(xs));
```

19.3: The most useful case-expression is probably the following.

```
case y mod 400 of
    0 => true | 100 => false | 200 => false | 300 => false
  | _ => y mod 4 = 0
```

Note that we might be tempted to nest case statements, but ML does not permit us to do so.

Solutions for Chapter 20

20.1: A solution appears in Fig. S23.

20.3: A solution is shown in Fig. S24. In function **sumInts1**, if the end of file has been reached **getInt(file)** raises the **Eof** exception and prevents the recursive call to **sumInts1** from taking place. We have not handled the exception **BadChar**, although we could do so in one of several ways.

```
exception Negative of int;

fun fact1(0) = 1
|   fact1(n) =
        if n<0 then raise Negative(n)
        else n*fact1(n-1);

fun fact(n) = fact1(n) handle Negative(n) => (
            print("error; n= ");
            print(n);
            print("\n");
            0
    );
```

Fig. S23. Solution to Exercise 20.1.

Solutions for Chapter 21

21.1a: Type = (int -> 'a) -> int -> 'a. Function compA1 takes as argument a function $F(x)$ and produces a function $G(x)$ such that $G(x) = F(x+1)$. Here, x must be an integer. Put another way, compA1 turns a function $F(x)$ into $F(x+1)$.

21.1b: Type = ((int -> 'a) -> 'b) -> (int -> 'a) -> 'b. The function compCompA1 takes a function F and turns it into F o compA1.

21.1c: Type = int -> int. Function f is defined by $f(x) = x + 2$. The explanation is that compA1 turns any $F(x)$ into $F(x+1)$, so if F is add1, $f(x)$ will be $add1(x+1)$, or $x+2$.

21.1d: Type = int, and $f(2) = 4$.

21.1e: Type = (int -> 'a) -> int -> 'a. Function g takes its argument function $F(x)$ and produces the function $F(x+2)$.

21.1f: Type = int -> int. Function h takes integer x and produces $x + 3$.

21.1g: Type = int, and $h(2) = 5$.

21.3: Here is a possible solution.

```
fun makeFnList F nil = nil
|   makeFnList F (x::xs) = F(x)::(makeFnList F xs);
```

If the higher-order function map of Chapter 11 is available, then we can get the effect of makeFnList by map(F,L).

```
exception BadChar and Eof;

fun white(c) = (c=" " orelse c="\n" orelse c="\t");

fun digit(c) =
        (ord(c)>=ord("0") andalso ord(c)<=ord("9"));

fun startInt(file) = (* get the first digit from file;
    raise Eof if there is none *)
        if end_of_stream(file) then raise Eof
        else let
                val c = input(file,1)
            in
                if digit(c) then ord(c)-ord("0")
                else if white(c) then startInt(file)
                else raise BadChar
            end;

fun finishInt(i,file) = (* return the integer whose first
  digits have value i and whose remaining digits are found
  on file, up to the end or the first white space *)
        if end_of_stream(file) then i
        else let
                val c = input(file,1)
            in
                if digit(c) then
                    finishInt(10*i+ord(c)-ord("0"), file)
                else if white(c) then i
                else raise BadChar
            end;

fun getInt(file) = (* read an integer from file *)
    let
        val i = startInt(file)
    in
        finishInt(i,file)
    end;

fun sumInts1(file) = (* sum the integers on file *)
        (getInt(file) + sumInts1(file)) handle Eof => 0;

fun sumInts(filename) = (* sum the integers on filename *)
        sumInts1(open_in(filename));
```

Fig. S24. Solution to Exercise 20.3.

```
(* ss1(L,M) tests whether list L is a prefix of list M *)
fun ss1(nil, _) = true
  | ss1(_, nil) = false
  | ss1(x::xs, y::ys) = (x=y andalso ss1(xs,ys));

(* ss2(L,M) tests whether list L is a sublist of list M *)
fun ss2(x, nil) = ss1(x,nil)
  | ss2(x, y::ys) = ss1(x,y::ys) orelse ss2(x,ys);

(* substring converts strings to lists and applies ss2 *)
fun substring x y = ss2(explode(x),explode(y));
```

Fig. S25. Part of solution to Exercise 21.5.

21.4:

```
fun applyList nil _ = nil
  | applyList (F::Fs) a = F(a)::(applyList Fs a);
```

21.5: A suitable function substring appears in Fig. S25. Note that the type of substring is string -> string -> bool. That is, substring takes a first string and produces from it a function that takes a string s and tells whether the first string is a substring of s. The desired function f is obtained by

```
val f = makeFnList(substring);
```

21.6:

```
val glist = f ["he","she","her","his"];
```

21.7: The result of applyList glist "hershey" is the list

```
[true,true,true,false]
```

That is, all but "his" is a substring of "hershey".

21.12a: fun curry F x1 x2 ... xn = F(x1,x2,...,xn)

Solutions for Chapter 22

22.1a: val IN = open_in("zap"). Technically, we are not required to retain the returned instream. However, if we do not bind it to some identifier, such as IN here, the token representing the instream is lost forever.

22.1c: val OUT = open_append("/usr/spool/mail/fred")

22.1e: close_in(in2)

22.1g: `output(out4,"super")`

22.1i: `can_input(std_in)`

22.3: A solution appears in Fig. S26. Function `getInt` acts like `digit` and `integer` of Fig. 22.3. However, `getInt` consumes a character after the integer that it reads.

Function `putInt1` is an auxiliary function for `putInt`. The latter calls the former and puts parentheses around the integer if it is multidigit. The purpose of `putInt` is to print an integer that is a single base-b digit. Similarly, `convert1` is an auxiliary for `convert`; the latter reads input and calls the former to do the real work of conversion.

Solutions for Chapter 23

23.1: Here is a function that prints the environment list, that is, the second of its two string-list parameters.

```
fun printEnv(_,nil) = ()
|   printEnv(y,x::xs) =
        (print(x:string); print("\n"); printEnv(y,xs));
```

We can follow this function by the `exportFn` call that places function `printEnv` in the file `printenv`.

```
exportFn("printenv",printEnv);
```

23.3: We can use the function `stringToInt` from Fig. 23.1. Then the following function takes a list of strings, converts them to integers, and sums those integers.

```
fun sum1(nil) = 0
|   sum1(x::xs) = stringToInt(x) + sum1(xs);
```

Then, the following function takes a pair of lists of strings, throws away the second and the head of the first, and calls `sum1` on the tail of the first. This tail is the list of arguments on a command line.

```
fun sum(L,_) = print(sum1(tl(L)));
```

Finally, we export the function `sum` into a file `foo`:

```
exportFn("foo",sum);
```

Solutions for Chapter 24

24.1a: Yes. Leaves 2 and 3 would be grouped first, and the tree printed would be $(1,(2,3))$.

```
(* read digits until a nondigit and return their value
   assuming i is value of previously read digits
   of digits *)
fun getInt(i,IN) =
    let val c = lookahead(IN)
    in
        if c = "" then i else (
            input(IN,1);
            if c <= "9" andalso c >= "0" then
                getInt(10*i+ord(c)-ord("0"),IN)
            else i
        )
    end;

(* print integer i in decimal *)
fun putInt1(i,OUT) =
        if i<10 then output(OUT, chr(i+ord("0"))) else (
            putInt1(i div 10, OUT);
            putInt1(i mod 10, OUT)
        );

(* print i, surrounding multidigit numbers by parens *)
fun putInt(i,OUT) =
        if i<10 then putInt1(i,OUT) else (
            output(OUT,"(");
            putInt1(i,OUT);
            output(OUT,")")
        );

(* convert i to a sequence of base-b digits and print *)
fun convert1(i,b,OUT) =
        if i<b then putInt(i,OUT) else (
            convert1(i div b, b, OUT);
            putInt(i mod b, OUT)
        );

(* read i and b and print i in base b *)
fun convert(IN,OUT) =
        let
            val i = getInt(0,IN);
            val b = getInt(0,IN)
        in convert1(i,b,OUT)
        end;
```

Fig. S26. Solution to Exercise 22.3.

24.2a: Give both the same precedence and make them left-associative. For example,

```
infix 6 +;
infix 6 *;
```

24.3a: We need to keep the precedences of the polynomial operators below 6, which is the precedence of the additive arithmetic operators. Thus, we could use something like

```
infix 2 padd;
infix 3 pmult;
infix 4 smult;
```

24.3b:

```
([~6.0,0.0,5.0,0.0,3.0] padd 2.0 smult [4.0,~3.0,2.0,1.0])
    pmult [1.0,1.0]
```

24.5a:

```
fun sumLeaves(x:real) = x
|   sumLeaves(T1 t T2) = sumLeaves(T1) + sumLeaves(T2);
```

Solutions for Chapter 25

25.1a: `fun f(x,y) = max(abs(x),abs(y));`

25.1c: A little trigonometry will show that if θ is the angle whose sine is x, then the tangent of θ is $x/\sqrt{1-x^2}$. Thus, we can use the built-in `arctan` function to compute:

```
fun arcsin(x) = arctan(x/sqrt(1.0-x*x));
```

25.1e: `fun expexp(x) = exp(exp(x));`

25.2a: `makestring(123)`

25.3: We start with the function `sumCodes` below, which sums the positions of a string s starting with position i.

```
fun sumCodes(s,i) =
        if i >= size(s) then 0
        else ordof(s,i) + sumCodes(s,i+1);
```

Then, a call to `sumCodes(s,0)` sums all the characters in string s.

25.5: The value is **true** for any L. The last position on list L is numbered one less than `length(L)`, as far as `nthtail` is concerned. Thus, the tail starting at position `length(L)` is the empty list.

25.7: `fun printList(L) = app print L;`

25.9: Start with the function `genList` below that generates the list of i terms $[y, xy, x^2y, \ldots]$.

```
fun genList(x:real,y,i) =
        if i <= 0 then nil
        else y::genList(x,x*y,i-1);
```

A call to `arrayoflist(genList(x,1.0,n))` does the desired job.

25.10a: The six-bit binary forms of 43 and 19 are 101011 and 010011, respectively. Thus, both strings have 1 in only the rightmost 2 bits, and the result is 3.

25.10c: The bit strings for 43 and 19 disagree in the first three positions and agree in the last three positions. Thus, their exclusive-or is 111000, or 56 in decimal.

25.11a: `"DEFG"`

Index